W9-AJC-873

New Testament

STUDY GUIDE

Chuck Smith

MATTHEW THROUGH REVELATION I verse by verse

THE WORD
FOR TODAY

P.O. Box 8000, Costa Mesa, CA 92628 • Web: www.twft.com • E-mail: info@twft.com • 1-800-272-WORD (9673)

NEW TESTAMENT STUDY GUIDE by Chuck Smith

© 1982, 2005 The Word For Today
Published by The Word For Today
P.O. Box 8000, Costa Mesa, CA 92628
(800) 272-WORD (9673)

Web Site: www.twft.com
E-mail: info@twft.com

ISBN 0-936728-33-7

Unless otherwise indicated, Scripture quotations in this book are taken from the King James Version of the Bible. Translational emendations, amplifications, and paraphrases are by the author.

Greek word definitions are paraphrased by the author.

Calvary Distinctive excerpts are taken from the book, Calvary Chapel Distinctives, written by Chuck Smith, copyright © 2000 by The Word for Today.

Biblical maps provided by www.ccel.org and www.bible.org from Biblical Studies Press, Copyright ©1996-2005 used by permission.

Printed in the United States of America

CONTENTS

THE NEW TESTAMENT
STUDY GUIDE

INTRODUCTION

Pastor Chuck Smith has been teaching the Bible for more than fifty years, and the New Testament study guides collected in this book are based upon his Bible commentaries delivered at Calvary Chapel of Costa Mesa.

These New Testament commentaries have also been broadcast on radio and the internet worldwide on *The Word For Today*, and were designed to help students of the Bible enhance their knowledge of the Scriptures.

As you read the Bible, we hope that this New Testament survey will help you grow in your personal reading and understanding of God's Word.

KEYS TO THE

NEW TESTAMENT STUDY GUIDE

The New Testament Study Guide is designed as a commentary outline to be read with a Bible.

The following icons will aid in your study of the New Testament.

KEY WORDS

Definitions of Greek words commonly found in the New Testament.

CALVARY DISTINCTIVE

Excerpts taken from the book, Calvary Chapel Distinctives, by Chuck Smith.

A CLOSER LOOK

Helpful charts or diagrams clarifying certain portions of the Bible.

BIBLE MAP AREA

Area maps relating to Scripture.

STUDY QUESTIONS

Questions pertaining to specific books of the New Testament.

THE GOSPEL ACCORDING TO
MATTHEW

AUTHOR OF LETTER:
Matthew, also known as Levi.

WRITTEN TO:
The Jews.

THEME:
The Gospel of Jesus, with special emphasis that He is the Messiah, the Lion of the tribe of Judah.

PURPOSE OF WRITING:
To prove that Jesus is the Messiah and fulfills the Old Testament prophecies.

NOTE:
The synoptic gospels: Matthew, Mark, and Luke cover the same subject matter.

CHAPTER 1:
GENEALOGY AND BIRTH OF JESUS CHRIST

•**SYNOPSIS OF VERSES 1-17** These verses deal with the genealogy of Jesus through the line of Joseph. Mary's lineage was the same as Joseph's from Abraham to David. Her genealogy is given in Luke 3. To establish His kingship, it was necessary that Jesus come from the line of Abraham and David.

•**VERSE 1** Jesus was often called "The son of David." God had promised a special son to Abraham and to David, and Jesus was the fulfillment of the promise.

•**VERSES 2-16** Women were not usually listed in genealogies, but Matthew includes:

(1) Tamar (verse 3): had children by her father-in-law.

(2) Rahab (verse 5): a prostitute in Jericho who protected the Hebrew spies.

(3) Ruth (verse 5): a Moabite, a nationality hated by the Jews.

(4) Bathsheba (verse 6): the wife David had stolen from another man.

God broke down the racial barriers in Jesus by including nations outside the covenant in His heritage. He broke down the sex barriers and made all people equal before Him, allowing Jesus to be identified with sinful man.

•**VERSE 16** Joseph was the husband of Mary, but she was the mother of Christ. Genealogies were very important to the Jews, and the scribes kept them carefully. Herod had all the genealogies destroyed, so that no man today can prove that he is a descendant of David and has a right to the throne of the Messiah.

• **VERSE 18** Children were often engaged to each other at three or four years of age. A year before the marriage was to take place, the couple entered a period of espousal where they were betrothed to each other, but not allowed to consummate the marriage. If the couple chose to break up during this time, they had to sign a bill of divorcement; if the groom died, the bride was considered a widowed virgin.

• **VERSE 19** A "just man" means he was straight and compassionate.

• **VERSE 20** Isaiah 7:14 says that a virgin shall conceive. Some versions of the Bible call her a "young woman," but every time this Hebrew word was used in the Old Testament, it referred to a virgin.

In 200 B.C., seventy Jewish scholars translated the Old Testament into Greek and used a Greek word here that could only mean virgin. It would not be a sign of any miracle if a young woman conceived and bore a son, yet a virgin bearing a son is a miracle.

• **VERSE 21** The name Jesus is the Greek for the name Joshua, which means "Jehovah is salvation." Joshua was a common name among the Hebrews, for the parents hoped their son would be the salvation of Israel.

CHAPTER 2:
THE VISIT OF THE WISE MEN

• **VERSE 1** Herod was appointed to his position by the Roman governor because he was so cruel he could keep the Jews in line.

• **VERSE 2** There were interesting conjunctions of planets at the time of Jesus' birth. The wise men had read the birth of a King in the stars.

• **VERSES 9-11** Jesus was a young child in a house, not a babe in a stable, by the time the wise men reached Him.

The gift of gold symbolized His kingly role, frankincense His priestly role, and myrrh His sacrificial death (myrrh was used for embalming).

• **VERSE 13** There was a great deal of angelic activity at this time. The angel had appeared to Mary, to Joseph, to the wise men in dreams, and to the shepherds in the field.

Joseph was not a dull man. The Lord used him to protect the baby Jesus.

• **VERSE 23** The phrase "that it might be fulfilled" occurs often in Matthew's gospel. He wanted the reader to see how many prophecies, some rather unlikely, Jesus fulfilled.

CHAPTER 3:
JOHN THE BAPTIST

There is a time gap of thirty years between Chapters 2 and 3, about which Matthew is silent.

• **VERSE 9** The people were trusting in their nationality for salvation.

• **VERSE 10** The Jewish branch was cut off and the Gentile branch was grafted in.

• **VERSES 16-17** The three Persons of the Trinity were manifested at the baptism of Jesus Christ.

CHAPTER 4:
A TEMPTATION AND A CALL

• **VERSE 1** After His baptism, Jesus began to be led by the Spirit. At first He was led out to the wilderness to be tempted by the devil. Temptation is a part of life on this earth.

• **VERSE 2** Jesus' hunger indicates He was beginning to starve to death after His long fast.

• **VERSE 3** The devil used the word "if" in the subjunctive case, which would mean "since," suggesting that Jesus use His divine power to fulfill the desires of the flesh.

• **VERSE 6** The devil tempted Jesus to use power from God to attract attention to Himself by performing miraculous acts.

• **VERSES 8,9** Satan used a powerful and subtle temptation when he offered the earth to Jesus, promising a shortcut to God's plan for the redemption of the earth through Christ.

• **VERSES 10-11** Jesus answered all the temptations with God's Word. When tempted, we should get into the Word to find the strength to resist, because prayer should not be our only defense in these times.

• **VERSE 17** "Repent" means to turn away from. It's more than being sorry.

• **VERSES 18-19** This was not the first time Peter and Andrew met Jesus (the other gospels tell of earlier meetings), but this was the first time He called them to follow Him.

CHAPTER 5:
THE RIGHTEOUSNESS GOD ACCEPTS

• **VERSES 1-2** The Sermon on the Mount was preached to the disciples.

• **VERSE 3** "Blessed" means "Oh, how happy!"

Poverty of spirit is the consciousness of ourselves when we meet God (Isaiah 6:5, Daniel 10:8, Luke 5:8).

• **VERSE 4** We mourn over our sinful state when we see ourselves.

• **VERSE 5** When we think we are strong, we are our weakest, because we are not leaning on His strength. The world tells us to be strong and assertive, but when we are meek and dependent on God we will inherit the earth.

• **VERSE 6** When we know we are weak, we hunger and thirst after righteousness.

• **VERSES 10-11** We are blessed when per-secuted for Jesus' sake or for righteous-ness sake, not for our own stupidity or fanaticism.

CALVARY DISTINCTIVE

Blessed are the merciful: for they shall obtain mercy (5:7).

It's interesting that, having received mercy, having received grace, the Lord emphasizes our need to show mercy and to show grace.

• **VERSE 13** Salt was used as a preservative to prevent putrefaction.

• **VERSE 16** We should let our works be done so that God is glorified when men see our works, rather than attracting attention to ourselves.

• **VERSE 18** "Jot and tittle" mean little marks in the Hebrew text.

• **VERSE 20** No one was more righteous than the scribes and Pharisees. Jesus was telling them that no one could be justified by the Law. The Law was given to show man's sin (Galatians 3:24).

Jesus was contrasting the teaching and practice of the Law by the scribes and Pharisees and the intention of God when He gave it.

The scribes and Pharisees told the people what the Law said, since it was in Hebrew and the people could not read Hebrew.

Jesus used the teaching method of setting a principle and giving illustrations or applications to make His meaning clear.

• **VERSE 22** "Raca" means vain fellow.

The scribes and Pharisees taught the commandment in a purely physical sense, but Jesus said that we should not harbor hatred for another in our hearts.

• **VERSES 27-30** Jesus did not want us to literally cut off a hand, but to realize that allowing sin to control us could lead us to hell.

• **VERSES 31-32** Some of the scribes and Pharisees were allowing men to divorce their wives for any reason.

Dowries were necessary to provide for the women in this situation (advance alimony).

• **VERSES 33-37** Jesus does not want us to swear, or take an oath that what we say is true, because He wants us to be people of our word.

• **VERSE 48** If we tried to make commandments out of these teachings we would be as guilty as the scribes and Pharisees.

Jesus was explaining the spirit of the Law so we would understand God's divine ideal for us and the impossibility of meeting His standard by our own efforts.

When we believe in Jesus, His righteousness is imputed to us and we are accepted by God.

CHAPTER 6:
OUR TREASURES

• **VERSE 1** The people used the words "alms" and "righteousness" interchangeably. Jesus is speaking of both.

• **VERSE 2** We receive our reward when our righteous acts are seen and praised by men, receiving their admiration.

• **VERSE 5** Prayers were very important to the Jews. They had to pray the shema twice a day and eighteen different prayers throughout the day.

• **VERSE 6** God wants us to pray when we desire true fellowship and open our hearts to Him.

• **VERSES 7-8** Long, elaborate prayers are not more effective than short, sincere prayers. Sincerity and faith produce answers.

• **VERSES 9-13** We should not rush through a repetition of a prayer in a ritualistic manner. Our words should be meaningful. Jesus gave us a good form to follow when we pray.

• **VERSE 9** Our prayers should be addressed to the Father in the name of Jesus, and should begin with praise.

"Hallowed" means sacred, holy.

• **VERSE 10** The first concern of our hearts should be the establishment of God's Kingdom on earth.

• **VERSES 11-13** The personal petitions should come next. Temptation is not always a solicitation to evil but is often a testing to prove our worth.

• **VERSES 14-15** If I want God to forgive me, it is imperative that I forgive others.

• **VERSE 16** "Hypocrite" was the Greek word for actor. Some people act spiritual because our flesh wants people to think we are more spiritual than we really are.

• **VERSE 18** Our service to God should be done for His attention, not for man's.

• **VERSES 19-21** Our hearts are with our treasures, and too often our treasures are material things.

• **VERSES 22-24** Our hearts are often divided between desire for God and desire for material things. Mammon is the god of power, represented by money.

• **VERSES 25-26** The word "anxious" should be inserted: "Take no anxious thought...."

• **VERSE 27** A cubit is eighteen inches.

• **VERSES 31-32** Our Father knows our basic needs and makes provision for us.

• **VERSE 34** God does not want us to worry about the possible situations, because He gives us the strength for each day's events on that day.

CHAPTER 7:
JUDGING, PRAYER, AND FALSE PROPHETS

• **VERSE 3** A mote is a sliver. When we judge another, we put ourselves on a spiritual scale above another, thereby manifesting our self-righteousness.

CALVARY DISTINCTIVE

We set the standard for our own judgment when we judge others.

•**VERSE 6** We need to be careful when we witness to people, using discernment as to whether they will scorn the precious things of God or listen with an open mind.

•**VERSE 7** When Jesus describes prayer here, He uses action verbs.

•**VERSES 8-11** The Father will not allow something terrible to happen to us if we open our hearts to Him.

•**VERSE 12** This verse sums up the message of the Law and the prophets.

•**VERSES 15-20** False prophets are not obviously wolves in sheep's clothing. They appear as "angels of light" and talk about love, but in their hearts they are seeking prey to devour.

We should examine the fruit of their lives and of their ministry to determine whether prophets are true or false.

•**VERSE 21** The will of the Father is that we believe in Jesus Christ and that we love one another. Jesus is to be the Lord of our lives in deed as well as in word.

•**VERSES 24-27** If the foundation of our work is sand, we will crumble when the storms come. Our foundation should be on the strong rock of faith in Jesus; and when the winds and storms of life hit us, we will stand firm.

•**VERSE 29** Jesus spoke with authority. The scribes quoted each other, because they were afraid to speak their minds.

CHAPTER 8:
THE CENTURION AND THE TEMPEST

•**VERSE 1** The Sermon on the Mount was over, so Jesus went down from the mountain.

•**VERSE 3** Jesus broke the Jewish law when He touched the leper, who was an outcast of society.

•**VERSE 5** The centurion was a Roman outside the covenant of the Jews, but Jesus had dealings with those outside the covenant and outside society.

•**VERSE 7** Jesus offered to go to the centurion's house, although the Jews did not go to the homes of Gentiles.

•**VERSE 11** "Many shall come" refers to the Gentiles.

•**VERSE 12** "The children of the kingdom" are the Jews.   *Interesting! Read Verse*

•**VERSE 17** Isaiah 53:4-5 refers to the physical healing Jesus provided for us when He suffered at the whipping post.

•**VERSE 21** The man who wanted to "bury his father" meant he wanted to stay with his family until his father died. Jesus was not being disrespectful.

•**VERSE 29** The demons recognized Jesus as the Son of God.

•**VERSE 30** It was against the Jewish law to keep pigs, but some of the tribe of Gad had begun to raise them.

•**VERSE 34** The people were more concerned with their swine industry than with the healing of the demon-possessed man.

CHAPTER 9:
JESUS PERFORMS HEALINGS

•**VERSE 1** The city of Jesus was Capernaum.

•**VERSE 2** Jesus took care of the man's spiritual needs first.

•**VERSE 9** Matthew was a tax collector and as such was hated by the people.

•**VERSES 12-13** Jesus ate with the sinners to show that His forgiveness extended to all people.

•**VERSES 16-17** Jesus did not come to rejuvenate the old religion, but to bring in a new relationship to God.

AREA OF JESUS' MINISTRY

• **VERSE 18** The man knew Jesus could bring his daughter back to life.

• **VERSES 21-22** The woman's faith was released when she touched the hem of Jesus' garment.

• **VERSE 34** The Pharisees hardened their hearts against Jesus. Since they had to acknowledge the miracles that He did, they chose to attribute them to devils rather than to God.

• **VERSE 35** Jesus taught in the synagogues and set the pattern that His disciples later followed.

CHAPTER 10:
THE APOSTLES ARE SENT OUT

• **VERSES 6-8** The apostles were to go out to prepare the way for the coming of Christ.

• **VERSE 15** "Verily" means very truly.

• **VERSE 23** Jesus refers to His first coming here, not the Second Coming.

• **VERSE 28** Hell here is Gehenna, the final place of punishment—not Hades the temporary place in the middle of earth.

• **VERSES 29-31** God is interested in every aspect of our lives.

• **VERSES 32-33** Our lives confess or deny the presence of Jesus.

• **VERSES 34-37** Jesus did not come to deliberately separate families, but He knew that division would occur because of faith in Him.

• **VERSE 39** This verse is the paradox of the Christian walk.

CHAPTER 11:
JESUS SPEAKS OF JOHN THE BAPTIST

• **VERSES 2-6** John expected Jesus to throw off the yoke of Roman rule and establish the kingdom of God on earth.

Jesus answered John's question by illustrating His fulfilling the prophecies, aware that John knew the Scriptures.

• **VERSE 14** John came in the spirit and power of Elijah, who will come again (Revelation 11:3-12) before Jesus' Second Coming.

• **VERSES 20-24** These cities that Jesus singled out for judgment are in ruins today, while other smaller cities from His day still stand and are inhabited.

• **VERSE 25** Men will be judged according to the light they have received.

• **VERSE 27** We can only know God when Jesus reveals Him to us.

• **VERSES 28-30** Other religions put heavy yokes upon the people, forcing them to earn their salvation, but Jesus' yoke is easy, giving us the strength and capacity for every task.

CHAPTER 12:
THE BLASPHEMY AGAINST THE HOLY SPIRIT

• **VERSE 1** The "ears of corn" may refer to stalks of wheat.

• **VERSES 2-8** Jesus explained that human need takes precedence over the Law.

God would rather that we were merciful than always giving sacrifices to Him (verse 7).

•**VERSES 22-32** The blasphemy against the Holy Spirit is the continual rejection of the work of the Holy Spirit in our lives and attributing His work to the devil (Romans 1:28).

•**VERSES 36-37** This does not apply to the Christians, though our works will be tried for our motivations and we will be rewarded accordingly.

•**VERSE 40** Jesus confirms the reality of the Jonah story, though some scholars deny the reality of it and consider it a Jewish myth.

Jesus was predicting His descent to Hades and His resurrection (Ephesians 4:8-10, Isaiah 61:1).

•**VERSES 46-50** The Bible does not teach us to pray to Mary for special favors.

CHAPTER 13:
THE PARABLE OF THE SOWER

•**VERSES 10-17** The purpose of the parables was to illustrate a truth and to make it more attractive.

Jesus noticed that the people were not listening to Him when He spoke the simple truth, so He began to tell stories to encourage the people to listen (Isaiah 6:9-10).

•**VERSES 18-30** The enemy planted "tares" in the Church causing perversions of the gospel and deceiving people.

•**VERSES 31-32** The birds are like the tares in the preceding parable, and the tree is the Church.

•**VERSE 33** Some have misunderstood this to mean that the Church will grow to encompass the whole earth, but leaven is always negative and has a bad influence when it is present; so, Jesus was saying that there is a leavening influence within the Church.

•**VERSES 44-46** The field is the world that Jesus gave everything He had to buy it, so that He could take His treasure (the Church) out of it.

•**VERSES 55-56** Jesus' four brothers and His sisters are mentioned, indicating that Mary was not a perpetual virgin, but that she and Joseph had a normal relationship after the birth of Jesus (Matthew 1:25).

•**VERSE 58** Our unbelief can limit the work of God in our lives.

CHAPTER 14:
FEEDING THE FIVE THOUSAND

•**VERSE 1** "Tetrarch" means Quarter-ruler, though he actually shared the kingdom with only two others. This king was Herod Antipas.

•**VERSE 8** "Charger" means platter. Herodias was an ambitious woman who wanted to silence John the Baptist.

•**VERSES 13-16** Even though Jesus wanted to get away for awhile, He felt compassion for the multitude and ministered to them.

•**VERSE 20** Here in the Greek, "filled" is translated more accurately as glutted.

•**VERSE 36** The woman had used the hem of Jesus' garment as a point of contact to release her faith.

We often have faith that God can do something, but we need to have a specific moment when we release that faith and accept what we have asked God to do.

CHAPTER 15:
THE CANAANITE WOMAN'S REQUEST

•**VERSE 2** The scribes and Pharisees followed a traditional ceremony when they washed their hands before meals.

•**VERSES 3-6** "Honor thy father and mother" meant that children should care for parents when elderly.

However, if the children said that everything they owned was dedicated to God (corban) as a gift, this tradition of the scribes and Pharisees allowed them to neglect their parents.

•**VERSES 10-20** What comes out of a man's mouth is in his heart and mind and declares what is in the man.

•**VERSE 21** Jesus stayed away from the Jews for awhile to avoid a confrontation with Herod, preventing premature attempts on His life.

•**VERSES 22-28** Jesus knew all along that He would heal the Canaanite woman's daughter. It seems He held back, drawing out her faith, demonstrating His greatness.

The word Jesus used for dogs (verse 26) was not the same word the Jews usually used to refer to Gentiles. Jesus used a word meaning "little puppies" indicating a household pet.

•**VERSE 31** The people glorified God when they saw the works of Jesus.

•**VERSE 37** The people were glutted this time also.

CHAPTER 16:
PETER'S CONFESSION

•**VERSE 13** Jesus was in the area of Caesarea Philippi.

•**VERSES 16-17** God's Spirit communicates truth to our spirit. When our spirit sends the message to our consciousness, we sometimes have difficulty discerning whether we are getting a revelation from God or are thinking our own thoughts.

Peter had a revelation from God, causing him to answer that Christ was the Son of God.

•**VERSE 18** Jesus called Peter "Petros," meaning a little stone, and then said that upon the "petra," giant rock, He would build His Church.

 KEY WORD

petros = little stone
petra = rock (16:18)

The Church is not built upon the man, Peter, but upon Peter's confession of faith in Christ as God's Son (1 Corinthians 3:11).

•**VERSE 19** We should exercise the power of binding and loosing that which Christ gave to His Church.

•**VERSES 22-23** Peter spoke to Christ out of love for Him, not understanding the plan of God; he was looking at things from the human aspect.

•**VERSES 24-26** If we deny ourselves and submit fully to Jesus, He will become the center of our lives as we follow Him.

The three requirements of discipleship are: 1) deny yourself, 2) take up your cross, and 3) follow Jesus.

•**VERSE 27** Jesus was speaking here of His Second Coming. Our heavenly position will be according to our works here on earth.

•**VERSE 28** This verse should be the first verse of Chapter 17 since Peter, James, and John saw Jesus glorified when they were on the mountain.

CHAPTER 17:
THE TRANSFIGURATION

•**VERSES 3-6** Moses stood for the Law and Elijah stood for the prophets.

God gave the preeminence to Jesus and told the disciples, "Hear ye Him."

•**VERSE 11** Jesus confirmed the prophecy that "Elijah will come again before the Kingdom of God is established upon the earth" (Revelation 11:3).

•**VERSE 20** The disciples had been so concerned by the manifestation of demon-possession of the boy that they could not cast the demon out.

They could not maintain their faith in the face of the evidence of Satan's power.

We need to meditate upon God's power in order to maintain our faith.

•**VERSES 24-27** Jesus and Peter weren't required to pay the tax that the tax collectors demanded, being citizens of Capernaum; but Jesus chose to pay it.

CHAPTER 18:
JESUS AND THE CHILDREN

•**VERSE 6** Millstones were huge and heavy.

•**VERSE 7** The world is full of filth and vulgarity that our children will be exposed to, in spite of our best efforts to protect them.

"Woe unto the world because of its offenses!"

•**VERSE 10** "Their angel faces do always behold the face of the Father" is another translation.

•**VERSES 15-17** We should follow the instructions of Jesus to go first to a brother that offends us, rather than going around to others and sharing the offense. His plan produces the greatest harmony in the Body of Christ.

•**VERSES 19-20** Two or three people gathered together in the name of Jesus comprise the Church, and He is there.

•**VERSE 24** Ten thousand talents is $16,000,000.

•**VERSE 28** A hundred pence is $15.

•**VERSE 35** God will enable us to obey, no matter how impossible it seems.

Only God can give us the power to forgive, and it is important that we have a forgiving spirit since He has forgiven us so much.

CHAPTER 19
THE KEYS TO THE KINGDOM

•**VERSE 3** The Pharisees attempted to trap Jesus into saying something contrary to the Law of Moses, because the Jews all recognized the Law as the Word of God.

•**VERSES 4-9** Jesus went further than the Law and its interpretations to the beginning and God's original intent and purpose for marriage. Jesus said that fornication is the only acceptable grounds for divorce.

•**VERSE 13** The disciples rebuked the parents for leading their children up to Jesus to be blessed.

•**VERSE 17** Jesus forced the young man to examine what he had said. Either Jesus was God and good, or He was no good. The young man had to decide.

•**VERSE 20** Though the young man was wealthy, a ruler, and led a moral life, he still felt a void.

•**VERSES 21-24** Jesus could see that the man had made a god of his possessions and that his love for material things kept him from following Him.

It is more difficult for a rich man to trust in God, because he is secure in his wealth.

•**VERSE 29** God will never be a debtor to us. He will increase one hundred times anything we give up for His sake.

CHAPTER 20:
A PARABLE AND AN ADMONITION

•**VERSES 1-16** The gift of God is eternal life, but we will be rewarded according to our faithfulness in the work He has called us to do.

He gives the gift of salvation freely to all who ask, no matter how late in their lives, nor how sinful they have been.

•**VERSE 19** Jesus even predicted His scourging. His disciples were so shocked whenever He said that He would be mocked, scourged, and crucified, that they did not hear Him say that He would rise on the third day.

It wasn't until after His resurrection that they remembered that Jesus had told them beforehand what would happen.

•**VERSES 20-28** It is comforting to see that the disciples were ordinary men with base human traits as we have.

God will hear our prayers just as He heard theirs.

CHAPTER 21:
THE FIG TREE

•**VERSES 4-5** Zechariah 9:9.

•**VERSE 9** "Hosanna" means save now (Psalm 118:25-26).

•**VERSES 19-21** Jesus' curse on the fig tree was symbolic of the nation Israel, which had failed to bring forth fruit.

Therefore, the vineyard was to be let out to the Gentiles to produce fruit for the Master.

•**VERSE 31** The publicans and the harlots had at first rejected the message of John the Baptist and Jesus, but they eventually came to believe.

The scribes and Pharisees claimed to believe in God all along but did not actually do His will.

•**VERSES 33-45** Isaiah 5 compared Israel to a vineyard, and Jesus was using the same analogy in His parable.

Jesus explained how Israel had beaten and scorned the prophets and would kill Him, the Son, and lose their inheritance because of their attitudes.

CHAPTER 22:
THE GREAT COMMANDMENT

•**VERSES 1-14** This parable demonstrated again that Israel had repeatedly ignored God's messages and would lose its favored status. Instead, God would raise up a people that would do His will.

The only requirement for entry to the marriage ceremony was to be clothed in the garment of Christ's righteousness.

•**VERSES 36-40** The two commandments Jesus gave were a summation of the Law and the messages of the prophets.

Jesus stated them in the form of positive commands rather than negative commandments.

CHAPTER 23:
MESSAGE TO THE SCRIBES AND PHARISEES

•**VERSE 2** The scribes and Pharisees interpreted the Mosaic Law to the letter of the outward observance, but they neglected the inward motivations. Jesus taught that God looks at our hearts.

•**VERSE 5** The phylacteries are little boxes containing slips with scriptures on them that tie onto the arm and forehead. The scribes and Pharisees wore them to appear more spiritual.

•**VERSES 6-12** We are all equal before Christ and should not exalt some people above others.

•**VERSE 23** According to the Law, the Jews had to give a tenth of their increase to God; the scribes and Pharisees even tithed a tenth of the produce from their spice garden.

•**VERSE 24** The Pharisees and scribes would strain and gag, coughing up a gnat they had accidentally swallowed, being unkosher to eat blood, yet they would ignore the important things.

•**VERSE 28** What we are on the outside makes no difference to God. He looks into our hearts (1 Samuel 16:7).

•**VERSE 39** Jesus won't return to Israel until after the terrible days of the Great Tribulation are over.

CHAPTER 24:
SIGNS OF HIS COMING

•**VERSE 2** This prophecy was fulfilled in forty years from the time Jesus spoke it.

•**VERSES 3-6** Jesus began to describe the world scene that would precede His Second Coming.

•**VERSE 7** This verse indicates world-wide war.

•**VERSE 9** Read Fox's Book of Martyrs for background information on Christian persecution.

•**VERSE 14** In Revelation 14:6-7 an angel preaches the gospel to the entire world in every language.

•**VERSE 15** Daniel 9:27, 11:31 and 12:11 are referred to in this verse.

•**VERSES 16-20** This chapter is addressed to the Jews, who will once more be God's elect nation, since the Church will be raptured by the time these prophecies come to pass (Ezekiel 39:23-29).

The applications to Israel are obvious: Judea is named, people are on their housetops, they will be concerned about breaking the law of the Sabbath.

•**VERSE 21** Revelation Chapters 6-19 have the details of the Great Tribulation.

•**VERSE 22** Once again, the elect is the nation of Israel since the Church will be with Christ.

•**VERSE 24** We have seen a proliferation of false cults in recent years.

•**VERSE 30** The people will mourn because they stubbornly rejected Jesus. The Jews will be especially saddened that they didn't recognize their Messiah.

•**VERSE 32** The nation Israel is symbolically referred to as a fig tree (Jeremiah 24; Hosea 9:10; Joel 1:7).

•**VERSE 34** The generation that sees Israel bud forth and become a nation again is the generation mentioned here.

🗝 KEY WORD

genea = generation; referring to an ethnic group or nation (24:34)

•**VERSES 40-41** Some feel these verses refer to the Rapture of the Church; others feel they refer to people being taken away to judgment.

•**VERSE 46** We should be doing what the Lord has called us to do—and wants us to do—when He comes for us.

•**VERSE 48** This philosophy produces slovenliness, or negligence, and is similar to those who believe Christians will go through all or part of the Tribulation.

CHAPTER 25:
THE PARABLE OF THE TEN VIRGINS

•**VERSES 1-13** The essence of the parable is that we must be ready for the coming of Christ.

•**VERSE 4** Some suggest that the oil symbolizes the Holy Spirit and that those who are walking in the Spirit will be raptured.

•**VERSES 11-12** Perhaps the foolish virgins symbolize the carnal Christians who walk in spiritual immaturity.

•**VERSES 14-15** "Talents" refers to money; not an ability to do something well.

•**VERSES 16-23** The way we handle the responsibilities God gives us here determines what we will be given in heaven.

•**VERSES 31-32** The first thing Christ will do when He returns to the earth in glory is judge those who lived through the Tribulation and refused to take the mark of the Beast.

•**VERSE 40** Many feel the words "my brethren" refer to the Jews, since they have been mistreated by many nations. Others think the brethren of Jesus are the Christians.

•**VERSE 46** The choice of where we will spend eternity is before each of us; everlasting punishment or eternal life with Jesus Christ.

CHAPTER 26:
THE LAST SUPPER

•**VERSE 2** Jesus was probably crucified on Thursday, not Friday, and rose on Sunday morning after spending three days and three nights in the tomb.

•**VERSE 3** Caiaphas was the high priest appointed by Rome, but the Jews recognized Annas, who had descended from Aaron, as their high priest.

•**VERSE 7** The ointment was worth a year's wages.

•**VERSE 8** Nothing we give to Jesus is ever a waste.

•**VERSE 9** Judas was not really concerned for the poor. Being the treasurer of the disciples' money, he had been stealing from the common purse.

•**VERSE 15** Thirty pieces of silver was the price of a servant under the Law (Zechariah 11:12).

•**VERSE 24** Some people think that Judas is the Antichrist since he and the Antichrist are both referred to as "the son of perdition" in Scripture. Jesus also called him a devil (John 6:70-71).

•**VERSE 39** Jesus asked that He be spared the death on the cross if salvation for mankind could be purchased any other way (Acts 4:12).

It wasn't Jesus' will to die on the cross, but He submitted His will to the Father.

•**VERSE 45** At this point the battle between God and Satan for Jesus' obedience to His redemptive death had probably been won, because Jesus told His disciples to sleep on. Perhaps He prayed for each of them as He sat there.

•**VERSE 49** The kiss of Judas was not a casual greeting but a passionate kiss, according to the Greek text.

•**VERSE 56** All the disciples fled and left Jesus alone to face the scribes, elders, and the high priest.

•**VERSE 61** Jesus was talking about the temple of His body.

•**VERSE 63** The high priest asked Jesus to take an oath and answer the question.

•**VERSE 67** Spitting was a sign of disdain in that culture.

•**VERSE 73** Peter had a Galilean accent.

CHAPTER 27:
THE CRUCIFIXION

•**VERSE 5** Peter went out, repented, and wept bitterly. Judas repented, went out, and hanged himself.

•**VERSE 9** Here either Matthew or a copyist made a mistake, because this verse that is attributed to Jeremiah was actually written by Zechariah in Chapter 11:13.

•**VERSE 16** Barabbas was a notorious criminal, and Pilate hoped the people would choose the release of Jesus over the release of a dangerous man.

•**VERSE 22** Pilate's question is one we all must decide.

Though Pilate was the judge, he was judged by his decision. What he chose to do with Jesus did not really affect Jesus, for the Scriptures had to be fulfilled that He would die.

Pilate's decision settled his own destiny.

•**VERSE 25** The consequences of this cry have been horrifying for the Jews as a people.

•**VERSE 26** The prisoners were to receive forty lashes, because that was the number of judgment—less one lash—because judgment was to be tempered with mercy.

The lashes became easier as the prisoner confessed his crimes and harder if the man remained quiet.

Since Jesus had no crime to confess, He took the full brunt of the scourging with a whip designed to tear the flesh (Isaiah 50:6, 53:2-7).

• **VERSE 31** Isaiah prophesied Christ will die on the cross in Chapter 52:13-14.

• **VERSE 51** God tore the veil from top to bottom. The veil symbolized the fact that God was unapproachable to sinful man, but the death of Christ made access to God open for every man.

• **VERSE 53** The bodies left the graves after the resurrection of Jesus, because He led the saints out of Hades after He spent three days there with them.

Luke 16:19-31 describes the two compartments in Hades where the dead, comforted by Abraham, waited for the death of Jesus to cover their sins (Hebrews 11:39; Isaiah 61:1).

• **VERSES 65-66** Pilate told the chief priests and Pharisees to make the tomb of Jesus as secure as they could; so they made it secure and then sealed it.

CHAPTER 28:
THE RESURRECTION

• **VERSE 2** The angel rolled back the stone from the door of the tomb, not to let Jesus out, but to allow the disciples to see inside.

• **VERSE 4** The guards were so frightened by the angel that they pretended to be dead.

• **VERSE 18** Jesus has all the power in heaven and in the earth.

• **VERSE 19** The ministry of the Church is to teach. The Church has plenty of preachers but not enough teachers.

• **VERSE 20** "Amen" means so be it.

CALVARY DISTINCTIVE

Peter answered and said unto him, Though all men shall be offended because of thee, yet will I never be offended (Matthew 26:33).

So whenever we think that we are the exceptions to the rule, the Lord allows us to stumble, to teach us our total reliance upon Him.

1. We read of Jesus' baptism in Matthew 3:13-17.

Describe how the Trinity is clearly seen during this event.

_____

_____

_____

2. Jesus taught much about prayer and even gave us a form or an example in the Lord's Prayer.

Which instruction or exhortation in Matthew 6:5-8 speaks to you the most and why?

_____

_____

_____

3. Jesus said to Peter that we are to forgive not just seven times, but seventy times seven.

According to the parable of the unmerciful servant in Matthew 18:21-35, why is it so important that we have a forgiving spirit?

_____

_____

_____

4. Describe the meaning and significance of the parable of the wedding banquet found in Matthew 22:1-14.

_____

_____

_____

5. What was the great commission Jesus gave to the disciples when He appeared to them after His resurrection from the dead? (See Matthew 28:18-20.)

_____

_____

_____

THE GOSPEL ACCORDING TO

MARK

AUTHOR OF LETTER:

Mark, also known as John Mark, a nephew of Barnabas.

WRITTEN TO:
The Romans.

THEME:
The Gospel of Jesus, with special emphasis that He is the Messiah, the Lion of the tribe of Judah.

DATE AND PLACE OF WRITING:

Probably while Mark was in Rome with Paul; one of the earliest gospels, thought to be written some time before the year 63 A.D.

PURPOSE OF WRITING:

To present the Gospel of Jesus, narrating more of what Jesus did rather than what He said.

THEME:

The Gospel of Jesus, with significance on the servanthood of Jesus Christ.

CHAPTER 1:
FISHERS OF MEN

•**VERSE 1** Mark wrote this gospel as Peter related the events to him. Mark himself wasn't an eyewitness to all that occurred, but he was present on some occasions (Mark 14:51-52).

•**VERSES 2-6** John the Baptist caught the attention of the people and began a revival among them.

•**VERSES 7-8** John prepared the way for Jesus in the hearts of the people (John 1:7-9).

•**VERSES 10-11** The Father, the Son, and the Holy Spirit were working together in harmony at the baptism of Jesus.

•**VERSE 15** This is the message of Jesus: "The kingdom of God is near. Repent and believe the good news!"

•**VERSES 16-18** Andrew and Peter knew Jesus before His ministry began (John 1:35-42). Jesus challenged them to leave what they were doing to follow Him.

•**VERSE 21** Capernaum became the center for the ministry of Jesus.

•**VERSE 22** The scribes who taught the Mosaic Law quoted extensively from the writings of other rabbis, rather than give their own interpretations.

•**VERSE 27** Demons are probably fallen angels who went with Satan when he was cast out of heaven (Revelation 12:4,9; Jude 6).

•**VERSE 28** At this time, 200 cities in Galilee had populations of 15,000 or more.

•**VERSE 35** Jesus found His strength in prayer.

CHAPTER 2:
A NEW RELATIONSHIP

•**VERSE 7** Sin is against God because it's the violation of His will (Psalm 51:4).

•**VERSE 14** "Levi" is Matthew, a tax collector Jesus called to be a disciple.

•**VERSES 18-20** Fasting doesn't obligate God to do what we ask Him. Whatever He gives us is by His grace, not as a reward for anything we've done.

We often pamper our flesh and starve our spirits. At the direction of the Holy Spirit, Christians should fast, strengthening the spirit as we deny the flesh.

•**VERSES 21-22** Jesus introduced a new relationship with God that would replace the old religious system of the Mosaic Law.

•**VERSE 27** God designed the Sabbath for us as a day of rest from daily pressures.

Certainly we weren't created for the Sabbath (Colossians 2:16-17; Romans 14:5).

CHAPTER 3:
THE TWELVE APOSTLES ARE CHOSEN

•**VERSE 2** The people watched Jesus approach the afflicted man, because they knew He always related to the man with the greatest need.

•**VERSE 5** When God commands us, He also enables us.

•**VERSES 21-22** His family was concerned about Jesus because He gave Himself to the crowds of people without even pausing to eat.

•**VERSE 29** The Holy Spirit convicts sin and draws us to Jesus for repentance.

The rejection of the Holy Spirit and His work in our lives is the only sin that condemns us to hell (John 16:7-11; Matthew 12:31-32).

🗝 KEY WORD

metanoia = repentance, turn from (3:29)

CHAPTER 4:
PARABLE OF THE SOWER AND SEEDS

•**VERSES 11-12** Jesus taught in parables to catch the attention of the people, since they had closed their ears to the teaching of straight doctrine.

The parables were stories that had the truth subtly worked into them. Those who listened carefully could understand the point of the parable, but those who listened casually only heard an interesting story.

•**VERSE 13** Expositional constancy is the consistent use of a symbol.

For example, if a field symbolizes the world in one parable, then it symbolizes the world in other parables. This exposition is a key, having many of the common symbols used throughout the Scriptures clearly explained by Jesus.

•**VERSES 14-20** Jesus explained that the Gospel touches people differently when they hear it.

•**VERSES 21-22** The light of God wasn't brought into the world to be hidden, but to enlighten every dark place.

•**VERSES 24-25** If we listen to the Lord, He'll give us even more to hear.

•**VERSES 26-29** When we walk with Jesus, fruit naturally results (John 15:1-5).

•**VERSE 32** Since the birds symbolized evil in the parable of the sower, they represent evil in this parable also.

This parable indicates that, although the Church will grow to a great size, evil forces will also come in.

•**VERSES 35-40** Jesus had told the disciples, "Let us pass over to the other side," even though the storm made the crossing difficult (Jude 24-25).

CHAPTER 5:
THE GIRL RESTORED TO LIFE

•**VERSE 1** The Gadarenes (or Gerasenes) were descendants of the tribe of Gad, who chose to settle on the eastern side of the Sea of Galilee when the Israelites first entered the Promised Land.

•**VERSES 2-4** The demons had given supernatural power to the man they inhabited.

•**VERSES 13-18** It was illegal for the Jews to raise swine since they were forbidden by the Mosaic Law to eat pork.

•**VERSE 20** "Decapolis" refers to the ten main cities in that area.

•**VERSE 28** The woman had set a goal in her mind that would release her faith when she touched Jesus' clothes.

•**VERSE 30** The "virtue" here was healing power.

•**VERSE 34** "Daughter" and other family terms didn't necessarily imply blood ties (Mark 3:34-35).

•**VERSE 38** It was a common practice to hire professional mourners to weep over the death of a loved one.

CHAPTER 6:
JESUS FEEDS THE FIVE THOUSAND

•**VERSE 1** Jesus and the disciples went to Nazareth.

•**VERSE 3** Jesus had lived in Nazareth and worked as a carpenter before He began His ministry, and His brothers are named here.

His brother James wrote the Epistle of James and His brother Judah wrote the short Book of Jude.

•**VERSE 13** The oil had no medicinal value. It provided a point of contact for the people to release their faith.

•**VERSE 14** This is Herod Antipas.

•**VERSE 46** Even though it had been a tiring day, Jesus took the time to pray before He rested. He was always strengthened by prayer.

•**VERSE 56** The woman with the issue of blood had started something in the minds of the people.

Many others also used the hem of Jesus' garment as the point of contact to release their faith.

CHAPTER 7:
JESUS HEALS THE DEAF MAN

•**VERSE 10** Honoring one's father and mother meant providing for their physical needs in their old age.

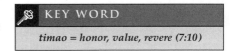
KEY WORD

timao = honor, value, revere (7:10)

•**VERSES 11-13** "Corban" was anything dedicated to God as a gift. Children would avoid helping their aged parents by calling their possessions corban, that is, dedicated to God.

•**VERSE 31** The man who had been possessed by the legion of demons witnessed of Jesus in Decapolis.

CHAPTER 8:
JESUS HEALS THE BLIND MAN

• **VERSE 15** Leaven is like sin—a small amount can permeate everything around it.

• **VERSE 29** "Christ" is a Greek translation of the Hebrew word for Messiah, which means anointed.

• **VERSE 31** Isaiah 53.

• **VERSE 33** Peter lacked spiritual discernment. He couldn't distinguish between the thoughts from God and those from his own heart.

• **VERSES 36-37** Our eternal souls are worth more than the entire world.

CHAPTER 9:
THE TRANSFIGURATION

• **VERSE 1** Matthew 16:28,17:1-9.

• **VERSE 3** The disciples were allowed to see Jesus in His glory (1 Corinthians 13:12).

• **VERSES 7-8** As God's Son, Jesus was able to reveal the nature of God and His intentions for man more fully than Moses (the Law) and Elijah (the Prophets).

• **VERSE 11** Malachi 3:1, 4:5-6.

• **VERSE 12** Jesus referred to Himself as the "Son of Man," one of the titles that the Old Testament prophets gave to the Messiah (Daniel 7:13).

At the first coming of Jesus, He was to sacrifice Himself as a ransom for our sins, fulfilling part of the prophecies relating to the Messiah. Before He returns to complete the prophecies, He will again be preceded by Elijah (Revelation 11:3-13).

• **VERSE 13** John the Baptist preached with the spirit and power of Elijah, but he wasn't Elijah (Luke 1:17; John 1:21).

• **VERSE 16** Jesus is the Good Shepherd, zealous in the protection of His sheep.

• **VERSES 18-20** Though the symptoms of the demon-possessed boy resembled epilepsy, it's totally wrong to equate epilepsy with demon-possession.

Satan probably caused the child to exhibit violent symptoms to frighten the disciples and render them powerless to help the boy. We must remember that the power of God is greater than the power of Satan (1 John 4:4).

• **VERSE 25** The demons are under the authority of Christ. They have no choice but to obey His commands.

• **VERSE 30** Jesus was anxious to be alone with His disciples since His days with them were coming to an end.

• **VERSE 35** In those days teachers sat down to teach. When Jesus sat down, the people knew He was going to teach them.

• **VERSES 43-44** "Hell" here is Gehenna, the final place of the dead.

The first two inhabitants of Gehenna will be the Antichrist and the false prophet (Revelation 19:20). Satan will join them there after a thousand years (Revelation 20:10).

• **VERSE 45** "Halt" here means lame.

• **VERSES 47** Jesus used shocking images to convey the importance of entering the kingdom of God.

CHAPTER 10:
DEFINITION OF THE MINISTRY

• **VERSE 1** "Coasts" refers to borders.

• **VERSE 4** Deuteronomy 24:1.

• **VERSES 6-9** Jesus answered the Pharisees by explaining that God instituted the principle of marriage before the Mosaic Law was ever written.

• **VERSE 21** Jesus wants us to give up whatever holds us back from a full surrender to Him.

• **VERSES 22-25** 1 Timothy 6:9-10.

•**VERSES 29-30** God will never be a debtor to us.

•**VERSE 43** The ministry means service to others. The minister is a servant, on call to meet peoples' needs.

•**VERSE 50** Some scholars suggest that the garment Bartimaeus took off was his begging coat. He knew that once he met Jesus, he wouldn't need to beg by the highway anymore.

✝ CALVARY DISTINCTIVE

"But Jesus called them to him, and saith unto them, Ye know that they which are accounted to rule over the Gentiles exercise lordship over them; and their great ones exercise authority upon them. But so shall it not be among you: but whosoever will be great among you, shall be your minister: And whosoever of you will be the chiefest shall be servant of all" (Mark 10:42-44).

It is essential to recognize that the ministry is not a place of being served — people waiting on you, honoring you, and respecting you because you're the minister. It's actually a place of serving people, even if that means going out of your way to do it.

CHAPTER 11:
THE BARREN FIG TREE

•**VERSE 9** "Hosanna" means save now (Psalm 118:25-26). Jesus' entry into Jerusalem was the fulfillment of prophecy (Zechariah 9:9; Daniel 9:25-26).

•**VERSES 13-14** The fig tree represents the nation Israel in the Scriptures (Jeremiah 24:1-10; Hosea 9:10; Joel 1:6-12).

When Jesus went to the fig tree, He knew it should have small, green figs by April. This demonstrated the nation of Israel's curse for not bearing fruit.

•**VERSE 16** People were using the temple grounds as a shortcut from one part of the city to another.

•**VERSE 17** If a man wanted to give an offering to God, he had to change his Roman currency for temple money. The moneychangers charged exorbitant interest for this transaction, thereby robbing God and lining their own pockets.

The doves sold in the temple were much more expensive than those sold outside. However, the priests only accepted temple doves, since they received a percentage from the sellers.

•**VERSES 25-26** There's a relationship between forgiveness and prayer.

When we've been forgiven by God, we're more inclined to forgive others. If we ask Him for forgiveness for ourselves, we cannot be harboring a grudge against someone else.

CHAPTER 12:
TEACHING THE TEACHERS

•**VERSES 1-9** "Winefat" means wine vat.

God sent prophets to the nation Israel. They were imprisoned, stoned, or otherwise executed.

Finally He sent His own Son, and the nation of Israel killed Him also (Isaiah 5:1-7).

•**VERSES 10-11** Since Israel rejected God's Son, the Gospel was taken to the Gentiles (Psalm 118:22,23).

•**VERSES 13-15** The people hated to pay taxes to Rome.

•**VERSE 28** This question refers to the commandment that is first in importance.

•**VERSE 29** Deuteronomy 6:4.

•**VERSES 35-37** A son would never call his father "lord" in that culture, for the father was always "master."

•**VERSE 42** A mite is worth about one-eighth of a cent.

•**VERSES 43-44** God doesn't look at the amount that we give Him, but at the cost to us to give to Him.

CHAPTER 13:
THE SECOND COMING FORETOLD

•**VERSE 1** The temple was a beautiful building of very large stones faced with white marble and trimmed with gold.

•**VERSE 2** This prophecy was fulfilled within 40 years when the Roman general Titus conquered Jerusalem in 70 A.D.

•**VERSE 6** Many cults have leaders who claim to be Jesus Christ.

•**VERSE 10** Revelation 14:6.

•**VERSES 14-18** The abomination of desolation will take place when the Antichrist goes into the Holy Place of the rebuilt temple declaring that he is God.

At this point the Jews will recognize that they have been betrayed by the Antichrist. They'll flee to Petra for protection (Revelation 12:14; Isaiah 16:4).

•**VERSE 20** The elect are the Jews, God's chosen people.

•**VERSES 21-23** False prophets will try to convince the Jews that they are the long awaited Messiah.

•**VERSE 26** Acts 1:11, Revelation 1:7.

•**VERSE 28** The fig tree symbolizes the nation of Israel.

•**VERSE 30** The generation that sees the rebirth of Israel as a nation will not pass until these prophecies are fulfilled.

CHAPTER 14:
EVENTS BEFORE THE CROSS

•**VERSE 3** Mary, the sister of Lazarus, was the woman who gave the ointment to Jesus (John 12:3).

•**VERSES 4-5** Judas complained about Mary's gift (John 12:4-6).

•**VERSES 22-25** Jesus gave new meanings to the old symbols of the Passover feast.

•**VERSE 26** The traditional songs sung after the Passover meal are Psalms 115-118.

•**VERSE 29** Giving ourselves too much credit can be self-deluding (Romans 12:3).

•**VERSES 30-31** It's dangerous to put confidence in our flesh (Romans 7:18).

•**VERSE 32** "Gethsemane" means olive press.

•**VERSES 33-34** The pressure of the sins of the world and His approaching death on the cross were beginning to weigh heavily on Jesus.

•**VERSE 36** "Abba" means father.

•**VERSES 51-52** The young man was probably Mark, the author of this gospel.

CHAPTER 15:
THE TRIAL AND CRUCIFIXION

•**VERSE 1** The night meeting of the Council was illegal, so the priests had to reconvene to confirm the decision made the previous night.

•**VERSE 13** A person often gets louder when they don't have a good argument for their case.

•**VERSE 15** The term "scourging" signifies a beating of 39 lashes, designed to force a confession from the prisoner.

•**VERSE 17** Jesus was crowned with thorns. Thorns resulted from the curse brought on earth by man's sins (Genesis 3:18).

•**VERSE 22** "Golgotha" is Hebrew for skull. "Calvary" is the Latin word for skull.

•**VERSE 28** Isaiah 53:12.

•**VERSE 34** Psalm 22:1.

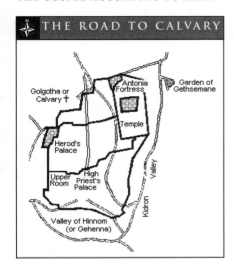

THE ROAD TO CALVARY

CHAPTER 16:
THE RESURRECTION

•**VERSE 7** This reference to Peter was probably intended to console the apostle after his denial of Christ.

Peter was very disappointed with himself, but Jesus wasn't surprised by the action since He knew what Peter would do.

•**VERSE 11** Unbelief robs the joy we should have in our victories in Christ.

•**VERSES 15-18** Jesus made these statements in the context of Christians reaching the world with the Gospel.

He protects us from dangers when we go into places in obedience to Him. He doesn't want us to purposely jeopardize ourselves to prove that we trust Him (Matthew 4:5-7).

•**VERSE 19** Ephesians 4:8-10; Romans 8:34.

•**VERSE 20** This is the proper order of evangelism. The Gospel should be preached first, with signs following as a confirmation of the Word that has been taught.

1. The key to understanding the parable of the sower (and other parables as well) is found in Mark 4:13-20. Describe Jesus' explanation of this parable.

_____

_____

_____

2. What did Jesus say is the greatest commandment? (See Mark 12:29-31.)

_____

_____

_____

3. In Mark 8:15-21, Jesus warns the disciples to beware of the leaven of the Pharisees. What does leaven symbolize in Scripture, and why is it important to guard against it? (See Matthew 16:6-12 and 1 Corinthians 5:6-8.)

_____

_____

_____

4. Many times we give the excuse that we are too tired or busy to pray. What example does Jesus set for us in that regard? (See Mark 1:35, 6:46, 14:32-41.)

_____

_____

_____

5. What was Jesus' definition of ministry in Mark 10:42-45? What did He say about His own ministry?

_____

_____

_____

THE GOSPEL ACCORDING TO
LUKE

AUTHOR OF LETTER:
Luke

WRITTEN TO:
Theophilus, "Lover of God," thought to be Luke's former master who freed the physician from his duties after both became Christians, that he might travel with Paul and tend to Paul's many infirmities.
All lovers of God.

DATE AND PLACE OF WRITING:
It is thought, and no doubt true, that Luke actually interviewed the eyewitnesses.

PURPOSE OF WRITING:
To instruct Theophilus and all Gentiles in the Gospel of Jesus Christ.
To confirm it and to let him know for certainty these things that happened.

THEME:
The Gospel of Jesus, with emphasis on the humanity of Jesus, the Son of Man.

CHAPTER 1:
THE ANNUNCIATOIN AND BIRTH OF JOHN THE BAPTIST

•**VERSES 1-3** Luke interviewed people who were eyewitnesses to the life of Christ.

•**VERSE 13** Zacharias had probably been praying for a son for many years. God answers our prayers in His time and for His purposes.

John means "God is gracious."

•**VERSES 14-19** Unbelief robs us of the joy we should experience in glad tidings.

•**VERSE 26** In the sixth month of Elizabeth's pregnancy, Gabriel was sent to tell Mary the news that she would give birth to the Messiah.

•**VERSE 27** The year before the wedding ceremony was a time of betrothal for engaged couples. If they decided to break up during this time, they had to obtain a divorce.

•**VERSE 31** Jesus is a Greek word for the Hebrew name Joshua.

•**VERSE 33** See Isaiah 9:6-7.

> 🔑 KEY WORD
>
> *Jesus = Greek for the Hebrew word Joshua, meaning "Jehovah is salvation."*

• **VERSE 34** Mary didn't question the word of God, she only questioned the method God would use to bring about His word.

• **VERSES 42-45** Elizabeth was anointed by the Holy Spirit to prophesy to Mary.

• **VERSES 52** "Seats" refers to thrones.

• **VERSES 67-69** This prophecy concerns the Messiah and His relation to the nation Israel during the time of His Second Coming (Romans 11:25-26).

CHAPTER 2:
THE BIRTH AND CHILDHOOD OF JESUS

• **VERSE 1** "Augustus" means of the gods.

• **VERSE 4** Micah 5:2.

• **VERSE 8** These were probably the temple shepherds who watched over the sheep used for sacrifices.

• **VERSE 14** Some translate this verse, "Peace among men who are approved by God" (Isaiah 57:20-21; John 14:27).

• **VERSE 24** The sacrifice of turtledoves indicates that Joseph and Mary were poor, since the sacrifice was supposed to be a lamb.

• **VERSE 34** The fall of Israel has already occurred. Now is the time for it to rise again.

• **VERSE 35** Simeon prophesied about the sorrow that Mary would feel at the crucifixion of her Son.

• **VERSES 48-49** When Mary referred to Joseph as "thy father," Jesus gently reminded her that He was doing the work of His Father.

CHAPTER 3:
THE MINISTRY OF JOHN THE BAPTIST

• **VERSE 2** The Roman government had appointed Caiaphas as the high priest, but the Jews recognized Annas as their high priest.

• **VERSE 8** John warned the Jews not to trust their ethnic heritage for salvation.

• **VERSE 17** Jesus would separate the wheat from the chaff in His ministry. The chaff will be destroyed.

• **VERSE 22** The three Persons of the Trinity are mentioned here: the Son praying, the Holy Spirit descending like a dove, and the Father speaking to His Son.

• **VERSE 23** Joseph was the son-in-law of Heli. Luke gives us Mary's genealogy.

CHAPTER 4:
JESUS BEGINS TO PREACH

• **VERSE 3** Satan wasn't questioning whether Jesus was God's Son. He was trying to tempt Jesus, knowing who He was.

• **VERSE 4** Satan tries to make the world believe that material things alone will satisfy their lives. Jesus reminds us that we have spiritual needs also.

• **VERSES 5-7** The world is in Satan's control at this time. It will be turned over to Jesus one glorious day.

Satan tempted Christ to bypass God's plan of redemption through the Cross by offering Him immediate fulfillment in exchange for worshiping him.

• **VERSE 10** Satan left out the last words, "to keep thee in all thy ways." If we're walking in the way of God, then He'll keep us.

• **VERSE 12** We're not to jeopardize ourselves to prove the existence or protection of God.

• **VERSE 17** Isaiah 61:1-2.

• **VERSE 19** Jesus stopped reading Isaiah's prophecy in the middle of the verse, for He was to fulfill only the first half in His first coming.

• **VERSES 25-29** The Jews were infuriated with Jesus because He attacked their racism and their presumption that they'd always be God's favored people.

CHAPTER 5:
A LEPER HEALED

•**VERSES 5-6** We often try to do the work of the Spirit in the energy of our flesh. Directed by the Lord, our work always bears fruit.

•**VERSE 10** Jesus called Peter to the ministry at the height of his success in the fishing industry.

•**VERSE 14** Sin causes a rotting effect in our lives like the rotting flesh caused by leprosy.

Sin and leprosy both lead to death.

•**VERSE 26** Our work for the Lord should be done so God receives the glory (Matthew 5:16).

•**VERSE 27** A "publican" was a tax collector.

The Jews hated the publicans because they gathered taxes for the Roman government. Their salaries came from any excess tax they could collect from the citizens.

Jesus later changed Levi's name to Matthew.

•**VERSES 36-39** The people felt comfortable with the traditional ways of the Pharisees. These were compared to old garments and old wineskins.

We have to stay flexible and open to change when the Holy Spirit directs us into new paths.

CHAPTER 6:
JESUS CHOOSES THE APOSTLES

•**VERSE 1** The "corn" here was actually kernels of wheat. The disciples were rubbing the kernels off the stalk and then blowing the chaff away.

•**VERSE 2** The Pharisees accused the disciples of working, and to work on the Sabbath was unlawful.

•**VERSE 11** Jesus disregarded the traditional ways, and this aggravated the Pharisees.

•**VERSE 12** Jesus prayed all night before choosing His apostles.

•**VERSE 13** Jesus had many disciples, but He chose only twelve apostles to take positions of leadership.

•**VERSE 19** "Virtue" here refers to healing power.

•**VERSE 20** This verse begins Luke's version of the Sermon on the Mount. Since Luke didn't hear it, he wrote down what was told to him by others.

•**VERSE 38** "Give, and it will be given to you" is one of the spiritual laws of God. We don't always understand how these laws work, but they do. We cannot out-do God in giving.

•**VERSE 42** A "mote" is a sliver. The "beam" is a log.

•**VERSE 48** When the storms of life come our way, we're not shaken, for our foundation is in Christ.

CHAPTER 7:
JOHN THE BAPTIST

•**VERSE 19** John thought that Jesus would take over the government and get rid of the wicked King Herod.

•**VERSE** 22 Jesus realized that John knew the Scriptures concerning the Messiah and that Jesus was fulfilling them all. John was in the king's prison.

•**VERSE** 33 John was a harsh prophet, and the Pharisees criticized him.

•**VERSE** 34 Jesus was kind, loving, and gregarious, and the Pharisees criticized Him.

•**VERSE** 44 It was customary to have one's feet washed by a servant when entering a home.

•**VERSE** 45 Friends would greet each other with a kiss.

•**VERSE** 46 It was customary to anoint a guest's hair with oil as a symbol of the joy to be shared together.

CHAPTER 8:
THE PARABLE OF THE SOWER

•**VERSE** 18 If we apply the Word of God to our daily lives, God will give us more guidance. If we hear His truths but choose to ignore them, we'll lose even the semblance of His hand on our lives.

•**VERSE** 31 "The deep" here refers to the abussos, the bottomless pit.

•**VERSE** 46 "Virtue" here again refers to healing power.

CHAPTER 9:
REQUIREMENTS FOR DISCIPLESHIP

•**VERSE** 1 Satan isn't the equal of Jesus Christ. Satan, a being created by God, isn't omniscient or eternal.

He's on the same level of power as the angel Michael, fully under the power and authority of Jesus.

•**VERSE** 2 When we submit to the lordship of Jesus Christ, we become members of His eternal kingdom with all its blessings and benefits (Isaiah 35:1-10).

This is the reason that healing often accompanies the preaching of the kingdom of God.

•**VERSE** 17 "Filled" here means that they ate until they were glutted.

•**VERSE** 18 Jesus made time for prayer, even after a tiring day.

•**VERSE** 20 The "Christ of God" means the Messiah, the Anointed One of God.

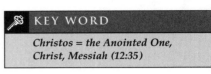

KEY WORD

Christos = the Anointed One, Christ, Messiah (12:35)

•**VERSE** 21 Jesus didn't want the people prematurely seeking to make Him their earthly king.

•**VERSE** 22 The Jews didn't think that their Messiah would suffer. They spiritualized those scriptures that spoke of the suffering of the Messiah.

They thought he'd reign over the Jews as He set up the Kingdom of God on the earth.

•**VERSE** 23 The three requirements for discipleship are:

(1) Denying ourselves of whatever stands between us and a full commitment to God.

(2) "Taking up the cross," or submitting our will to the will of God (Mark 14:36).

(3) Following Jesus.

•**VERSE** 27 The mention that some standing there would not taste of death until they saw the kingdom of God was a reference to the transfiguration that Peter, James, and John would witness.

•**VERSE** 29 This transformation took place as Jesus was praying.

•**VERSE** 30 "Elias" is Elijah. Moses represents God speaking to man through the Law. Elijah represents God speaking to man through the prophets.

•**VERSE 40** Jesus gave His disciples authority over demons. They should have been able to cast the demons out of the boy.

The symptoms of possession in this child were so frightening that the disciples were overwhelmed.

•**VERSE 51** Jesus had a set purpose in going to Jerusalem.

•**VERSE 54** Jesus called James and John the "sons of thunder."

•**VERSES 55-56** Jesus didn't seek revenge upon those who reviled Him (1 Peter 2:23; Matthew 5:44; 2 Samuel 22:2-3; Isaiah 54:17; John 3:17).

Our Lord brought a message of hope and salvation.

•**VERSE 58** Jesus warned the man to consider the cost of following Him.

•**VERSES 59-60** The man's father wasn't necessarily dead yet. The man wanted to wait until his father died before he would follow Jesus.

•**VERSES 61-62** When we follow Jesus, He has to be first in our lives.

CHAPTER 10:
A HARVEST OF SOULS

•**VERSE 12** The "day" here is the Day of Judgment.

•**VERSE 17** We must deal with Satan only through the powerful name of Jesus Christ.

•**VERSE 33** The Jews hated Samaritans and would have no dealings with them.

•**VERSES 41-42** Sometimes we get so busy serving Jesus that we don't take time to sit and listen to Him.

CHAPTER 11:
JESUS ADDRESSES THE PHARISEES

•**VERSE 13** If we ask the Father for a spiritual gift, He won't give us something evil.

•**VERSE 14** The demon had inhibited the speech of the possessed man.

•**VERSE 22** Jesus is stronger than Satan and has destroyed his defenses.

•**VERSE 31** The "queen of the south" is the Queen of Sheba.

CHAPTER 12:
THE FAITHFUL STEWARD

•**VERSE 7** We're God's children and we're very valuable and precious to Him.

•**VERSES 22-32** We're to establish our priorities so that we put spiritual needs first in our lives, then the Lord will provide our material needs.

•**VERSES 35-46** We're to watch expectantly for the coming of our Lord Jesus while we continue in the ministry He has given to us.

CHAPTER 13:
THE KINGDOM OF GOD

•**VERSE 1** The shadow of the Cross looms over this part of Christ's ministry.

•**VERSE 2** The Jews often considered sickness and misfortune as judgment for unrighteousness.

•**VERSES 6-9** The fruit of love should be working in our lives (John 15:1-5; 1 John 4:20).

•**VERSE 14** The ruler of the synagogue was blinded by tradition to the miracle of God's healing power.

•**VERSE 16** Jesus used the term "daughter of Abraham" in the spiritual sense to denote a woman of faith (John 8:39-44).

•**VERSE 19** In biblical interpretations, the tree represents the Church and birds symbolize evil. Many evil influences permeate the Church today.

•**VERSE 21** Leaven always symbolizes evil in scriptural interpretation (1 Corinthians 5:6-7).

•**VERSE 23** Though multitudes of people went to see Jesus, not all of them accepted His teachings.

•**VERSE 24** "Strive" here means agonize (Philippians 3:14; 1 Corinthians 10:12, 11:31; 2 Peter 1:10).

⚷ KEY WORD

"Strive" is the translation of a Greek word meaning agonize

•**VERSE 25** Jesus knocks at the door of a man's heart, asking to come in (Revelation 3:20).

•**VERSES 31-32** Jesus knew that Herod wouldn't be able to kill Him prematurely.

•**VERSE 34** Romans 11:25.

CHAPTER 14:
A DINNER WITH THE PHARISEES

•**VERSES 13-14** God has great concern for the poor.

He watches our actions, and He'll reward us for giving to the poor (Proverbs 19:17).

•**VERSES 16-24** The Gospel of the kingdom of God was presented to the Jews first and they rejected it, just as the invited guests in this parable refused the nobleman's invitation.

The Gospel was then taken to the Gentiles. They accepted it readily, just as the people in the street accepted the invitation to the nobleman's house.

The last few people are now being brought into God's kingdom.

•**VERSE 26** Our love for Christ has to be above our love for anyone else.

We must count the cost which a total commitment to Christ requires.

CHAPTER 15:
THE PRODIGAL SON

•**VERSE 2** The Pharisees were very careful about the people with whom they ate, because eating a meal together made them one with each other.

•**VERSE 3** Jesus tells us three parables. All three concern something once lost and now found.

•**VERSES 4-6** Jesus is the Shepherd who sought us when we were lost and saved us from the consequences of our sins (John 10:14).

He rejoices whenever He brings a lost sheep home (Zephaniah 3:17).

•**VERSE 12** Everything we own has been given to us by the Father.

•**VERSE 17** The servant of God has more than any person in the world.

God doesn't call us to be servants, though, for He makes us His children (Romans 8:16-17).

•**VERSE 20** The father smothered him with kisses.

•**VERSES 22-24** God joyfully welcomes us into His kingdom.

•**VERSES 25-32** The Pharisees were like the older brother who was angry and jealous when the lost son returned.

Jesus was reaching the lost, but the Pharisees, rather than rejoicing that the unrighteous were turning to God, criticized Him for associating with sinners.

CHAPTER 16:
THE RICH MAN AND LAZARUS

•**VERSE 8** The dishonest steward was shrewd because he took advantage of his present position to arrange a comfortable future.

•**VERSE 9** We're to use the money God has given us for spiritual investments, so that we'll have treasures in heaven (Matthew 6:20).

•**VERSES 10-13** We're to control the money God gives us, rather than allow the money to master us.

•**VERSE 15** The favor and admiration of man doesn't add anything to our standing with God.

•**VERSES 22-26** Before the sacrifice of Jesus, the dead went to Hades (called "Sheol" or grave in the Old Testament). There were two sections in Hades. Abraham presided over the section of the just, and he comforted those waiting for the promised Savior, who would lead them out of their captivity (Ephesians 4:8-10; 1 Peter 3:18-20; Isaiah 61:1).

The unjust were sent to the other section where they were punished. There was a great gulf between the two sections that couldn't be crossed.

•**VERSES 27-31** Even if unbelievers could see miracles, they would rationalize them away and wouldn't believe. The Word of God is the only basis for faith.

CHAPTER 17:
THE HEALING OF THE LEPERS

•**VERSE 1** When we make a stand for godliness, the world will attack us.

•**VERSE 2** The millstones in Israel were large and heavy. A millstone cast into the sea is a symbol of destruction (Revelation 18:21).

•**VERSE 4** We need help from God to forgive people repeatedly.

•**VERSE 10** We don't obligate God to us by serving Him.

•**VERSE 14** Healed lepers were to show themselves to the priests, who would examine them to determine whether they were fully cured (Leviticus 14:2-4).

•**VERSES 15-19** The man who gave thanks for his healing was given more than physical restoration; he was made whole in body, soul, and spirit.

•**VERSE 21** "Within" is a poor translation of the Greek word. It actually means among or in the midst of.

•**VERSE 26** When Jesus comes for His church, the world will be conducting business as usual, without any awareness of God's impending judgment.

•**VERSE 29** The church will be taken away from the destruction that will come, just as Lot was removed from Sodom before it was destroyed.

•**VERSE 37** Job 39:27-30.

CHAPTER 18:
THE RICH YOUNG RULER

•**VERSE 1** Jesus used this parable of a persistent widow to teach us to continue in prayer until we receive an answer.

•**VERSES 6-8** If an unjust judge would be moved to help a poor widow, how much more would a loving, heavenly Father be moved to help His children.

•**VERSE 19** By addressing Jesus as "Good Master," the young ruler had unknowingly recognized that He was God.

CHAPTER 19:
JESUS ENTERS JERUSALEM

•**VERSE 5** "Abide" here means to settle down and make oneself at home.

•**VERSES 12-27** We're to continue working and living normal lives, being good stewards of those things which God has entrusted us until Jesus returns.

•**VERSES 35-38** This was the day that the prophets had foretold—when the King would enter Jerusalem (Daniel 9:24-25; Zechariah 9:9; Psalm 118:24-26).

CHAPTER 20:
THE PARABLE OF THE VINEYARD

•**VERSES 9-18** The vineyard is the nation Israel (Isaiah 5:1-7).

The vineyard hadn't produced the fruit that God wanted, so He sent prophets to Israel, but the people wouldn't hear them.

Finally, he sent His Son, but the people rejected and killed Him. After this, the Gospel was taken to the Gentiles.

•VERSE 27 The Sadducees didn't believe in the resurrection, angels, or spirits. They were materialists.

•VERSES 41-44 The son was always subordinate to the father in Israel's social structure. A father would never call his son "my lord."

David was prophesying of His Lord, the Messiah Jesus Christ.

•VERSE 46 Jesus warned the disciples against the proud, self-righteous attitude of the scribes.

CHAPTER 21:
THE DESTRUCTION OF JERUSALEM

•VERSE 2 Two mites equal about one quarter of a cent.

•VERSES 3-4 God doesn't measure our gifts by the amount, but by the sacrifice.

•VERSE 6 In 70 A.D., Titus attacked Jerusalem and his soldiers tore the temple apart stone by stone.

•VERSE 8 One of the signs of the return of Jesus Christ will be a proliferation of false messiahs.

•VERSE 11 "Divers" means diverse, different.

•VERSES 12-13 God allowed the disciples to get into situations where their testimonies for Jesus Christ would be delivered to large, captive audiences.

•VERSES 14-15 Acts 7.

•VERSE 16 Many of the apostles and early Christians were martyred for their faith in Christ.

•VERSE 18 Matthew 10:28.

•VERSE 24 More than one million Jews were killed by the army of Titus, and

the remaining Jews were dispersed among the Gentile nations (Daniel 9:26).

In 1967, the Jews took Jerusalem from the Gentiles again.

•VERSE 25 This section of the prophecy deals with the end times and the Tribulation.

"With perplexity" means with no way out.

•VERSE 29 The fig tree refers to the nation of Israel.

•VERSE 32 "Generation" here may refer to the Jews as a race of people, or the generation living at the time when these prophecies are fulfilled.

•VERSE 34 "Surfeiting" means over-eating.

Three traps that men in the last times can fall into are: (1) overeating, (2) drunkenness, (3) the cares of our busy lives.

•VERSE 36 We should pray that we'll be allowed to escape the judgment of God about to be poured upon the earth and to stand before the Son of Man (Revelation 5:9-10).

CALVARY DISTINCTIVE

"Watch ye therefore, and pray always, that ye may be accounted worthy to escape all these things that shall come to pass, and to stand before the Son of man" (Luke 21:36).

I firmly believe that the Church will not go through the Great Tribulation. Now if Jesus tells me to pray for something, believe me, I will do it!

CHAPTER 22:
THE LAST SUPPER

•VERSE 3 At this point Satan entered Judas. Judas opened himself to possession by Satan when he surrendered to greed.

•**VERSES 15-16** Jesus had celebrated previous Passovers with His disciples, but He had been looking forward to this one.

It would be the last one He would share with them until the Kingdom Age.

•**VERSES 19-20** Jesus gave new meanings to the symbolism of the Passover feast.

•**VERSE 27** Jesus set the example for our conduct by serving the disciples. The true minister is a servant.

•**VERSES 31-32** Our Lord knew what Peter would have to learn, and how he would encourage the others after he truly changed.

•**VERSE 37** Isaiah 53:12.

•**VERSE 39** "Wont" means accustomed to.

•**VERSE 42** The Cross of Jesus Christ is an offense to people because it affirms there is only one way of salvation (Galatians 5:11).

People don't like the narrowness of coming to God on His terms. They would rather believe that many roads lead to God.

CHAPTER 23:
THE CRUCIFIXION

•**VERSES 1-2** The chief priests and rulers deliberately lied (Luke 20:22-25).

•**VERSE 8** Herod wanted Jesus to entertain him by performing a miracle.

•**VERSE 23** How many horrible crimes have been committed when the voice of the crowd prevailed.

•**VERSE 34** Jesus prayed for those who were nailing His hands and feet to the cross (Isaiah 53:12).

•**VERSES 35-39** Jesus had many temptations to save Himself.

•**VERSE 43** Even in the hour of death, Jesus experienced the joy of granting forgiveness to a lost sinner (Hebrews 12:3).

Paradise was a part of Hades where Abraham and the other saints waited for Jesus Christ to come and set them free.

•**VERSE 45** The darkness couldn't have been caused by an eclipse, since the Passover was held during a full moon.

CHAPTER 24:
THE RESURRECTION

•**VERSE 11** The disciples were afraid to believe at this point, since they were so grieved and discouraged by the death of Jesus.

•**VERSE 13** "Threescore furlongs" is about eight miles.

•**VERSE 16** The two disciples were spiritually blind because of their grief.

•**VERSE 21** Their hope in Jesus was gone.

•**VERSE 27** Jesus fulfilled the Old Testament prophecies concerning the Messiah, which present the strongest proof that He is the Son of God (2 Peter 1:16-21).

•**VERSE 44** Many psalms also prophesied of Jesus Christ (Psalms 2,22,110).

•**VERSE 45** A man who believes in Jesus and is Spirit-filled can give instruction in the Scripture far superior to the teaching of a highly educated nonbeliever (1 Corinthians 2:14; Romans 1:22; Psalm 14:1).

•**VERSE 48** Our lives are a witness for Jesus Christ to those around us.

1. Details about the birth of John the Baptist are only found in Luke's Gospel. What is the description of John, that the angel gave to Zechariah in Luke 1:15-17?

_____

_____

_____

2. What is the description of Jesus that the angel Gabriel gave to Mary in Luke 1:32-33?

_____

_____

_____

3. During the Last Supper with His disciples, Jesus gave new meanings to the old symbols of the Passover Feast. What were these new meanings? Why are we to partake in communion? (See Luke 22:19-20.)

_____

_____

_____

4. Jesus had been scourged, brutally beaten, and mocked. What was His response when they hung Him on the cross? (See Luke 23:34.)

_____

_____

_____

5. Jesus fulfilled the Old Testament prophecies concerning the Messiah. In Luke 24:46-47, after Jesus rose from the dead, what did He remind the disciples concerning the Scriptures?

_____

_____

_____

THE GOSPEL ACCORDING TO
JOHN

AUTHOR OF LETTER:
John

WRITTEN TO:
The world.

DATE AND PLACE OF WRITING:

The Gospel of John was the fourth and last gospel to be written.

The date of writing is not known for certain, possibly between 85 and 90 A.D., probably written from Ephesus.

PURPOSE OF WRITING:

For the purpose of convincing people that Jesus is the Christ, and that by believing in Him they might have life in His name (John 20:31).

To counteract some of the false concepts and heresy concerning Jesus Christ that had developed in the very first century, the Apostle John found it necessary to set forth in his gospel the deity of Christ.

THEME:

The Gospel of Jesus, with emphasis on Jesus being the Son of God.

CHAPTER 1:
JESUS CHRIST AS GOD IN THE FLESH

•**VERSE 1** Before anything was ever created there was the Word (Genesis 1:1). "The Word was God" literally means that Jehovah God was the Word.

•**VERSE 3** Jesus Christ is the Creator of this universe. All things are held together by Christ (Colossians 1:15-17).

•**VERSE 5** The darkness didn't understand the light of Jesus Christ.

•**VERSES 6-8** This is in reference to the ministry of John the Baptist.

•**VERSE 9** A better translation would be, "Who was the true Light, who by His coming into the world has brought light to every man."

•**VERSE 11** "His own" refers to the Jewish people.

•**VERSE 13** We have been born again by the will of God, not by our own will.

In John 15:16 Jesus said, "Ye have not chosen me, but I have chosen you" (Romans 8:30; Ephesians 2:8). This shouldn't be carried to the extreme of continuously resisting His grace.

•VERSE 14 The purpose of the incarnation is that God might communicate to us the truth about Himself. Jesus Christ is God come in human flesh (Philippians 2:7).

•VERSE 15 Although John the Baptist was Jesus' older cousin, John states that Jesus came before him.

•VERSE 17 The Law was given to the nation Israel to establish fellowship between God and man.

This "old covenant" was based upon man's faithfulness. Because man couldn't keep the Law, his fellowship with God was destroyed (Isaiah 59:1-2).

God established a "new covenant" with man which is based upon God's faithfulness: the finished work of Christ. Through Him we have continual fellowship with God by His grace (God's unmerited favor).

•VERSE 21 Malachi 4:5; Revelation 11:3-12; Matthew 17:11; Deuteronomy 18:15.

•VERSE 34 This is John the Baptist's testimony of Jesus Christ.

•VERSE 36 John the Baptist even sought to point his own disciples to Jesus Christ and not to draw attention to himself. 1 Peter 1:18-19.

CHAPTER 2:
WATER INTO WINE

•VERSES 1-12 Jesus isn't condoning the drinking of wine (Proverbs 20:1, Proverbs 23:29-35, Ephesians 5:18, 1 Corinthians 6:12).

•VERSES 14-17 The high priests owned the stalls for the animals. The money changers were charging a 25-percent exchange rate.

God hates the merchandising of religion.

•VERSES 19-20 The Jews thought Jesus was referring to the temple that Herod had started to build.

CHAPTER 3:
BORN AGAIN

•VERSES 1-7 By all natural standards of salvation, Nicodemus had it made. He was a Jew, God's chosen people. He was a Pharisee, a man who spent his whole life endeavoring to keep the righteousness of the Law. He was a ruler among the Jews.

In spite of these things he still needed to be born again.

•VERSE 2 Acts 2:22; John 14:11.

•VERSE 5 "Born of water" refers to physical birth, as the protective liquid is brought forth from the mother's womb at birth.

•VERSE 14 This is a type of crucifixion (Numbers 21:7-9). Moses took the symbol of sin (serpent) and the symbol of judgment (brass) and put it upon a pole.

All who looked upon it were healed of the poisonous snakebite. Those who didn't acknowledge it would die.

•VERSES 15-18 We can be born again and escape the judgment of God by simply believing in Him.

•VERSE 17 Jesus doesn't condemn us; man condemns. Jesus came to save us, and He is praying to the Father on our behalf (Romans 8:34).

•VERSES 19-21 We're condemned when we reject God's offer of salvation by not coming to the Light.

•VERSE 29 John was content just to be a friend of the Bridegroom.

•VERSE 34 The fullness of the Spirit was upon Christ.

CHAPTER 4:
JESUS AND THE SAMARITAN WOMAN

•VERSES 7-13 Jesus is talking about the thirst in man's spirit for God.

You will never be satisfied by trying to

quench your spiritual thirst with physical experiences.

•**VERSE 20** This refers to Mount Gerizim where the blessings of God were to be called out (Joshua 8:30-35).

•**VERSE 24** God wants us to worship Him in spirit and in truth.

•**VERSE 34** The will of Him who sent Jesus was to seek and to save that which was lost (Luke 19:10).

•**VERSE 38** "Other men" refers to the Old Testament prophets.

•**VERSE 41** Philip went to Samaria later, and there a great revival that took place (Acts 8:5-8).

•**VERSES 46-49** The distance from Cana to Capernaum was 12 to 15 miles. The nobleman was asking Jesus to take a day's journey to heal his son.

🗝 KEY WORD

basilikos = nobleman, an officer of the king; so this man was no doubt one of the officials in Herod's government. It is suggested by some that maybe it was Chuza (4:46).

CHAPTER 5:
THE POOL OF BETHESDA

•**VERSE 1** Under the Jewish law all adult Jewish males were required to go to Jerusalem three times a year to participate in the following feasts: (1) Feast of Passover, (2) Feast of Pentecost, and (3) Feast of Tabernacles.

•**VERSE 4** Stepping into the water was a point of contact, as faith in God was released to make the person whole.

•**VERSE 10** Exodus 31:14-15.

•**VERSE 14** In this man there was a cause and effect relationship between a continuing sin in his life and his illness. This isn't always the case.

•**VERSE 17** God cannot rest when there is human need. A man in need supersedes the Law.

•**VERSE 18** The literal Greek meaning is "continuing to make himself equal with God."

•**VERSE 25** Ephesians 4:8-10.

•**VERSES 28-29** These two resurrections are separated by 1000 years (Daniel 12:2; Revelation 20:6).

•**VERSE 31** Deuteronomy 19:15.

These four bore witness of Jesus:

•**VERSE 33** (1) John the Baptist.

•**VERSE 36** (2) Jesus' own works are a witness that the Father has sent Him (Acts 2:22; Matthew 5:16).

•**VERSE 37** (3) The Father has borne witness of Him.

•**VERSE 39** (4) The Scriptures. There are over 300 prophecies in the Old Testament that refer to the first coming of Christ (Psalm 40:7; 2 Peter 1:19).

•**VERSE 40** 1 John 5:11-12.

•**VERSES 46-47** The books of the Law testify of Jesus Christ.

CHAPTER 6:
JESUS IS THE BREAD OF LIFE

•**VERSES 1-14** This is the one miracle recorded in all four gospels.

•**VERSE 12** "Filled" literally means glutted.

•**VERSE 15** This was a premature effort to make Him their king.

•**VERSE 29** Man had already failed in doing the works of God by the Law (Micah 6:8; Matthew 5:48).

All that God requires of us now is to believe on Jesus Christ (Romans 4:5-8).

•**VERSE 35** Our souls can only find rest by faith in Christ.

•**VERSE 37** The purposes of God will still be accomplished; they aren't dependent upon man (Esther 4:13-14; Acts 13:48).

•**VERSE 44** This shows the fallacy of our own arguments and efforts to draw others to Christ.

Our requirement is to bear witness of Jesus Christ, and the Holy Spirit will do the rest.

•**VERSE 63** "Quickeneth" means makes alive.

CHAPTER 7:
THE PROMISE OF BELIEVING ON CHRIST

•**VERSE 1** "Jewry" means Jerusalem.

•**VERSES 3-5** These were Jesus' own brothers, the sons of Mary.

•**VERSE 15** Only scholars could speak Hebrew, yet Jesus, who didn't have any formal education, was speaking Hebrew.

•**VERSE 37** In those days a teacher would sit and the people would stand. (John 8:2).

A herald, an evangelist to the people, would stand and the people would sit.

Here Jesus is standing, heralding a glorious new age and proclaiming the simple Gospel.

•**VERSE 38** This literally means, "there shall gush forth torrents of living water." Jesus was describing how the Holy Spirit would flow from our lives.

•**VERSE 39** The Holy Spirit couldn't come upon the disciples until Jesus had ascended into heaven and was glorified.

The descent of the Holy Spirit was proof of Christ's ascension and glorification (Acts 2:32-33).

•**VERSE 40** Deuteronomy 18:15,18.

CHAPTER 8:
THE WOMAN TAKEN IN ADULTERY

•**VERSE 5** Under the Law, the Jews should have also brought the man to be stoned.

In those days there was active discrimination against women. Christianity has freed women and set them on equal footing with men before God (Galatians 3:28).

•**VERSE 10** Jesus didn't come to condemn, but to save (John 3:17-18; Romans 8:1-4).

•**VERSE 24** Jesus is actually using the name of God, "I AM." The word "He" was inserted by the translators (Exodus 3:14; John 8:58).

•**VERSE 28** "Lifted up" refers to the Cross.

•**VERSE 33** These are the unbelieving Jews who are answering Jesus.

In reality, they were under Roman rule, but they wouldn't acknowledge it.

God has placed a beautiful spirit of strength, independence, and nationalism in the Jews.

•**VERSE 44** The desire of their father, Satan, was to destroy Jesus.

•**VERSE 56** There are two different instances when Abraham may have seen Jesus: (1) As Melchizedek (Genesis 14:18; Psalm 110:4; Hebrews 5-7), (2) While Abraham was interceding (Genesis 18). These manifestations of God are called theophanies.

•**VERSE 58** I AM is the name of the eternal God.

CHAPTER 9:
THE MAN BORN BLIND IS HEALED

•**VERSES 1-2** The disciples associated the man's blindness with either his sin or the sin of his parents.

•**VERSE 3** It would be better for this verse to end after "parents." As it stands, the verse reads as though the man was born blind just so Jesus could heal him.

•**VERSE 4** It would be better for this verse to start with "but" from verse 3.

•**VERSE 7** Jesus used different methods of healing.

•**VERSE 16** Jesus broke the law by making a man well on the Sabbath

•**VERSE 34** The Pharisees also related the man's blindness to sin (verse 3).

•**VERSES 35-38** Jesus plainly told the man that He was the Son of God (John 4:6-13).

•**VERSE 39** Jesus is using a physical healing to make a spiritual analogy. Jesus came to heal the sick (Matthew 9:12).

CHAPTER 10:
THE GOOD SHEPHERD

•**VERSES 1-7** A sheepfold had only one entrance. The shepherd would sleep in front of that entrance, making himself the door. He'd protect the sheep from wolves, wind, and storms.

Jesus is our Shepherd protecting us from Satan.

•**VERSE 8** There were men who claimed to be the Messiah before Christ.

•**VERSE 10** Thieves don't have a beneficent interest in the sheep.

•**VERSES 12-13** Many ministers are hirelings who don't care for the sheep (Philippians 2:19-20).

•**VERSE 16** "Other sheep" refers to Gentile Christians. Jesus brings Jewish and Gentile Christians together into one fold.

•**VERSE 18** Nobody killed Jesus. He laid down His life (Matthew 27:50).

•**VERSE 22** This feast called the Feast of Lights, falls around the winter solstice.

•**VERSES 27-28** Romans 8:35.

•**VERSE 30** "One" here literally means one in substance and nature.

•**VERSE 33** The Jews accused Jesus of continually making Himself God.

•**VERSE 34** "Gods" here is a reference to the judges (Exodus 22:8-9).

CHAPTER 11:
THE RAISING OF LAZARUS

•**VERSE 1** These two sisters had different personalities.

Mary showed her love by devotionally sitting and visiting with Jesus. Martha showed her love by actions and being busy (Luke 10:38-42).

•**VERSE 3** Here the word "lovest" in the Greek is phileo, to be fond of, to admire.

•**VERSE 4** Jesus is saying that Lazarus' death wasn't a final one.

•**VERSES 5-7** Here the word "loved" in the Greek is agape, to have a deep, divine, fervent love.

Lest we prejudge and question Jesus' purpose, the writer stresses the fact that Jesus loved them with a divine love.

•**VERSE 9** "Twelve hours" refers to the sunlight period of the day. "Day" here means daylight.

•**VERSE 11** The term "sleep" is used later in the New Testament to refer to the death of a Christian. The experience of death for a believer and a nonbeliever is vastly different.

•**VERSE 14** Literally, "Lazarus died."

•**VERSE 15** Jesus said this so that the faith of His disciples might be increased and that God might be glorified.

•**VERSES 19-20** In the Jewish culture, the depth of the love for the deceased was demonstrated by the amount of mourning, even to the point of hiring professional mourners.

•**VERSE 21** Death seems to be an opportunity for natural man to blame God. Death is the result of man's sin.

•**VERSE 25** Matthew 27:52,53; Ephesians 4:8,9; 1 Peter 3:19,20.

•**VERSE 26** The moment a Christian dies, he moves out of his earthly body and into his incorruptible body (1 Corinthians 15:51-53; 2 Corinthians 5:1-8; Philippians 1:23).

•**VERSE 33** This "weeping" in the Greek is wailing.

The Greek word for "groaned in the spirit" signifies wrath or anger.

As Jesus was looking at the anguish in the faces of those around Him, He was angry over the issue of sin which had caused man such death and sorrow.

•**VERSE 35** "Wept" here means that tears began to pour down His cheeks.

•**VERSE 38** Jesus was "groaning in Himself" because He was angry at sin.

•**VERSE 55** To prepare for worshiping God during the holy feast days, the Jews had to perform certain rites of purification.

•**VERSE 56** The chief priests and Pharisees had probably issued a warrant for Jesus' arrest.

CHAPTER 12:
THE TRIUMPHANT ENTRY

•**VERSE 2** Martha isn't complaining anymore. She has learned to serve Jesus from the heart (1 Peter 5:2; 2 Corinthians 9:7).

•**VERSE 3** Mary must have sensed that Jesus was troubled, as He knew that He'd be crucified soon. Anointing Him was her expression of love.

•**VERSE 6** Judas had stolen from the treasury. The word "bare" should be translated pilfered.

•**VERSE 13** "Hosanna" in Hebrew means save now (Psalm 118:25).

•**VERSE 23** John 2:4.

•**VERSES 24-26** Jesus here is speaking of Himself. Through His death, the Church would be multiplied.

•**VERSE 31** "The judgment of this world" was to fall upon Jesus.

"The prince of this world is to be cast out," meaning that Satan will be brought down or destroyed.

Through Jesus' death on the cross for our sins, victory has come over Satan's power (Colossians 2:14-15).

•**VERSE 32** "Lifted up" refers to the Cross. This verse doesn't mean that if we exalt Him then He'll draw all men to Himself.

•**VERSE 38** Isaiah 53:1.

•**VERSE 39** It's possible to harden your heart to Jesus Christ once too often so that you "could not believe" (Genesis 6:3; Jeremiah 14:10-12).

•**VERSE 40** When the Lord hardens the heart, the literal meaning is "to make firm stout, or strong" (Exodus 7:13-14:8).

•**VERSE 43** Man's opinion had a stronger hold on their lives than did God's thoughts about them.

•**VERSE 45** John 14:9.

•**VERSE 50** Jesus is placing Himself in total unity and identity with the Father. You cannot have one to the exclusion of the other.

CHAPTER 13:
THE LAST PASSOVER

•**VERSE 1** "Unto the end" can also be translated "unto the uttermost."

•**VERSE 4** In girding Himself with a towel, Jesus took the position of a bondslave.

•**VERSE 14** In those days the washing of feet was the lowliest act a bondslave could perform.

•**VERSE 15** Jesus is saying this to the apostles, the leaders of the early

Church. They were to take the position of servants.

Three criteria are used in establishing something for general Church practice:

(1) It must be taught by Christ.

(2) There must be an example in the Book of Acts.

(3) There must be practical teaching on it in the epistles.

Thus, we hold water baptisms and practice the Lord's Supper. Foot washings aren't mentioned in the Book of Acts or epistles, and thus are not considered to be a continuing church practice.

⚜ CALVARY DISTINCTIVE

"A new commandment I give unto you, That ye love one another; as I have loved you, that ye also love one another" (John 13:34).

God's supreme desire for us is that we experience His love and then share that love with others.

•**VERSE 19** Here Jesus used the prophetic utterance "I AM" to prove who He was.

•**VERSE 23** This disciple was John.

•**VERSE 26** Giving a sop is like making a toast to the person or offering him friendship.

Judas may have been Satan incarnate (John 6:70, 17:12; Acts 1:25).

•**VERSE 27** Jesus was giving Judas the opportunity to back out. Man makes his own choice, and God ratifies that choice.

•**VERSE 31** Jesus is referring to the Cross.

•**VERSE 34** Rather than a new commandment, a new emphasis is given in the degree we are to love one another.

This can only be fulfilled as we yield to the work of the Holy Spirit in our lives.

•**VERSES 37-38** Peter wanted to die for the Lord, but he had trouble living for the Lord. To live for Christ is sometimes harder than to die for Him.

CHAPTER 14:
THE PROMISE OF THE SPIRIT

•**VERSE 1** This verse should be a continuation of the previous verse.

Because Peter was to fail, Jesus went on to say in this verse, "Let not your heart be troubled." God cannot be disappointed in our failures, because He knows what is in us. We expect more out of ourselves and become discouraged.

•**VERSE 2** "Mansions" literally means abiding places.

•**VERSE 3** Jesus promises to come again.

•**VERSE 6** Jesus rules out every other religious system. He isn't "a" way but "the" only way to the Father (Matthew 7:13-14).

•**VERSES 7-9** Jesus was such a perfect witness of the Father that He could make this claim.

•**VERSE 11** The works of Christ were the proof of His origin (Acts 2:22).

•**VERSE 12** "Greater works" could possibly mean greater in number. Jesus was going to the Father; the Holy Spirit was to descend and would touch lives throughout the world.

•**VERSE 14** This is a beautiful promise for prayer. The purpose of prayer is to get God's will done, not our own.

•**VERSE 15** The proof of love is obedience to the command of Christ (1 John 4:20).

•**VERSE 16** God has given us the Holy Spirit to enable us to do His work. The Greek word is parakletos, one called alongside to help (John 15:5; Romans 7:18).

KEY WORD

*parakletos = comforter; kletos is to be
called, and para is alongside or with;
one who is called alongside (14:16).*

•**VERSE 17** We can have a twofold relationship with the Holy Spirit.

(1) "With you" in the Greek is para. Prior to conversion, the Holy Spirit convicted you of sin and drew you with loving kindness to Jesus.

(2) When you open the door to Jesus the Holy Spirit comes in and begins to dwell "in you" (en in the Greek) (1 Corinthians 12:3; 1 Corinthians 3:16; Ephesians 5:18).

A further relationship a person can have with the Holy Spirit is "upon or over you" (epi in the Greek) (Acts 1:8). This is where the Holy Spirit flows out of your life like a torrent of living water.

•**VERSE 18** Matthew 18:20, 28:20; Revelation 1:13,16.

•**VERSE 19** They saw Him after He rose from the dead.

The resurrection of Jesus Christ gives us living hope (1 Peter 1:3) for eternal life; it's the affirmation that all Jesus said is true.

•**VERSE 21** Possessing the commandments but not keeping them condemns a man (Romans 2:12,13; James 1:22).

If you love the Lord and prove it by obedience, God will manifest Himself to you.

•**VERSE 23** "Abode" is the same as abiding places in John 14:2.

God can only dwell in an atmosphere of love (Revelation 2:4-5).

•**VERSE 26** This is an illustration of the Trinity. The Holy Spirit is promised to be the teacher.

If you feed on the Word of God, the Holy Spirit will bring it to your remembrance when it is needed.

•**VERSE 27** This is more than peace with God (Colossians 1:20). We can have the same peace of God that Jesus had.

•**VERSE 28** The Father was greater than Jesus at that time, because of Christ's limitations with His body of flesh.

We shouldn't be troubled when Christians die, because they go to the Father and receive a new body from Him.

•**VERSE 29** Jesus shows us that prophecy proves that He speaks the truth.

•**VERSE 30** "Prince of this world" refers to Satan. This world is currently under the power and authority of Satan (Matthew 4:8,9).

We shouldn't blame God for tragedies in this world.

•**VERSE 31** God's commandment to Christ was that He demonstrate His love by dying for this world (Philippians 2:6-8).

CHAPTER 15:
THE VINE AND THE BRANCHES

•**VERSES 1-5** The Jews were familiar with the symbol of the vine. (Isaiah 5:1-7; Matthew 21:33-41).

•**VERSE 2** Christians who bring forth fruit are purged so that they'll bring forth more fruit.

•**VERSE 3** The Word of God acts as a cleansing agent when we read it.

•**VERSE 4** Galatians 5:17-24.

•**VERSE 5** Philippians 4:13.

•**VERSE 6** You are eternally secure as you abide in Christ.

•**VERSE 7** "Ask" in the Greek is "you will demand."

•**VERSE 11** Joy is a quality of man's spirit, independent of outward circumstances, and the result of keeping God's commandments (John 16:24; 1 John 1:4).

• **VERSE** 12 The fruit of the Spirit is love. The only way to love in the spirit is to abide in the Spirit.

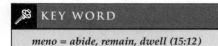

KEY WORD

meno = abide, remain, dwell (15:12)

• **VERSE** 16 God has the right to choose, and He has chosen us to enter into His eternal love. God doesn't turn anyone away who wants to enter. Through our prayers God can give us what He has always wanted to give us.

• **VERSES** 18-21 Persecution from the world will come upon Christians because the world doesn't know God.

• **VERSE** 22 Man will be judged by the amount of light given him. With knowledge comes responsibility (Luke 12:42-48).

• **VERSE** 27 Acts 1:21-22.

CHAPTER 16:
THE DISCIPLES WARNED OF PERSECUTION

• **VERSE** 2 Acts 8:1-3, 9:1-2.

• **VERSE** 4 Jesus didn't reveal these things until now because the disciples couldn't have accepted them.

• **VERSE** 6 This is an attitude we often take toward death. The disciples should have been happy that Jesus was going to the Father.

• **VERSE** 7 Acts 2:37-38.

• **VERSE** 8 The Spirit makes us conscious of sin, righteousness, and judgment.

• **VERSE** 9 The only sin man will be condemned for is rejecting Christ.

• **VERSE** 10 Jesus fulfilled the only righteous standard God will accept. In order to be righteous, we must believe on Jesus.

• **VERSE** 11 Satan was judged and defeated at the Cross.

Because Satan was defeated, we can enter into the victory of Christ.

• **VERSE** 13 The purpose of the Holy Spirit is to be the spokesman for God; He leads us to Jesus.

• **VERSE** 16 In the first part of this verse Jesus talks about seeing Him literally. In the second part He talks about seeing Him with spiritual eyes.

• **VERSE** 20 He's talking about the three-day period after His death.

• **VERSE** 21 We as Christians are in travail now, but we'll have complete joy when we enter into heaven.

• **VERSE** 23 We should be praying to God in the name of Jesus.

• **VERSE** 24 Joy is related to our prayer life (James 4:3).

• **VERSES** 26-27 We can ask the Father ourselves, because He loves us.

• **VERSE** 32 The time was coming when the disciples would go through their most severe trials. We're never alone, because the Father is with us always.

• **VERSE** 33 Jesus wants us to have peace. The source of this world's tribulation comes from Satan who is trying to antagonize us.

The source of the Great Tribulation at the end of the world is from God who will send judgment against the Christ-rejecting world.

CHAPTER 17:
CHRIST'S INTERCESSORY PRAYER

• **SYNOPSIS** This is truly the Lord's prayer. Jesus is interceding for His disciples and all future believers. This prayer is offered just before He enters the Garden of Gethsemane.

• **VERSE** 1 The first petition is that the Son might be glorified. Jesus' hour had come; He was to be glorified through the crucifixion. We glory in the work of the Cross (Galatians 6:14).

•**VERSE 2** This is divine election (John 6:44).

•**VERSE 3** There is only one true God; there are many false gods.

•**VERSE 4** God's work of salvation for lost man was finished at the Cross.

•**VERSE 6** "Thy name" refers to the name Jehovah-shuah which means "Jehovah is salvation." This was the mission given to Jesus.

•**VERSES 6-8** Jesus is talking about His disciples.

•**VERSE 10** We belong to both the Father and the Son. We are God's inheritance and His treasure (Ephesians 1:18; 1 Peter 2:9; Matthew 13:44).

•**VERSE 11** 1 John 1:3.

•**VERSE 12** "The son of perdition" refers to Judas Iscariot. In 2 Thessalonians 2:3 "son of perdition" is also used; Judas may be the Antichrist.

•**VERSE 14** We are to be in this world, but when the world starts getting into us, we're in trouble.

•**VERSE 17** "Sanctified" means to be set apart for God's exclusive use. The Word of God sanctifies us. Sanctification is a gradual process and a work of the Holy Spirit.

•**VERSE 20** Jesus is praying for future believers.

•**VERSE 23** "Perfect" here means complete.

•**VERSE 24** Jesus desires to deliver us out of this world and for us to behold His glory.

CHAPTER 18:
JESUS BEFORE THE HIGH PRIESTS AND PILATE

•**VERSES 5-8** Jesus is using the eternal name of God, I AM, which is Jehovah and means the becoming one.

•**VERSE 11** Jesus had resigned completely to the will of the Father.

•**VERSE 13** At this time in Jewish history, there were two high priests, Annas and Caiaphas.

•**VERSE 15** "Another disciple" refers to John.

•**VERSE 23** Instead of turning the other cheek, Jesus rebuked him (Matthew 5:39).

•**VERSE 28** Pilate's judgment hall was in the court of the Gentiles and would make a Jew ceremonially unclean prior to the Passover.

In the name of religion the Jews were careful to observe their traditional law, yet they wanted to see Christ crucified.

•**VERSE 32** The Jews didn't use crucifixion; it was a Roman way of putting people to death.

•**VERSES 33-34** Jesus was questioning Pilate's sincerity in asking Him who He was.

•**VERSE 37** Jesus answered, "You said it" literally, "The inference of what you are saying is correct" (Isaiah 9:6-7).

•**VERSE 38** In asking "What is truth?" Pilate was being cynical. Pilate was living near the end of the age of Greek philosophy, a time when all hope in ever discovering truth was gone.

•**VERSE 40** Jesus was too much of a threat to the security and position of the religious leaders.

CHAPTER 19:
THE CRUCIFIXION OF JESUS CHRIST

•**VERSE 1** Pilate was caught in a political vise and had to lay aside his own principles.

He knew that Jesus was innocent, and he tried to avoid making a decision he knew was wrong (Isaiah 53:5; Matthew 27:4; Luke 23:41).

A historian of that time recorded that Pilate ultimately committed suicide (Matthew 16:25).

The purpose of scourging was to make prisoners confess their crimes (Acts 22:24).

• **VERSE 2** Purple was a royal color.

• **VERSE 3** Isaiah 52:14.

• **VERSE 7** Literally, "He is continually making himself the Son of God."

• **VERSE 8** Matthew 27:19.

• **VERSE 17** "Golgotha" is rendered as "Calvary" in Latin.

• **VERSE 24** Psalm 22:18.

• **VERSE 25** Luke 2:34-35.

• **VERSE 27** John took Mary into his own home.

• **VERSE 31** Breaking their legs hastened their deaths.

• **VERSE 34** "Blood and water" indicates death by a ruptured or broken heart.

• **VERSE 36** A lamb offered as a sacrifice could not have any broken bones or blemishes (Exodus 12:46). Jesus, God's sacrificial lamb for our sins, didn't have a bone broken.

CHAPTER 20:
THE RESURRECTION OF JESUS CHRIST

• **VERSE 6** "Seeth" in the Greek means to study the situation.

• **VERSE 7** The napkin was wrapped as if Jesus was still in it.

• **VERSE 8** "Saw" in the Greek is comprehended. John understood that Jesus had risen from the dead.

• **VERSE 13** Mary still calls Jesus "Lord" even though she thinks He's dead.

• **VERSE 14** Mary turned from the angel because she was looking for her Lord.

• **VERSE 17** In the Greek Jesus said, "Don't cling to Me."

• **VERSE 18** Mary was the first witness of the risen Christ.

The Resurrection of Christ is the central message of the Gospel.

• **VERSE 19** The disciples were still fearful of the Jews.

• **VERSE 21** As God sent Jesus to earth, so Jesus was sending them to be witnesses for Him.

As He talked to them, He showed them His pierced hands, designating how difficult it would be to live as a Christian in the world

• **VERSE 22** Jesus demonstrated the power in which the disciples should walk by breathing on them the Holy Ghost (Acts 2:4).

• **VERSE 23** If a person confesses his sin and turns to Christ, we can tell him that his sins are forgiven by God.

If he refuses to confess his sin, we can tell him he will face the judgment of God.

• **VERSE 25** Thomas was very frank and straightforward (John 14:5).

• **VERSE 27** Jesus wanted the disciples to realize that He was with them even though they couldn't see Him.

• **VERSE 28** Thomas called Jesus his God (Titus 2:13; Hebrews 1:8).

• **VERSE 29** Jesus was talking about us (1 Peter 1:8).

• **VERSES 30-31** John chose certain events to write about in order to prove that Jesus Christ is truly the Son of God.

CHAPTER 21:
THE RISEN CHRIST

• **VERSE 1** Jesus makes one last appearance at the Sea of Galilee.

• **VERSE 2** The two other disciples probably weren't of the twelve.

• **VERSE 3** Simon was somewhat of a leader, and the others followed.

The first time he met Jesus, Peter was fishing, as this was his trade (Luke 5:1-11). The men caught no fish, because their work wasn't ordered by the Lord.

•VERSE 6 The full net of fish showed that the Lord directed their fishing here.

•VERSE 11 This showed Peter's physical strength. It also shows what we can have when we follow the Lord's orders.

•VERSE 15 Jesus uses the word agape here. Peter uses phileo.

"These" could mean the fish, since fishing was Peter's life, or it could refer to the other disciples (Matthew 26:31-35).

•VERSE 16 Jesus uses agape; Peter uses phileo. "Feed" means to shepherd.

•VERSE 17 Jesus uses phileo here. Peter was grieved by this.

Earlier, he felt that the Lord didn't know him (John 13:36-38; Luke 22:31-34). This time Peter realized that Jesus knew all things about him (John 14:21).

Jesus told the disciples to wait in Galilee for Him, but they didn't. If they had waited, they would have shown agape love; instead they went fishing.

•VERSE 18 Jesus foretold Peter's crucifixion.

•VERSE 19 Jesus told Peter to follow Him regardless of the cost.

•VERSE 21 Peter took his eyes off the Lord and worried about John. We need to keep our eyes on Jesus, not on others.

CALVARY DISTINCTIVE

"He saith to him again the second time, Simon, son of Jona, lovest thou me? He saith unto him, Yea, Lord; thou knowest that I love thee. He saith unto him, Feed my sheep" (John 21:16).

My job is just to love the sheep, take care of them, watch over them, feed them, tend them, and trust the Lord to build the church and add those that should be saved.

STUDY QUESTIONS FOR JOHN

1. What do you learn about Jesus in John 1:1-3?

_____

_____

_____

2. Jesus taught Nicodemus the way of salvation in John 3:3-21. What did Jesus say we must do to have eternal life? What does this mean to you?

_____

_____

_____

3. According to John 6:29 what is the only work that God requires of us?

_____

_____

_____

4. We know that we will go through many trials in this world. Write out John 16:33 and memorize it.

_____

_____

_____

5. In John chapter 15 Jesus tells us that He is the vine and we are the branches. What is the only way we can bear fruit? (See John 15:4-5.) What is that fruit? (See Galatians 5:22-23.)

_____

_____

_____

THE ACTS
OF THE APOSTLES

AUTHOR OF LETTER:

Luke

He took care of Paul's medical needs while he was going through the rigors of extensive travel in taking the Gospel into Asia Minor, Greece, and Rome.

WRITTEN TO:

Theophilus, "Lover of God," thought to be Luke's former master who freed the physician from his duties in order that he might accompany Paul.

All lovers of God.

DATE AND PLACE OF WRITING:

Sometime near 65 A.D.

PURPOSE OF WRITING:

A continuation of the Gospel According to Luke.

To tell of the continued work of Jesus through the apostles who had been anointed by the Holy Spirit.

CHAPTER 1:

THE ASCENSION OF JESUS

• **VERSES 1-2** The Book of the Acts of the Apostles was written by Luke, the beloved physician. He also wrote the Gospel of Luke. Both books are addressed to Theophilus ("lover of God").

• **VERSE 3** Second Peter 1:16.

• **VERSES 4-5** We don't have to attain a certain degree of holiness to receive the power of the Holy Spirit in our lives (Acts 8:15-17; John 7:37-39).

• **VERSE 8** The word "power" comes from the Greek word dunamis also meaning dynamic. The Holy Spirit gives us the power to be a witness of God. Before we were Christians the Holy Spirit was **with** us (Greek: para), convicting us of sin and drawing us to Christ.

Once we became Christians the Holy Spirit was **in** us (en), dwelling in us (John 14:17; 1 Corinthians 12:3, 6:19).

The third experience of the Holy Spirit is when He comes **upon** us (epi) and overflows from our lives.

✞ CALVARY DISTINCTIVE

"But ye shall receive power, after that the Holy Ghost is come upon you" (Acts 1:8).

Jesus made three promises to us about the Spirit—He is with you, He shall be in you, and you will receive the power when He comes over you, or upon you.

• **VERSE 11** Jesus went to heaven in a body and will return to earth in a body ("in like manner").

• **VERSE 14** This is the last mention of Mary, the mother of Jesus.

• **VERSE 20** Peter quoted liberally from the Psalms with knowledge and understanding.

• **VERSES 21-22** These are the requirements for apostleship.

• **VERSES 24-26** After the Holy Spirit came upon the Church, the believers didn't have to cast lots to determine the will of God because the Holy Spirit directed them.

In the Old Testament the people often went to the priests who would cast lots for direction from God. David used to have the priests cast lots before every battle.

CHAPTER 2:
GOSPEL PREACHED FOR THE FIRST TIME

• **VERSE 1** The Feast of Pentecost celebrated the harvest. The people offered the first fruits to God.

• **VERSE 4** The Holy Spirit gives us the power to live the life that God wants us to live. Other religions tell men to live a good life but give them no power to do so.

The Spirit gives us the ability to speak in tongues, but we have the control of when and how loudly to speak.

• **VERSE 11** The Christians were praising God in various languages. When we speak in unknown tongues we're speaking to God.

• **VERSE 14** When Peter stood up to speak to the people, he spoke in a known language. Those who were speaking in other tongues no doubt stopped so the message could be heard.

• **VERSES 16-21** Peter quoted Joel 2:28-32 as the scriptural basis for what was taking place.

God's Word must be the basis for our faith and practice. Experience alone is not a solid basis for our faith.

The events described in Joel are to take place in the last times just prior to the return of Jesus Christ.

Therefore, we believe that the gifts of the Spirit are for the Church until Christ returns.

• **VERSE 23** God sent Jesus to die for us.

• **VERSE 24** The resurrection of Christ is the heart of the Gospel message.

• **VERSE 27** When Jesus died, His soul went into hell (hades) for three days and three nights. He preached to the captives there (Matthew 12:40; Isaiah 61:1; 1 Peter 3:18-19).

• **VERSE 28** 1 Corinthians 13:12.

• **VERSE 37** This was the first message preached under the anointing of the Holy Spirit, where men's hearts were convicted ("pricked").

• **VERSE 38** Infant baptism cannot save, since baptism follows repentance.

• **VERSE 42** The four activities of the early Church were: (1) Bible study, (2) fellowship, (3) ordinance of the Lord's Supper, (4) prayer.

• **VERSE 47** The Holy Spirit adds to the Church those whom He chooses. It is not the work of the Church to increase its membership.

CHAPTER 3:
THE LAME MAN HEALED

•**VERSE 1** The "ninth" hour is 3 p.m.

•**VERSE 2** "Lame from his mother's womb" indicates a congenital malformation.

•**VERSE 7** Luke, as a physician, gives a medical description of a lame man's healing.

•**VERSE 12** The men of Israel should not have been surprised that their God could heal a man, since He had done so many miracles for their nation, but they had lost the awareness of the power and might of God.

Also, they were ready to honor a man for the healing rather than give God the glory.

•**VERSE 13** "Son" in the Greek is "servant" (Isaiah 53).

Peter's message is made up largely of quotes from the Old Testament, as he knew the Scriptures well.

The man God uses is a man who is:

(1) One who does not seek his own glory, but has come to the cross and is dead to self.

(2) One who is thoroughly knowledgeable in God's Word.

(3) A man of prayer.

•**VERSE 15** "Prince" is also translated Author.

•**VERSE 16** There is power in the name of Jesus Christ (John 14:13).

Peter didn't even take credit for his faith, necessary to heal the man, for he recognized that Christ deserved all the glory.

•**VERSE 17** Luke 23:34.

•**VERSES 22-25** Peter again quotes freely from the Scriptures.

CHAPTER 4:
THE PRAYER OF THE CHURCH

•**VERSES 1-2** Though the Pharisees were the instigators of Christ's death, the Sadducees were the persecutors of the early Church.

The Sadducees were materialists and didn't believe in spirits or resurrection, and the Church was preaching resurrection through Christ.

•**VERSE 8** The Holy Spirit gave Peter the courage to speak boldly to the religious council.

•**VERSES 19-20** The laws of God always supersede the laws of man.

•**VERSE 29** The Christians prayed for boldness to continue witnessing rather than for an end to the threats.

•**VERSE 32** "One soul" refers to the Christians being of one mind. They had all things in common ("in fellowship").

•**VERSES 34-37** This communal living isn't the same as the atheistic communism of today. The Christians chose to give up their personal possessions and to share among themselves.

This choice perhaps wasn't inspired by the Holy Spirit, because serious financial difficulties resulted for the church in Jerusalem.

CHAPTER 5:
THE APOSTLES GO TO PRISON

•**VERSES 3-4** These verses, as well as many others, are used as proof texts to support our belief that the Holy Spirit is God, the third Person of the Trinity.

•**VERSES 5-10** The environment of the early Church was so pure that the Holy Spirit purged the leaven.

•**VERSE 13** People became a bit leery of the apostles when they heard of the deaths of Ananias and Sapphira.

•**VERSE 15** The people had made Peter's shadow a point of contact for the release of their faith.

•**VERSE 17** The high priest was a Sadducee. "Indignation" would be better translated jealousy.

•**VERSE 19** God doesn't always deliver us from difficult circumstances, but in this case, He did deliver them from prison.

•**VERSE 28** It is glorious that Jerusalem was filled with the doctrine of Christ.

The people had asked for Jesus' blood to be upon them when they sought His crucifixion (Matthew 27:25).

•**VERSE 29** "Ought" would be better translated must.

•**VERSE 30** The shape of the cross Jesus died upon may not have been the T-shaped cross. The Greek word used in the gospels can mean post or pole.

•**VERSE 32** The obedience required to receive the Holy Spirit is to repent (Acts 2:38).

•**VERSE 34** Gamaliel was one of the most respected Jewish teachers of his day. Paul the Apostle was one of his young students.

CHAPTER 6:
THE ACCUSATION OF STEPHEN

•**VERSES 1-5** The "Grecians" in Acts were those Jews who practiced Grecian culture rather than orthodox Judaism.

The deacons chosen were Grecian Jews.

CHAPTER 7:
THE WITNESS OF STEPHEN

•**VERSE 8** The twelve patriarchs were the beginning of the twelve tribes of the nation of Israel.

•**VERSES 9-10** Though it appeared that Joseph was forsaken by God because of all the trials he had to endure, God was with him working things out for his good.

At first he was rejected by his brothers, later they bowed before him.

•**VERSE 17** The "promise" is that the children of Israel would leave Egypt to return to the land God had promised to them.

•**VERSES 26-28** Stephen pointed out that even Moses was rejected by the children of Israel and was cast out from them when he first visited them.

The Jews later had a great reverence for Moses, and recognized him as God's appointed leader.

•**VERSE 34** God sees and hears when we suffer and He will come to our aid.

•**VERSE 38** The "church in the wilderness" was the tabernacle. The "lively oracles" are the living Word of God.

•**VERSES 39-43** The people turned away from Moses again.

•**VERSE 45** "Jesus" is a reference to Joshua from the Old Testament. (Jesus is the Greek word for Joshua.)

•**VERSE 51** The true circumcision is of the heart, not of the flesh alone.

Even as their fathers did not recognize Joseph and Moses the first time around, so also they failed to recognize Jesus at His first coming.

•**VERSE 52** The prophets of the Old Testament were speaking of Jesus.

The Jews wouldn't receive the words of the prophets and persecuted them (John 5:39; Hebrews 10:7).

•**VERSE 53** The Jews believed they were properly following the law of God.

•**VERSE 58** Saul was renamed Paul.

•**VERSE 60** Stephen "fell asleep" because a Christian goes to be with Jesus when he leaves the earth and doesn't "die" in the sense that a non-Christian does (John 11:25,26; 2 Corinthians 5:1-4).

The Christian moves to a new home.

CHAPTER 8:
PHILIP'S MINISTRY

•**VERSE 1** Saul's consent to Stephen's death implies that he was voting for the stoning as a member of the Sanhedrin. As a member of the Sanhedrin he had to be married, but the Bible doesn't mention his wife.

•**VERSE 4** The persecution of the Church only served to expand it as the people were scattered to various places.

•**VERSES 5-7** Philip, like Stephen, had been faithful in waiting on tables and now God used him for bigger things.

•**VERSE 8** Great joy always comes with revival.

•**VERSES 15-17** The Holy Spirit was indwelling the believers but hadn't yet come upon them. Philip's ministry was evangelism but probably didn't include the ministry of the Holy Spirit.

•**VERSES 18-24** This was the first time that someone tried to buy position and power in the Church, but the Church was still pure enough to resist this temptation.

•**VERSE 26** Philip could have waited for God to explain why he was to leave Samaria in the midst of a great revival and go out to the desert, but he simply obeyed God and took the first step.

•**VERSES 27-28** The relation between Israel and Ethiopia dates back to the Queen of Sheba's visit with King Solomon.

The eunuch was searching for spiritual answers. God saw his heart and sent Philip to help him. God will always meet the need of a searching heart.

•**VERSE 29** This was the second step Philip was directed to take.

•**VERSES 32-35** The passage from Isaiah 53:7-8 was a prophecy about Jesus Christ (John 5:39; Hebrews 10:7).

•**VERSES 38-39** It appears that this baptism was a full immersion into the water, symbolizing the burial of the "old man."

CHAPTER 9:
THE CONVERSION OF SAUL

•**VERSE 5** The Holy Spirit had been pricking and goading Saul's conscience.

•**VERSE 6** Saul was instantly converted. The first step Saul was told to take was to go into the city.

•**VERSE 7** The men with Saul could hear the sound of a voice but couldn't distinguish the words.

•**VERSE 9** These three days of blindness must have been difficult for Saul while he reassessed his life and his new commitment to Christ.

•**VERSE 11** Saul's prayers now had a new meaning as he truly communed with God.

•**VERSE 15** God had thoroughly prepared Saul for the work He had for him to do.

Born in Tarsus, Saul was a Roman citizen with the right to appeal to Caesar. The culture in Tarsus was predominately Grecian, so Paul learned to understand the Greek mind.

Then Saul's parents sent him to school in Jerusalem, so Saul had an education in Jewish religion and culture as well.

•**VERSE 22** Saul left for Arabia for three years immediately after his conversion (Galatians 1:17-18).

•**VERSE 27** Barnabas means "the son of consolation" (Acts 4:36), and here he shows himself to be aptly named.

•**VERSE 32** Lydda is the present Israeli city of Lod.

•**VERSE 40** Peter sent everyone out of the room before he prayed for Dorcas to be revived.

CHAPTER 10:
PETER VISITS CORNELIUS

•**VERSE 4** God had taken note of the prayers and offerings Cornelius had made.

•**VERSES 9-22** God was beginning to break down the walls of prejudice in Peter.

•**VERSE 28** The Jews would not eat or lodge with Gentiles.

•**VERSE 35** The "fear" of the Lord is to hate and depart from evil and to do righteousness.

•**VERSE 42** Jesus is the Judge and the standard of righteousness by which all are to be judged.

•**VERSE 44** Here the Holy Spirit fell on the people before they were baptized in water. God demonstrated that He doesn't follow any set pattern.

•**VERSE 45** The Jews were amazed that God poured out His Spirit on the Gentiles too.

CHAPTER 11:
PETER'S VISION, AND THE GOSPEL SPREADS

•**VERSE 2** "Contended" means criticized.

•**VERSES 4-11** The fact that Luke here repeated the story of Peter and the Gentiles demonstrated the importance of the event to the Jews, who had previously thought that the Gospel was only for the Jews.

•**VERSES 12-17** Peter explained that the Spirit told him to go to Cornelius; it wasn't Peter's idea to take the Gospel to the Gentiles.

•**VERSE 18** More walls of prejudice were broken down as other Jewish Christians realized that the Gospel was for everyone.

•**VERSE 20** The Grecians were again the Jews who were following and practicing the Greek culture.

•**VERSE 22** Barnabas was a brother with a ministry of bringing people together.

•**VERSE 23** The gift of exhortation is very important in the Body of Christians to encourage believers in the practical application of spiritual principles.

•**VERSE 25** At this point Saul had been a Christian for nine years, but he had dropped out of sight for awhile.

If Barnabas hadn't sought him and exhorted him to go to Antioch, perhaps Saul wouldn't have had the ministry he did.

•**VERSE 26** The term "Christian" was first used by the world to designate the followers of Christ.

Though the world applied the name in derision, the Christians liked the term and began to use it.

 KEY WORD

Christianos = Greek word Christos with a Latin ending antios = Christianity, like Christ (11:26)

CHAPTER 12:
KING HEROD MOVES AGAINST THE CHURCH

•**VERSE 1** This King Herod is Herod Agrippa, the First. He was half-Jewish, so he often tried to ingratiate himself with Jews.

•**VERSE 2** This James was one of the sons of Zebedee.

•**VERSE 4** The word "Easter" is the King James translation of the word Passover.

The Easter holiday originated as a pagan holiday featuring colored eggs, to celebrate the new beginnings of spring (fertility).

•**VERSES 6-7** One chain was customary, but Peter was under double guard. The angel hit Peter on the side to awaken him.

•**VERSE 9** Peter thought he was dreaming or seeing a vision.

•**VERSE 11** Peter suddenly realized that he was indeed awake and had actually been freed from prison by the angel.

•**VERSE 12** This John Mark wrote the Gospel of Mark. He was the nephew of Barnabas and went on the missionary journey with Paul and Barnabas.

•**VERSE 17** God delivered Peter at this time because He still had work for Peter to do.

Our lives are in God's hands, and He takes us home in His own time.

CHAPTER 13:
THE FIRST MISSIONARY JOURNEY

•**VERSE 1** The prophets were itinerants, traveling from church to church. The teachers were usually settled in one area.

Manaen had been part of Herod's household.

•**VERSE 2** We have a blessed privilege to minister to the Lord.

The direction of the Holy Spirit probably came through the prophets who were there.

•**VERSE 4** How wonderful that the Holy Spirit was guiding the expansion of the Church, rather than men directing it.

•**VERSE 5** John Mark went along as a servant to Paul and Barnabas.

•**VERSES 7-8** Rulers often had wizards to advise them.

•**VERSE 9** Paul means "little one."

•**VERSE 13** It upset Paul that John Mark left them to return home.

•**VERSE 22** God called David a man after His own heart, because David sought to fulfill God's will.

•**VERSE 30** Once again, the resurrection of Jesus Christ is the central theme of the message.

•**VERSE 35** "Suffer" means allow.

•**VERSE 38** The forgiveness of sins is necessary if we're to have fellowship with God.

•**VERSE 39** We're justified through Christ no matter what we've done. It's just as if we had never committed a sin.

•**VERSE 48** It's not up to us to prove the truth of salvation to people.

God ordains those whom He wants to save, so the pressure isn't on us to convince people. We're to present the love and truth of the Gospel to them, and the Holy Spirit does the work in their hearts.

•**VERSE 52** Joy is an accompanying emotion when God's Spirit is working.

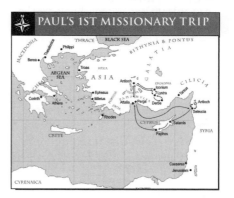

PAUL'S 1ST MISSIONARY TRIP

CHAPTER 14:
THE JOURNEY CONTINUES

•**VERSE 1** Paul and Barnabas went to the Jews first with the Gospel.

•**VERSE 8** "Impotent in his feet" means that the man was lame.

•**VERSE 9** The Holy Spirit was working in the man's heart, giving him the gift of faith.

•**VERSES 15-17** Paul's messages to the Gentiles were on a spiritual level they could understand. He spoke of the evidences of God in nature.

•**VERSE 19** The same people who wanted to worship Paul a few days earlier decided to stone him when the Jews stirred them up.

It's possible that Paul experienced death at this time, for he later described a time when he didn't know if he was dead or alive and was caught up to heaven (2 Corinthians 12:2-4).

•**VERSE 26** This was the end of the first missionary journey.

CHAPTER 15:
A MEETING OF THE CHURCH ELDERS

•**VERSES 1-5** Circumcision symbolized the cutting away of the flesh-dominated life in order to lead a spirit-dominated life.

The Jews felt very strongly about circumcision. Many believed that to be a Christian one had to convert to the practices of Judaism (such people were known as Judaizers).

Christianity might have become another Jewish sect if the Judaizers had prevailed.

•**VERSE 6** This first meeting of the Church elders to decide the Gentile question was very important for setting policy for the teaching of new converts.

•**VERSE 13** This again is James, the half-brother of Jesus, also known as James the Just and the leader of the church in Jerusalem.

•**VERSES 14-15** What Peter had said about the work of God among the Gentiles was confirmed by Scriptures (Luke 21:24; Romans 11:25).

•**VERSE 18** God is omniscient.

•**VERSES 19-20** This decision is an excellent example of the word of wisdom being spoken through James.

•**VERSE 28** This verse confirms the fact that the Holy Spirit was operating in James to bring forth the word of wisdom.

•**VERSE 29** The eating of blood was the eating of meat from animals that had been strangled and left with blood in them, rather than being butchered and bled.

The Jews were meticulous about eating only kosher meat. This rule would make it easier for the Christian Jews and Gentiles to eat together.

The elders didn't need to cover all the Law because much of it would naturally be obeyed by those who loved God. They sought to settle the questions that could bring the Jews and Gentiles into a closer fellowship in Christ.

•**VERSES 39-41** The contention between Paul and Barnabas resulted in two missionary teams going out.

CHAPTER 16:
PAUL CALLED TO MACEDONIA

•**VERSE 3** Paul wanted to tutor and train Timothy in the ministry but had him circumcised to avoid problems with the Jews.

•**VERSES 6-7** The Holy Spirit forbade them to preach in Asia and wouldn't allow them to go to Bithynia. He dealt strongly with Paul because he was such a strong-willed man.

•**VERSE 10** Luke begins to use the pronoun "we" because he joined Paul's missionary journeys at this point.

Some think perhaps Luke was the man Paul saw in the vision, while others speculate that Paul's "thorn in the flesh" required constant attention of a physician.

•**VERSE 13** Ten men were required to form a synagogue, so not even ten Jewish men were in the area.

•**VERSE 14** Those who dealt in purple were of the wealthy classes.

•**VERSE 15** Lydia was a clever saleslady.

•VERSE 25 The prayer and praises of Paul and Silas in their difficult circumstances put us to shame when we complain to God over petty things.

•VERSE 31 Paul wasn't saying that the jailer's family would be saved if he alone believed, but that the children under the age of accountability would be saved through their father's faith. Others would have to believe for themselves (1 Corinthians 7:14).

•VERSES 37-38 A Roman citizen wasn't to be beaten by the authorities unless he was judged and condemned.

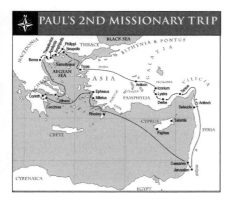
PAUL'S 2ND MISSIONARY TRIP

CHAPTER 17:
PAUL'S MESSAGE ON MARS HILL

•VERSES 2-3 Paul explained that the Messiah had to suffer and die, but that He would eventually set up the Kingdom of God.

The Jews had great difficulty reconciling the prophecies that spoke of the Messiah, for some prophecies told of His suffering while other verses prophesied of the Kingdom He would establish.

•VERSE 6 We are "turned upside down" when we're born again, for we now give the higher place to the spiritual part of our nature rather than to the flesh.

•VERSES 7-8 This situation marked the beginning of the Roman government's displeasure with the Christians.

•VERSE 9 The "security" was a fine that Jason was forced to pay.

•VERSE 10 Berea was a small town off the beaten track.

•VERSE 11 1 Thessalonians 5:21.

•VERSE 18 The Epicureans lived for pleasure. The Stoics believed that everything happened by fate and that one should accept whatever happened without emotion.

•VERSE 22 "Too superstitious" would be better translated very religious.

•VERSE 24 The Athenians believed that the gods dwelt in the temples that had been built for them.

•VERSE 27 "Haply" means by chance.

•VERSES 28-29 Man was created in the image and likeness of God, so we are His offspring. We become like the God we serve (Psalm 135:15-18).

•VERSE 30 "Winked" means overlooked. "Repent" means have another mind or turn from.

•VERSE 32 Some people rejected Paul's message, while others postponed making a decision.

•VERSE 34 Some accepted Paul's message.

The Areopagite was one of thirty judges set over Athens.

A woman in the company of men would not have been an honorable woman, for the honorable women in the Greek culture stayed at home.

God reaches people from the highest and the lowest walks of life.

CHAPTER 18:
PAUL'S VISIT TO CORINTH

•VERSE 1 Corinth was a busy port and a wicked city.

• **VERSE 3** The rabbis were to learn a trade so they wouldn't have to accept money from the people. Thus, Paul learned a trade.

• **VERSE 7** "Joined hard" means the house was right next door to the synagogue.

• **VERSE 9** These visions that Paul received were important in the direction of his ministry.

• **VERSES 12-16** Gallio was newly appointed by Rome. He was an honest magistrate and interested in properly administering Roman justice.

• **VERSE 17** Sosthenes probably took over the synagogue when Crispus became a Christian. Gallio wouldn't let himself become involved in the Jews' disputing because it wasn't under his jurisdiction.

• **VERSE 21** It is good to make our plans subject to the will of God (James 4:15).

• **VERSE 25** Apollos didn't know yet about the work of the Holy Spirit, but he taught what he knew.

• **VERSE 26** "Perfectly" means completely.

• **VERSES 27-28** Apollos went to Achaia and watered the seeds that Paul had planted in the hearts of people.

CHAPTER 19:
AN UPROAR IN EPHESUS

• **VERSE 1** Paul now watered the seeds that Apollos had planted.

• **VERSE 2** Paul probably noted that something was lacking in the body of believers in Ephesus.

• **VERSE 9** "Divers" means many. Christianity is described as "that way" or "the way" throughout the Book of Acts.

• **VERSE 11** The special miracles were a sign of Paul's apostleship.

• **VERSE 12** The "handkerchiefs" were sweatbands that tied around the forehead.

The people activated their faith at the point of contact when Paul's articles were placed on them. The articles themselves had no power to heal but triggered the release of faith.

• **VERSE 14** The seven sons of Sceva were exorcising evil spirits in the name of Jesus "whom Paul preacheth." They didn't have a personal relationship with Jesus.

• **VERSE 23** "That way" again refers to the way of life the Christians practiced in following Jesus.

• **VERSES 27-28** Demetrius and the other idol craftsmen were afraid that they would lose their business if the people converted to Christianity and left the worship of other gods.

CHAPTER 20:
PAUL'S MESSAGE TO THE CHRISTIAN ELDERS

• **VERSE 1** Macedonia was the northern part of Greece.

• **VERSE 2** Paul's plan was to collect an offering from the Gentile churches to help the suffering church in Jerusalem. The area then known as Greece was the area around Corinth.

• **VERSE 4** Several men from the various churches were accompanying Paul, probably carrying the offerings from their individual churches, to present to the church in Jerusalem as a sign of Christian love and solidarity.

• **VERSE 6** Luke uses "we" to indicate that he also accompanied Paul.

• **VERSE 7** The early Church believed that Sunday was the best day to observe communion, since Jesus was resurrected on a Sunday. Jesus didn't specify how often to have communion or what day was best to gather for worship.

Anything practiced often becomes a ritual and grows meaningless. We want our worship to be deeply felt in our hearts.

•**VERSE 8** The "lights" in the room were candles. They probably made the room very smoky and stuffy.

•**VERSE 9** Eutychus was sitting in the window getting fresh air, but the gases and smoke from the candles were escaping out the window, which may have caused him to fall asleep. He fell out the window backwards into the courtyard three floors below the upper room where they were meeting.

•**VERSE 12** God preserved the life of the young man, to the comfort of all the Christians gathered there.

•**VERSE 19** All our work and service should be done as unto the Lord. Knowing we are working unto Him makes many tasks more bearable.

•**VERSE 20** Paul's preaching was by word and example.

•**VERSE 23** "Abide" means await.

•**VERSE 24** Paul wasn't moved by the afflictions he had to endure from following God's will. He was willing to serve God faithfully until he'd finished all that God had for him to do on the earth.

Paul's ministry was to testify of the good news (gospel) of God's grace.

•**VERSES 26-28** Paul had shared and taught everything God had put on his heart to tell them, so he had done his duty toward them.

Now they were responsible to God for the flocks of God in their churches (Ezekiel 3:18,19).

The Holy Spirit—not men on a board or committee—had made these men the elders in their churches. The continuing obligation of the elders and pastor of a church is to feed the flock of God. We only grow by feeding on the Word of God.

This verse speaks of Jesus as God, for Jesus purchased the Church with His own blood.

•**VERSE 29** There are still wolves going around trying to draw lambs away from the flock in order to devour them.

•**VERSE 31** Paul was upset when he thought of men coming in and tearing up the work that had been done.

•**VERSE 32** God's Word is able to build and strengthen us and to bring us into the inheritance.

PAUL'S 3RD MISSIONARY TRIP

CHAPTER 21:
PAUL'S ARRIVAL AND ARREST IN JERUSALEM

•**VERSE 3** "Unlade her burden" means unload her cargo.

•**VERSES 4-5** Wherever we go and find Christians, we find family, for we are brothers and sisters in Christ.

•**VERSE 8** This is the same Philip who was one of the original seven deacons chosen to resolve the Grecian dispute (Acts 6:1-6) and later used mightily as an evangelist (Acts 8).

•**VERSE 11** Paul was continually warned by the Holy Spirit not to go to Jerusalem.

•**VERSE 15** "Carriages" here means luggage or baggage.

•**VERSE 20** Many of the Jewish Christians were still carefully practicing the ordinances of the Law.

•**VERSE 24** Paul was asked to conform to the Jewish laws for purification and to pay for four young men's sacrifices.

•**VERSE 26** Paul graciously complied with the request of the Church elders in order to avoid upsetting or offending anyone.

•**VERSE 29** Paul hadn't taken Trophimus into the temple as the Jews falsely assumed he had.

•**VERSE 32** The Jews stopped beating Paul when the Roman soldiers arrived.

•**VERSE 34** The "castle" was a fortress.

CHAPTER 22:
PAUL'S MESSAGE TO THE JEWS

•**VERSE 14** God has chosen us to know His will, see Jesus, and to hear God's Word.

•**VERSES 17-18** This refers to Paul's visit to Jerusalem three years after his conversion and after his stay in Damascus.

•**VERSE 24** The Romans solved many crimes when they questioned the prisoners during a beating (scourging).

•**VERSE 28** The chief captain had purchased his Roman citizenship, but Paul was born a citizen.

•**VERSE 29** The Roman citizens were well protected by Roman law. No one wanted to be found guilty of violating the rights of a Roman citizen.

Roman citizens were not even to be bound except under certain conditions.

•**VERSE 30** The chief captain wanted to learn what the Jews were accusing Paul of doing.

CHAPTER 23:
PAUL SPEAKS TO THE SANHEDRIN

•**VERSES 1-3** Paul had a zeal for righteousness and the Law. He knew that it was unlawful for someone to order him to be slapped, yet they were judging him by the Law they did not keep.

•**VERSE 5** Paul apologized to the high priest because it was against the law to speak evil against him.

There is a hint here that perhaps Paul's "thorn in the flesh" that he referred to in his epistles was an eye disease. Certainly Paul should have recognized Ananias, for Paul had worked closely with him in the days when he was still prosecuting the Church.

•**VERSE 11** Paul could easily have been discouraged at this point since his great dream of preaching to the Jews had proved to be disastrous.

Paul had been warned by the Lord about going to Jerusalem, and none of the Christians there stood by him. Still, Jesus told him to be cheerful, for a witness had been preached.

Our job is only to bear witness. The Holy Spirit convicts hearts and brings people to repentance. We don't have to worry about seeing results, as long as we have done our part.

•**VERSES 16-21** God often works in our lives in such a natural way that we don't realize something supernatural is happening.

•**VERSE 23** Paul was conducted from Jerusalem with a guard of 470 soldiers. The Roman government took excellent care of its citizens.

•**VERSE 31** Antipatris was about 25 miles from Jerusalem through the Judean hills.

•**VERSE 32** The way from Antipatris to Caesarea was less dangerous to travel, so only the cavalry escorted Paul on this stage of the journey.

CHAPTER 24:
PAUL'S DEFENSE

•**VERSES 2-3** The Jews hated Felix, a former slave and a wicked man.

• **VERSE 5** The charges against Paul were serious. He was a "pestilent fellow" which means "a man who is stirring up insurrection." Tertullus claimed that Paul was going from place to place inciting the Jews.

• **VERSE 10** Paul showed his knowledge of Roman law when he made his defense.

• **VERSE 14** Paul believed everything the prophets had foretold.

• **VERSE 17** Paul had collected money from the Gentile churches to help the Jews at the church in Jerusalem, since they were living in difficult, turbulent times.

• **VERSE 22** "That way" again refers to the Christian faith.

• **VERSE 24** Felix and Drucilla were living in open adultery, but Felix apparently had a hunger for God since he asked Paul to tell him about his faith in Christ.

• **VERSE 25** The Christian walk of righteousness and self-control is very reasonable.

• **VERSE 27** These two years in custody were a time when Paul could relax from his busy and trying life.

He was a political pawn used by the rulers to please the Jews.

CHAPTER 25:
PAUL APPEALS TO CAESAR

• **VERSES 10-11** Paul appealed to Caesar since he wasn't getting fair treatment from Festus.

• **VERSE 13** Bernice was a sister to Drucilla and Agrippa. The power of the Herodian kings was greatly diminished, but Agrippa and Bernice still paid this courtesy call on the new governor.

• **VERSES 20-27** Festus would look bad as a judge if he sent Paul to Caesar without any clear charges against him.

Festus hoped that Agrippa would come up with some charges if he listened to Paul.

CHAPTER 26:
PAUL SPEAKS BEFORE AGRIPPA

• **VERSE 3** Agrippa was part Jewish and a scholar of Jewish law and culture in order to better deal with the Jews.

Paul probably hoped that Agrippa would be converted to Christianity when he heard the Gospel.

• **VERSE 5** "Straightest" means strict.

• **VERSE 6** The "hope of the promise" was the Messiah. Jesus fulfilled over 300 prophecies concerning the Messiah.

• **VERSE 8** We often carry over our human restrictions and limitations to our concept of God. Nothing is too difficult for God!

• **VERSES 10-11** Paul confesses his persecution of the Christians.

• **VERSES 13-17** Paul's conversion was one of the most dramatic, for he turned completely around from persecuting Jesus to following Him.

• **VERSE 18** Paul's ministry to the Gentiles was: (1) To open their eyes. This indicates that Satan has blinded the eyes of unbelievers to the truth. We need to ask God to bind the work of Satan in their lives (2 Corinthians 4:4).

(2) To turn them from darkness to light. The flesh-dominated man walks in the kingdom of darkness. When he is born again and spirit-dominated, he walks in God's light (Colossians 1:13).

(3) To turn them from the power of Satan unto God. We are to lead unbelievers from the control of Satan to the control of God.

(4) To tell them that the inheritance we have by faith is eternal life.

• **VERSE 20** When a person is born again, evidences are present in his life of a change of heart and a turn to God.

•**VERSE 24** Paul was a scholar, so Festus told him that too much knowledge was forcing him to lose touch with reality.

•**VERSE 26** Paul began to address King Agrippa again, probably sensing that Agrippa was more receptive to his message.

•**VERSE 28** Agrippa's response was more of a question than a statement of his attitude.

CHAPTER 27:
THE PERILOUS JOURNEY

•**VERSE 1** Augustus was the title of Caesar. A centurion of Augustus' "band" was one of the elite soldiers of the Roman army.

All centurions in the New Testament were outstanding men, and Julius was among them.

•**VERSE 3** Julius was kind to Paul in allowing him to see his friends.

•**VERSE 7** "Suffering" means allowing.

•**VERSE 8** The city of Lasea was very small and the sailors would be bored there.

•**VERSE 9** The "fast" that year took place between October 10-17, so it was a dangerous time to sail.

•**VERSE 12** The sailors wanted to winter in Phenice since it was a bigger city.

•**VERSE 17** They would bind the ship tightly to hold it together during the storm.

•**VERSE 20** They were probably all gloomy and seasick at this point.

•**VERSES 22-26** Paul brought consolation and hope to the men through his faith in God.

•**VERSE 28** At fifteen fathoms they knew that they were closer to shore.

•**VERSE 30** The sailors were planning to flee in the lifeboat while pretending to be dropping the anchor.

•**VERSES 31-35** Paul had taken control of the situation.

•**VERSE 36** Paul's encouragement gave them all hope.

CHAPTER 28:
PAUL REACHES ROME

•**VERSE 1** "Melita" is the island of Malta.

•**VERSE 2** "Barbarous" refers to people who don't speak Greek, not that they were primitive or uncultured.

It was still cold and rainy.

🔑 **KEY WORD**

barbaros = barbarous; barbar was a Greek slang word for anybody who couldn't speak Greek, but really barbaros was just a native of Malta (28:2).

•**VERSES 4-6** Apparently the snake that bit Paul was very poisonous, because the people expected him to swell up and die.

•**VERSE 13** Puteoli was the best port near Rome (100 miles away), connected to Rome by the Appian Way.

•**VERSE 15** The Christians traveled thirty to forty miles out of Rome to welcome Paul.

•**VERSES 17-19** Paul wanted the Jews to know that he was not there to make an accusation against them to Caesar, but that he was a prisoner because of his belief in the Messiah.

•**VERSES 26-27** Romans 11:25.

•**VERSES 30-31** "Hired" means rented.

Paul was chained to a soldier day and night. Each soldier assigned to Paul probably received a heavy witness about Christ.

Paul's confinement to Rome for two years gave him the opportunity to write his epistles to the churches.

Luke ends the story here. Secular history says that Paul was freed by Caesar, since there were no real charges against him. Paul went back to Ephesus, where he lived until he was again arrested. This time Caesar had Paul beheaded.

1. What was Jesus' instruction to the apostles in Acts 1:4-5? When and how was this fulfilled? (See Acts 2:1-4.)

_____

_____

_____

2. What were the four activities of the early church as found in Acts 2:42?

_____

_____

_____

3. Throughout the book of Acts we see the apostles boldly preaching the name of Jesus. Write out the powerful testimony given in Acts 5:30-32.

_____

_____

_____

4. The disciples healed many through the power of God. What is the reaction of the people toward Peter and Paul in Acts 3:11-16 and Acts 14:11-18 when they each healed a crippled man? How do Peter and Paul respond?

_____

_____

_____

5. Through the work of the Lord at Cornelius' house, it was now accepted that Gentiles could also be saved. But many Jews believed that the Gentile believers needed to convert to the practices of Judaism. What did the council at Jerusalem decide about the Gentiles? (See Acts 15:7-20.)

_____

_____

_____

THE EPISTLE OF PAUL THE APOSTLE TO THE
ROMANS

AUTHOR OF LETTER:
Paul the Apostle

WRITTEN TO:
The church at Rome.

DATE AND PLACE OF WRITING:
Written during Paul's third visit to Corinth, around 60 A.D.

THEME:
Righteousness through faith in Jesus Christ.

PURPOSE OF WRITING:
To express his desire to come to Rome, and lay out the Gospel and God's plan of salvation.

INTRODUCTION:
The New Testament is divided into three categories. The first contains the Gospels, the first four books of the New Testament, which deals with the life of Christ.

Next is the Book of Acts, which continues Christ's ministry through His apostles.

The rest of the New Testament is made up of epistles, which emphasize matters of doctrine. Romans is the first epistle.

In determining scriptural conduct for the Church, we use hermeneutics, or scriptural interpretation, as our guide. If something was taught by Christ, practiced in Acts, and taught in the epistles, then we feel that it can be properly practiced by the Church.

CHAPTER 1:
GOD'S ATTITUDE TOWARD SIN

•**VERSE 1** "Servant" means bondslave. The slave was completely at his master's disposal. His one goal in life was to serve.

Paul was called to be an apostle and sent by the Holy Spirit to witness to the Gentiles. "Gospel" means Good News.

KEY WORD

apostolos = apostle, messenger, sent out by the Lord (1:1)

•**VERSE 2** The message of the Gospel was promised in the Old Testament.

•**VERSE 3** The name Jesus is the Greek word for Joshua, which in Hebrew means "Jehovah is salvation." Christ is Greek for the Hebrew word "Messiah" which means Anointed One.

Jesus is His name, Christ is His distinction, and Lord is His title, signifying our relationship with Him.

Mary was a descendant of David, to whom God had made the promise that the Messiah would come through him.

•**VERSE 7** All those in the body of Christ are saints. After we experience the grace of God and make our peace with Him, we can know the peace of God in every situation.

•**VERSE 11** Paul's desire to go to Rome was to minister to the church there.

•**VERSE 14** "Barbarians" refers to those who didn't speak Greek. They weren't necessarily wild, coarse people as the name implies today.

•**VERSE 16** This verse speaks of the power of God.

•**VERSE 17** This verse speaks of the righteousness of God and introduces the theme of this epistle: righteousness comes by faith, not by works.

•**VERSE 18** This verse speaks of the wrath of God.

"Ungodly" means not in the right relationship with God. "Unrighteous" means not in the right relationship with man. We cannot have the proper relationship with God and have the wrong relationship with man.

Holding the truth in unrighteousness is believing that there is a God, yet living as though He didn't exist.

•**VERSE 20** We can see God in His creation.

•**VERSE 21** 1 Thessalonians 5:18, Psalm 37:23, Romans 8:28.

•**VERSE 23** The idols which men create often look like grotesque forms of men and beasts.

•**VERSES 24-28** When men create their own god, they become like the god they serve and are rapidly degraded. God gives them up to their own base desire.

Homosexuality is the result of moral depravity; people are not "born" homosexuals but have been given up to their own lusts.

•**VERSES 29-31** Our society has sought to rule God out of its conscience and now evidences the evils of reprobate minds.

•**VERSE 32** Movies and television programs that glorify lying, cheating, stealing, murder, and adultery can cause us to take pleasure in these sins and make us guilty.

CHAPTER 2:
GOD'S JUDGMENT

•**VERSE 2** God will not only judge a person's actions but also his motivations. He knows the truth about each of us.

•**VERSE 4** People mistake God's mercy and long-suffering for weakness or indifference to their sin and rebellion. God's goodness, not the threat of judgment and hell, leads a man to repentance.

•**VERSE 6** We ask for God's mercy, not justice—for our sins deserve punishment.

•**VERSE 11** God will judge us without regard to our nationality.

•**VERSES 12-15** We'll be judged according to the knowledge that we have. God has given every man a conscience, so that he knows good and evil.

•**VERSES 17-29** Rituals will not save us if we're not walking according to God's will, whether we're circumcised, baptized, or members of a church.

Obedience to God, not rituals, counts for salvation.

CHAPTER 3:
NO MAN IS RIGHTEOUS BY THE LAW

•**VERSE 2** The Word of God was given to the Jews, who preserved the Scriptures with diligence and accuracy.

•**VERSE 3** Our belief in God doesn't add to Him, nor does our unbelief detract from Him.

•**VERSE 5** Since God has said that all men have sinned, some people say they sin to prove that God spoke the truth. This is evil reasoning.

•**VERSE 7** Some people tell untrue stories to sway people's emotions and bring them to salvation, but this is wrong.

•**VERSES 10-18** Every man is guilty before God. There's not one man who dares to stand before God in his own righteousness.

•**VERSE 20** No man can be justified by keeping the Law. The Law was intended to show us our sin, not to justify us. "Justified" means "Just as if I'd never sinned."

KEY WORD

dikaioo = justified, rendered innocent

•**VERSES 21-22** There was a righteousness apart from the Law that was spoken of in the Old Testament. This righteousness was the justification through faith in God's grace and mercy.

Our salvation is based on God's faithfulness rather than the variability of our goodness.

•**VERSE 23** We all have sinned, some more than others; but all of us have fallen short of the goal God has for us.

•**VERSES 24-26** God has a righteous basis for our justification through the sacrifice of Jesus for our sins.

•**VERSE 27** All we can do to gain salvation is to believe in the salvation God provided for us.

•**VERSE 31** The Law is established because it has done its work of showing us our sin and driving us to the redemption we have in Jesus.

CHAPTER 4:
ABRAHAM WAS RIGHTEOUS BY FAITH

•**VERSE 1** What did Abraham discover?

•**VERSE 2** Abraham didn't trust in his works to save him (Romans 7:18).

•**VERSE 3** God imputes righteousness to us when we believe Him.

•**VERSES 4-5** If we try to approach God on the basis of our works, we nullify His grace.

When we have a right relationship with God, our natural response that flows from our hearts is to do anything He wants. Our works are thus motivated by love (2 Corinthians 5:14).

•**VERSE 7** "Blessed" means "Oh, how happy!"

•**VERSES 9-11** God considered Abraham righteous before he had ever been circumcised.

•**VERSES 13-14** Abraham was accounted righteous before the Law was ever given.

•**VERSE 15** There is no way to break a law before it exists.

•**VERSE 16** Our salvation is not variable, i.e., dependent on our works, but is as sure as God's promise to us.

•**VERSE 17** God talked about Abraham's son as if Isaac existed before he was even conceived.

•**VERSES 18-21** The four keys to Abraham's faith:

(1) Abraham ignored the human impossibilities and trusted God to keep His promises (Isaiah 55:8,9).

(2) Abraham did not stagger at the promises of God (Philippians 4:19).

(3) Abraham praised God before the evidence was there.

(4) Abraham believed God was able to do what He had said He would (Isaiah 40:15; Ephesians 3:20).

CHAPTER 5:
THE EFFECTS OF ADAM'S SIN

•VERSE 2 We have access to the Father any time our righteousness is based on faith. When our righteousness is based on our keeping the Law, access to the Father depends on our works.

•VERSE 3 The trials that come into our lives promote spiritual growth.

•VERSES 6-8 Christ died for sinners, not "righteous" people (Mark 2:17).

•VERSES 9-10 Christ died for us when we were sinners and reconciled us to God. Now He establishes our relationship with God through His life.

•VERSE 11 The word "atonement" in the Old Testament meant covering.

The blood of the sacrifices was to cover the sins of the people, but it couldn't put away their sins.

In the New Testament, "atonement" means at one-ment, because Christ's death put away our sins and made us one with Him.

•VERSES 12-14 When Adam sinned he brought sin into the world, and every man after him was born a sinner.

•VERSE 15 One man brought sin into the world, and one Man died for the forgiveness of the world's sins.

•VERSE 18 Adam's sin brought condemnation on us; Christ's death bought justification for us.

CHAPTER 6:
WE ARE DEAD TO SIN

•VERSE 2 "God forbid" means "perish the thought." When we're born again, our spirits are put in control of our bodies and minds.

In the spiritual dimension we fellowship with God and we are conscious of Him.

•VERSES 3-4 We buried the old flesh-dominated nature in baptism, and the new creature is free from sin.

•VERSE 6 "Destroyed" is the Greek word *katargeo* which means "to put out of business."

This should read in the past tense, "Our old man was crucified."

•VERSE 11 God didn't intend for our bodily appetites to rule over us, but as long as we're in these bodies, we'll have a struggle with the flesh. We must daily go before God to reckon our old nature dead and faithfully claim the victory (Galatians 5).

•VERSES 12-13 We don't have to sin anymore. We now have the choice to yield to the flesh or to God.

•VERSES 14-17 We've been freed from being servants of sin. Now that we're free from the bondage of sin and under grace, it doesn't make sense to sin.

Instead, we can yield ourselves to God as His instruments for righteousness.

•VERSE 21 The fruit (or product) of sin is death.

•VERSES 22-23 The fruit of holiness is eternal life.

CHAPTER 7:
THE SPIRIT VERSUS FLESH

•VERSE 1 When Paul uses the word "brethren" he's referring to his Jewish brothers. The principle Paul begins to establish here is that death brings freedom from the Law.

•**VERSES 4-6** The Jews who had become Christians thought they still had to keep the Law.

Paul explained that they had died in Christ. Once freed from the Law, we can serve God from the motivation of love.

•**VERSE 7** Paul here states that the purpose of the Law was to show men their sins.

•**VERSE 14** We're in agreement with the Law because it is good and just. Our problem is that the Law is spiritual and we are carnal.

Jesus explained God's intention when He gave the Law, because the Pharisees had misinterpreted it (Matthew 5-7).

The new covenant we have with God depends upon our belief in His righteousness. The old covenant depended on our obedience in keeping the Law.

•**VERSE 15** This is the struggle Paul had before he realized that the Law was spiritual.

•**VERSES 17-20** Only the Christian has this conflict between the flesh and the spirit. The non-Christian lives in harmony with the desires of his flesh, but we Christians are trying to bring our flesh into conformity with the will of God.

Now our will and desire is to serve God. So, when we sin, it's because we still have the sinful nature.

•**VERSE 22** My spiritual, inward self loves God's law and wants above all to obey Him.

•**VERSE 23** Our flesh always seeks to gratify itself and struggles with our spirit to bring it under the control of sin.

•**VERSE 24** We're dragging the body of our dead man (our flesh) around with us, hoping for the day when we'll be released.

•**VERSE 25** With God's help through Jesus, there's a way that we don't have to continue to be defeated by the flesh.

CHAPTER 8:
LIFE IN THE SPIRIT

•**VERSE 1** Because in our hearts we desire to serve God, He doesn't condemn us when we fail.

•**VERSE 2** The law of sin and death is still in effect, but the new law of life in Christ Jesus supersedes the old law.

•**VERSES 3-4** The law of sin and death couldn't make us righteous, but the new law of life is fulfilled in us by Christ (not by us) as we walk after the Spirit. Through Him we're accounted righteous.

•**VERSE 5** The main concerns of the flesh are: What shall we eat? What shall we drink? What shall we wear?

•**VERSE 6** The mind of the flesh is death; the mind of the Spirit is life and peace.

As we allow the Spirit to govern our minds, we think in conformity to the will of God.

•**VERSES 7-8** The flesh is in rebellion to God's laws, so we cannot please God when we're in the flesh.

•**VERSE 9** We're not in the flesh when we allow God's Spirit to dwell in us.

•**VERSE 11** The Holy Spirit brings us into the resurrected life of Christ.

•**VERSE 12** We don't owe the flesh anything!

•**VERSE 13** Through the power of the Spirit, we're enabled to put to death the deeds of the flesh.

•**VERSE 15** "Abba" means Father.

•**VERSE 17** Matthew 25:34.

•**VERSE 18** 2 Corinthians 4:17.

•**VERSE 19** All of creation waits expectantly for the redemption of our bodies when we'll finally be in a body that is in harmony with our spirit.

•**VERSE 20** "Vanity" means emptiness.

•**VERSE 23** "They" refers to the world around us.

•VERSES 24-25 Our hope is for that new body from God.

•VERSES 26-27 "Infirmities" means weaknesses. The purpose of prayer is never to get our will done, but to get God's will done. It's a waste of time to pray for things that are contrary to God's will.

Sometimes we don't know God's will in a certain situation; then the Holy Spirit interprets our groanings and intercedes for us, according to God's will.

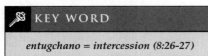

KEY WORD

entugchano = intercession (8:26-27)

•VERSE 28 This beautiful verse sustains us in times of painful trials.

•VERSE 29 God predestined those He knew would respond to His love and grace. When God watches our lives, it's as if He were watching a rerun, because He knows what we would do (Psalm 90:9).

Christ was the firstborn.

•VERSES 30-31 God chose us, called us, justified us, and glorified us. He is for us. The world, the flesh, and the devil are against us, but they're no match for God.

•VERSE 33 Satan accuses us, but God justifies us.

•VERSE 34 The difference between Satan's condemnation and the Holy Spirit's conviction is that the condemnation makes us want to pull away from God, because we feel unworthy; yet the conviction helps us go to God to make things right. Jesus doesn't want to condemn us. He pleads our case for us.

CHAPTER 9:
THE SOVEREIGNTY OF GOD

•VERSES 1-3 Paul continually sorrowed that the Jews didn't accept Jesus as the Messiah.

•VERSE 4 God adopted the children of Israel as His special people. The glory of God's presence filled the tabernacle and the temple.

God made a covenant with the people that He would be their God and they would be His people. God gave the Law and the order for service to Him (Leviticus). God gave numerous promises to Israel, some that are still in effect today.

•VERSE 5 The great patriarchs belonged to Israel.

This text should read "...Christ came, who is God over all, blessed for ever." Jesus is God (Titus 2:13).

•VERSES 6-9 Paul here demonstrates that not all of the children of Israel were acknowledged by God as His people.

•VERSES 10-13 God had chosen Jacob, because He knew that Jacob would be a spiritual man and Esau would be a fleshly man.

•VERSE 14 The choices God has made haven't closed the door to one individual. He loves and accepts all who come to Him.

•VERSES 15-18 Since God is supreme, He can choose and act as He pleases. His ways are beyond our human understanding.

•VERSE 24 God has called the Church out from among the Jews and Gentiles that He might display His mercy through us.

•VERSE 27 Only a remnant of Israel will be saved, so being Jewish doesn't guarantee salvation.

•VERSE 30 The Gentiles, who didn't follow the Law, gained righteousness through faith.

•VERSES 31-33 Jesus was the stumbling stone. The idea of righteousness by faith was difficult for the Jews to accept after the years they'd spent seeking righteousness by the Law.

CHAPTER 10:
RIGHTEOUSNESS BY FAITH

•VERSES 1-3 Paul wasn't bitter against the Jews for fighting his attempts to bring Christ to them. He was longing to release them from their futile attempts to become righteous by following the Law.

•VERSE 4 Christ brings an end to the Law for those who believe.

•VERSE 5 The righteousness of the Law is based on man's doing; the righteousness of faith is based on the work Christ has done.

•VERSES 8-10 We only have to speak and believe the words of faith in Jesus to attain all His righteousness.

•VERSES 11-13 God delights to show mercy and will not turn away any who come to Him. He doesn't take more pleasure in a Jew coming to salvation than a Gentile.

•VERSES 14-15 This passage contains the reason we send missionaries out.

•VERSE 17 This "word" refers to the spoken word.

•VERSE 18 Psalm 19:4. Nature testifies to God's existence.

CHAPTER 11:
OUR ATTITUDE TOWARD THE JEWS

•VERSES 1-4 God hasn't cast off Israel. He defended them when Isaiah complained to Him.

•VERSE 5 God has a remnant among the Jews today who believe in Jesus as their Messiah.

•VERSE 6 We're accepted by God either by our works or by grace; it cannot be both.

•VERSES 7-8 God has blinded those who reject His grace.

•VERSE 11 Through the cutting off of the Jews, an opening was made for the Gentiles.

•VERSE 12 When God restores the Jews to His favor, the Kingdom Age will begin.

•VERSE 17 The Gentiles are the wild olive branches grafted into the good olive tree of Israel, with the blessings of the covenant and the promises.

•VERSES 21-22 God grafted us by our faith in Christ. The Jews were cut off because of their unbelief, not merely to make room for us.

•VERSE 25 The "fullness of the Gentiles" indicates that there is a number of Gentiles who will be saved, after which God will turn back to Israel, drawing His people unto Himself.

•VERSE 28 God calls the Jews His "elect" (Matthew 24).

•VERSE 32 The Jews are now in unbelief of God, so that He can extend His mercy to them.

•VERSE 33 God doesn't ask us to reconcile the various truths about His relations with man. He only wants us to believe, trusting Him with simple faith.

•VERSE 36 Everything is centered around God.

CHAPTER 12:
EXHORTATIONS

•VERSE 1 "Reasonable" means logical. It makes sense to let God direct our lives.

 KEY WORD

logikos = reasonable, logical (12:1)

•VERSE 2 God leads us in very natural ways when we make ourselves available to Him.

•VERSE 3 First Corinthians 4:7, Ephesians 2:8,9.

•VERSE 6 God gives us a gift suitable for our ministry in the Body.

•**VERSE 8** The exhorter gives us a little shove in the right direction.

•**VERSE 9** Show love without partiality; love all equally.

•**VERSES 10-21** These verses are exhortations from Paul on the way we should live as Christians.

•**VERSE 20** Heaping coals of fire on someone's head refers to the fact that people often carried coals in a container and were given live coals by friends. It was a gracious act.

CHAPTER 13:
BEING SUBJECT TO AUTHORITIES

•**VERSE 1** Sometimes God ordains an evil ruler because He plans to bring judgment on a country.

•**VERSES 3-4** People who obey the law need not fear the police. They're here to protect us, and we should have an appreciative attitude toward them.

•**VERSES 6-7** "Tribute" means taxes.

•**VERSES 8-10** Love for one another sums up the Law and makes it a positive command, rather than a list of negatives.

•**VERSE 13** This verse lists the works of darkness we're to cast off.

•**VERSE 14** The armor of light is Jesus Christ.

CHAPTER 14:
JUDGING OTHERS

•**VERSE 1** We shouldn't judge those who are weak in faith but accept them with love.

•**VERSES 2-3** Paul here talks of vegetarians who were weak in the faith because they felt convicted about eating meat.

•**VERSES 5-6** Others who were weak in the faith felt that there were certain days when the Lord should be worshiped.

CALVARY DISTINCTIVE

"Who art thou that judgest another man's servant? to his own master he standeth or falleth. Yea, he shall be holden up: for God is able to make him stand" (Romans 14:4).

I would hate to err on the side of judgment, to judge someone falsely who had truly repented.... So, again, if I err, I want to err on the side of grace because I know that God will be much more gracious towards me than if I err in judging a person wrongly.

•**VERSE 7** Paul encouraged the Christians to allow each other their personal convictions without trying to put them on everyone else.

•**VERSE 10** To "set at nought" a brother is to say that he isn't a Christian.

•**VERSES 11-12** When we stand before God for judgment, it won't be to determine our salvation, for that is already secure.

He'll judge our works and the motivation behind our works, then give us our place in His kingdom (Philippians 2:10,11).

•**VERSES 13-15** Paul warns against enjoying our freedom in Christ to the detriment of our weaker fellow Christians.

•**VERSE 18** God and men accept us if we're walking in the Spirit.

•**VERSE 20** We shouldn't destroy the work of God in a person's life because we disagree about eating meat.

We can do something that isn't wrong in itself, but is evil because it offends someone else.

•**VERSES 22-23** It's wrong to try to argue someone out of his convictions, since his conscience will condemn him if he is committing sin.

CHAPTER 15:
PAUL'S MINISTRY TO THE GENTILES

• **VERSE 1** We that are strong in the faith should be helping the weaker brothers to stand.

• **VERSE 3** Christ took reproaches on Himself that were aimed at God, because He didn't live to please Himself.

• **VERSES 5-7** We should seek unity in the Body, accepting one another.

• **VERSE 8** Jesus ministered to the Jews, the "circumcision," because He came to fulfill God's promises to the Jews.

• **VERSES 9-12** Paul gives the Scriptures that prophesied the inclusion of the Gentiles in God's grace.

• **VERSE 13** Paul begins an extended benediction and series of prayers to close the epistle.

• **VERSES 16-19** Paul says his ministry to the Gentiles was proper because the Holy Spirit ordained it.

• **VERSES 22-24** Paul hadn't visited the church in Rome before.

• **VERSE 26** The saints in Jerusalem were poor because they had sold their possessions to share everything in common.

• **VERSE 30** Paul asked the Christians to strive and persevere in their prayers for him—interesting words relating to prayer.

• **VERSES 31-32** Paul asked them to pray for three things:

(1) That he be delivered from the unbelievers in Judea.

(2) That the offering would be accepted by the Jerusalem church.

(3) That he could visit Rome with joy and be refreshed.

CHAPTER 16:
PERSONAL GREETINGS FROM PAUL

• **VERSES 1-2** "Servant" here means deaconess. Phebe carried this epistle from Paul to Rome.

• **VERSES 3-5** Paul met Priscilla and Aquila when he first went to Corinth. Wherever they lived, they opened their home for Bible studies and helped to establish new believers.

• **VERSE 7** Junia is a feminine name and, some believe, she was a woman apostle, while others believe she was well-known by the apostles.

• **VERSES 17-18** Differences over doctrinal matters were too dangerous to overlook. Paul warns the Christians to take note of those who brought divisions into the Church and to avoid them.

• **VERSE 19** Their obedience to Christ was well-known. Paul wanted the Christians to be wise in spiritual things but unlearned in evil things.

• **VERSE 20** Genesis 3:15.

• **VERSE 25** "Mystery" refers to something now revealed that had previously been unknown, not something that couldn't be known.

1. Read the list of sinful behavior found in Romans 1:29-32. Which one of these is the most surprising to see, or perhaps the most convicting to you today and why?

_____

_____

_____

2. We clearly see in Romans that we have all sinned and come short of the glory of God. How then are we justified according to Romans 3:20-22, 28 and 5:1-2?

_____

_____

_____

3. As long as we are in these bodies, we will struggle with our flesh. What must we do in order to claim victory over our flesh? (See Romans 6:11-14.)

_____

_____

_____

4. Many people think that God is just waiting for us to mess up so that He can condemn us. What does Romans 8:31-34 say about Him?

_____

_____

_____

5. Paul gives many exhortations on the way we should live as Christians in Romans 12:10-21. Pick three that speak to you the most today and why.

_____

_____

_____

THE FIRST EPISTLE OF PAUL TO THE
CORINTHIANS

AUTHOR OF LETTER:
Paul the Apostle

WRITTEN TO:
The church in Corinth.

DATE AND PLACE OF WRITING:
In Ephesus about 59 A.D.

THEME:
A corrective epistle.

PURPOSE OF WRITING:

To respond to a letter that he received with questions concerning different issues.

To correct carnal abuses that were existing in the Corinthian church.

To talk to them about spiritual things: the operation of the gifts of the Spirit, the supremacy of love, and the power of the resurrection.

To bring them into the consciousness of the universal church of God in Jesus Christ.

INTRODUCTION:

Paul went to Corinth in Greece on his second missionary journey. Corinth was a thriving commercial center and a very corrupt city. The church in Corinth had several problems, so Paul wrote this epistle to correct them.

CHAPTER 1:
GOD'S WORK IN US

•**VERSE 2** In the phrase "called to be saints," the words "to be" were inserted by the translators. All Christians are called saints—not just the especially devout.

This epistle is addressed to those of us who call upon the name of Jesus, as well as to the church that was in Corinth.

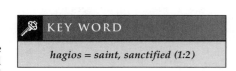

KEY WORD

hagios = saint, sanctified (1:2)

•**VERSE 3** After we accept the grace of God, we're able to experience the peace of God.

•**VERSE 5** "Enriched" comes from the Greek plutocrat. It means lavishly wealthy.

•**VERSE 6** Their lives were a confirmation of the truth of the Gospel.

•**VERSE 7** There was an abundant use of the spiritual gifts in the Corinthian church. Christ wants us to live in anticipation that He may come at any time.

•**VERSE 8** He will complete His work in us so that we will be blameless when we're presented to God. The "day" of Jesus is the day of His coming.

•**VERSE 9** "Fellowship" means communion or oneness.

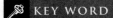
KEY WORD

koinonia = fellowship, oneness, unity, communion (1:9)

•**VERSES 10-12** Some of the people were taking sides in disputes that had arisen. Carnality, not spiritual maturity, leads to division in the Body of Christ.

•**VERSES 14-17** If a person had to be baptized in order to be saved, Paul would never have made these remarks about baptism.

Baptism is the outward symbol showing that the filth of the flesh has been washed from our hearts, but it is our faith in Christ that saves us.

•**VERSE 18** The death of Christ isn't meaningful to those who are dying in their sins (Hebrews 12:25).

•**VERSES 19-20** Romans 1:21.

•**VERSE 21** Preaching appears foolish to those who are wise in the world.

•**VERSES 26-27** Not many of the wise and powerful have been chosen by God.

He has chosen the humble so that He will be glorified in them.

•**VERSES 30-31** Jesus is our wisdom and deserves all the glory.

CALVARY DISTINCTIVE

"For ye see your calling, brethren, how that not many wise men after the flesh, not many mighty, not many noble, are called: But God hath chosen the foolish things of the world to confound the wise; and God hath chosen the weak things of the world to confound the things which are mighty; And base things of the world, and things which are despised, hath God chosen, yea, and things which are not, to bring to naught things that are:" (1 Corinthians 1:26-28).

The whole purpose of God is to choose those who really aren't qualified, but to anoint them with His Spirit. Then, when the results are forthcoming, it's an amazement and a wonder to the world.

CHAPTER 2:
THE WISDOM OF GOD

•**VERSE 2** This verse gives us the message of Paul's preaching.

•**VERSE 4** Paul's preaching was a demonstration of God's Spirit and power.

•**VERSE 6** "Perfect" means complete.

•**VERSE 9** The wisdom of the world hasn't revealed to man the glorious things God wants to do for us. We who have received His grace are experiencing the blessings of being His children.

Many people misinterpret this verse as referring to future things God will do for us, but the next verse shows Paul's intention more clearly.

•**VERSES 10-13** The Spirit brings us to an understanding of God and His plans for our lives.

•**VERSE 14** The natural man is blinded to spiritual things.

•**VERSE 15** "Judgeth" means understands. The Holy Spirit gives us knowledge beyond our experience.

•**VERSE 16** Philippians 2:5.

CHAPTER 3:
DIVISIONS IN THE BODY

•**VERSE 1** Many of the Corinthian Christians hadn't entered the spiritual dimension yet. They were still living the carnal lives of babes in Christ (2 Peter 1).

•**VERSE 2** Babes in Christ aren't able to digest a message that contains basic doctrine. They look more to testimonies and stories.

•**VERSE 4** The party spirit was the mark of carnality, for God was responsible for the work done in their lives.

•**VERSE 6** In the church at Ephesus, Paul planted and Apollos watered the seed.

•**VERSE 11** Jesus is the foundation for our faith.

•**VERSES 13-15** Matthew 6:1.

•**VERSES 21-23** Though Bible commentaries can add to our knowledge, the best study is the time we spend reading the Bible with the Holy Spirit as our teacher.

CHAPTER 4:
MINISTERS OF CHRIST

•**VERSE 1** "Ministers" in the Greek means under-rowers or galley slaves.

Just as the galley slave heard and obeyed the voice of his master, so the minister should be in submission to the Lord Jesus.

The steward was the housekeeper who protected the treasures of the house and drew from them for the needs of the family.

The truths of God are treasures which the ministers hold and share with the members of God's family.

•**VERSE 2** God requires that we be faithful to the ministry to which He has called us.

•**VERSE 4** "By" means against.

•**VERSE 5** God will judge the secret motivations of our hearts.

•**VERSE 7** We're all alike as sinners before God, and anything of value that we have has been given to us by God.

•**VERSE 9** God used the patriarchs, kings, priests, and prophets to minister His truth to the people.

Paul felt that the apostles were the last in this long line of God's spokesmen.

•**VERSES 10-13** Paul here describes the difficulties of apostleship.

CHAPTER 5:
THE CASE OF INCEST

•**VERSE 5** God protects us from many attacks of Satan (Job 1:10).

The man involved in incest would reap the consequences of his sin when the church separated him from the protection of fellowship.

•**VERSE 6** The church had been proud of its tolerance toward the man.

•**VERSE 9** The word translated "fornicators" in the Greek means male prostitutes.

•**VERSES 10-11** Paul knew the Christians would be around wicked people as long as they existed in this world, but he warned that evil men shouldn't be allowed to remain in the church.

CHAPTER 6:
CHRISTIANS AND THE LAW

•**VERSES 1-6** Members of the Corinthian Church were suing each other in the civil court. Paul told them to settle their disputes within the church, because the least-esteemed man in the church could judge better than a man in the worldly court.

•**VERSE 9** The "abusers of themselves with mankind" are homosexuals.

•**VERSE 11** Christ washes, sanctifies, and justifies us when we turn our lives over to Him.

•**VERSE 12** We shouldn't exercise our freedom in such a way that we're brought into bondage to something.

•**VERSE 15** Since our bodies belong to Christ, we involve Him in everything we do.

•**VERSE 20** God purchased us at a tremendous price from the old life of sin. Now we're obligated to glorify Him with our bodies and our spirits which belong to Him.

CHAPTER 7:
CHRISTIAN MARRIAGE

•**VERSES 1-2** The Corinthians had written to Paul for advice about marriage and physical relationships.

The Corinthian society was evil and exerted an amoral influence on the people. Paul wanted to help the believers to resist the temptations of the world.

•**VERSE 9** It's better to marry than to burn with lust.

•**VERSE 14** A believing husband or wife sanctifies the home and the marriage.

•**VERSES 20-23** If a man was a servant when he became a Christian, he should continue in service unless the opportunity arose to purchase his freedom.

If a man was free when he came to Christ, he should not sell himself into slavery.

•**VERSES 25-31** Paul felt that Christ would return soon and he didn't want the Christians to be involved in things of the world.

•**VERSES 32-35** Carefulness means worries. Paul realized that married people were distracted from service to God by their concerns for each other.

He felt that if people could remain single, they would be spared the problems and worries of marriage and could devote themselves wholeheartedly to God.

•**VERSE 39** Paul reaffirmed that marriage is for life. Widows were free to remarry as long as they married Christians.

CHAPTER 8:
CHRISTIAN LIBERTY

•**VERSE 1** Edifieth means builds up.

•**VERSES 2-3** The knowledge of God is the most important knowledge.

•**VERSES 4-7** Though most Christians could eat meat sacrificed to idols without feeling guilty, some Christians suffered pangs of conscience if they ate it.

•**VERSES 8-13** We're to practice our liberty in Christ in submission to the law of love, so that we don't destroy our brothers by offending their consciences.

CHAPTER 9:
MORE ON CHRISTIAN LIBERTY

•**VERSE 1** One of the requirements of apostleship was to have seen the resurrected Christ.

•**VERSE 2** The Corinthian Church was another proof of Paul's apostleship.

•**VERSE 6** The apostles weren't required to work at regular jobs, since they were busy with God's work.

•**VERSES 10-11** Paul was explaining the right of the minister to be supported by those he ministered to.

•**VERSE 13** The Old Testament priests were allowed to partake of the offerings.

•**VERSE 14** God ordained the support of ministers.

•**VERSE 15** Paul didn't want the Corinthians to send money to him.

He just wanted to make the point that he didn't allow any people to support him, and he'd rather die than become a financial burden to them.

•**VERSE 18** Paul gladly preached the Gospel without charge.

•**VERSE** 19 Though Paul wasn't obligated to the Christians, he offered himself as a servant to them.

•**VERSES** 20-23 Paul sought to win people to Jesus Christ by being sensitive to their needs and identifying with them. We should try to reach people where they are today and expect to see changes later.

•**VERSES** 24-27 Paul encouraged the Corinthians to put all they had into living the Christian life. He said he blackened his eyes and beat and bruised his body to keep it "under," that is, so the Spirit might rule.

✌ CALVARY DISTINCTIVE

"But I keep under my body, and bring it into subjection: lest that by any means, when I have preached to others, I myself should be a castaway"
(1 Corinthians 9:27).

Seek to bring glory to Jesus Christ and the Lord will use you.

CHAPTER 10:
LESSONS FROM THE WILDERNESS

•**VERSES** 1-5 Paul teaches here that the experiences of the children of Israel have spiritual applications for us.

•**VERSE** 6 The lessons we're to learn from the children of Israel are: (1) We're not to desire evil things.

•**VERSE** 7 (2) We're not to worship anything or anyone other than God.

•**VERSE** 8 (3) We're not to commit fornication.

•**VERSE** 9 (4) We're not to challenge the work of God in our lives.

•**VERSE** 10 (5) We're not to murmur complaints about the circumstances God puts us in.

God wants us to trust Him to work it out for our good.

•**VERSE** 13 God won't allow us to be tempted beyond our endurance. He'll always provide a way out for us.

•**VERSE** 16 "Communion" means fellowship or oneness.

•**VERSE** 17 In the Asian culture, eating the same food together brought people into oneness, for the food they ate became part of all their bodies.

•**VERSE** 20 The idols were inhabited by demons, so eating food sacrificed to idols would bring Christians into fellowship with demons.

•**VERSE** 23 All things are lawful to us, but some things can tear us down and hurt our Christian walk.

•**VERSE** 24 We're not to think only of ourselves but of others as well.

•**VERSE** 25 "Shambles" means market. It was better not to ask whether the meat had been offered to idols when they went to the meat market, so they could eat it with a clear conscience.

•**VERSES** 29-33 When we're thinking of others, our liberty is bound by their needs.

CHAPTER 11:
THE COMMUNION SERVICE

•**VERSE** 3 The chain of authority is set up here.

•**VERSE** 4 The Jews pray to God with their heads covered as a symbol of their unworthiness to approach Him.

Since Jesus opened the door for us to approach God freely, it would nullify His work if a Christian man covered his head for prayer.

•**VERSES** 5-6 The prostitutes in Corinth went about unveiled.

A wife who didn't wear her veil dishonored her husband, since people might think she was a prostitute.

•**VERSE 8** The woman was made from part of the man (Genesis 2:21-23).

•**VERSE 13** This rule applied only to the women in Corinth because of the prostitutes in that city. The other churches didn't have any customs concerning veils.

•**VERSES 21-22** Some of the people were eating and drinking greedily at the agape feasts, leaving very little for the others.

•**VERSE 27** "Unworthily" also means "in an unworthy manner."

•**VERSE 30** Those asleep were dead. Paul was either saying that the Christians were sick and dying because they had celebrated the Lord's Supper improperly, or because they hadn't appropriated the healing that Christ had for them.

CHAPTER 12:
THE BODY OF CHRIST

•**VERSE 1** The word "gifts" isn't in this verse in the Greek. Paul was moving away from the carnal issues to discuss spiritual things.

•**VERSE 4** There are different gifts but one Holy Spirit.

•**VERSE 5** People can have the same gift, but it works differently in their lives.

•**VERSE 7** The gifts of the Spirit are given to profit everyone in the Body of Christ.

•**VERSE 8** The word of wisdom isn't a reservoir that can be drawn upon at any time, but a spontaneous prompting of the Spirit.

How to discern between our own heart and the voice of God:

(1) Anything that modifies or contradicts God's already revealed truth isn't from God, for His truth doesn't change.

(2) If something is ridiculous, it isn't from Him.

(3) We can wait and see if it comes to pass.

The word of wisdom is knowledge applied. Sometimes we're given knowledge so that we'll pray. No other action may be necessary.

•**VERSE 10** The gift of prophecy is more a speaking forth of God's message than a foretelling of events.

Discerning of spirits is the ability to discriminate between the Spirit of God and the spirit of Satan (Revelation 2:2).

•**VERSE 13** The whole Church is one body. We need the unifying power of the Holy Spirit to bring us together in love.

•**VERSES 22-26** All the parts of the body are vitally important.

•**VERSE 31** Our place in the body determines what the best gifts are for our ministry.

We desire the power of the Spirit in our lives, but love demonstrates a deeper walk with God than the exercise of spiritual gifts.

CHAPTER 13:
AGAPE LOVE

•**VERSES 1-3** The gifts of power are nothing if we don't exercise them in love.

•**VERSE 4** The description of agape love ("charity") begins here.

"Vaunteth" means boasts. "Puffed up" means blows itself up.

•**VERSE 5** Love is gracious and doesn't misbehave. Love doesn't seek its own way. Love isn't provoked (the word "easily" isn't in the Greek manuscripts). Love doesn't keep a record of evil.

•**VERSE 7** "Bears all things" means covers as a shield to protect.

•**VERSES 8-9** We won't need spiritual gifts when we have our heavenly bodies.

KEY WORDS

eros = love on a physical level, lust
phileo = love, fondness, friendship
agape = a giving love, a divine love, a
self-sacrificing love

AGAPE LOVE

1 CORINTHIANS 13

Suffers Long	Does Not Envy
Is Kind	Does Not Parade Itself
Rejoices in The Truth	Is Not Puffed Up
Bears All Things	Does Not Behave Rudely
Believes All Things	Does Not Seek Its Own
Hopes All Things	Is Not Provoked
Endures All Things	Thinks No Evil
Never Fails	Does Not Rejoice In Iniquity

•**VERSE 10** Most Greek scholars agree that "that which is perfect" refers to the coming of Jesus Christ. Some say that this refers to the full revelation of the Bible, but the context doesn't bear this out.

The gifts of the Spirit are helpful and should be in operation until Christ returns (Acts 2:16-20).

•**VERSE 12** We're looking through a dark glass, and it's hard to understand the things of the Spirit. We still need Him to speak the words of God to our hearts.

We'll know each other in heaven, for we'll know more, not less, than we know now.

•**VERSE 13** If we read verses 4-7 and substitute the name of Jesus for "charity," the verses flow easily.

However, when we put our own name in the place of "charity" we see how much we need the work of the Spirit in our lives.

CHAPTER 14:
PROPER OPERATION OF SPIRITUAL GIFTS

•**VERSE 1** We shouldn't close the door to God's work in our lives.

"Prophesy" here again refers to speaking God's truth by the anointing of the Holy Spirit.

•**VERSE 2** The tradition of a "message in tongues" followed by an interpretation in which God is seemingly speaking to the congregation is unscriptural.

In this situation, the "interpretation" is usually a prophecy addressed to the congregation, since tongues are addressed to God (Acts 2:5-13).

"Mysteries" means divine secrets.

•**VERSE 3** Prophecy builds up, encourages, and consoles.

•**VERSE 4** When the Holy Spirit edifies us, He builds up Christ in us.

The Holy Spirit helps us to praise God without the limitations of our intellect. He also helps us to pray for things according to God's will and to intercede in a situation when we're not sure how to pray.

Prophecy builds up Christ in the whole Church.

•**VERSE 13** This verse doesn't apply to our personal prayer lives, but to those times when we might be in a group and pray in tongues.

•**VERSE 15** We have control whether we speak aloud or keep quiet when the Spirit tells us something.

Therefore, if we interrupt a service, we're responsible—not the Holy Spirit.

•**VERSE 26** The first rule for church service is that everything should build up Christ.

•**VERSES 27-33** Paul here gives some suggestions for orderly services.

•**VERSES 34-35** The men and women were separated and seated on either side of the assembly during services. The women were calling to their husbands to ask questions during the service, so Paul asked the women to wait until they were home to discuss the message.

•**VERSE 40** The second rule of the church service is that everything be done with dignity and order.

CHAPTER 15:
THE RESURRECTION OF CHRIST

•**VERSES 12-19** Most Greeks didn't believe in the resurrection of the dead, and some of the Corinthian Christians were led astray by the Greeks' worldly doctrine.

•**VERSES 20-26** Whereas Adam's sin brought death to the whole world, Christ's righteousness brought life to the whole world.

•**VERSE 29** Baptism for the dead is a practice that was common in the pagan religions of Greece and is still practiced today by some cults; but it doesn't change a person's eternity, for that is determined while he lives (Luke 16:26).

•**VERSE 36** "Quickened" means made alive.

•**VERSES 37-38** Resurrection is demonstrated in nature all the time by plants. The seed dies and later comes forth in a new body.

•**VERSES 39-44** The bodies we "plant" in the grave aren't the bodies we'll have when we're resurrected. Our new bodies will be spiritual, incorruptible, and perfectly adapted to heaven.

•**VERSES 52** Greek scholars say that this "trumpet" isn't the seventh trumpet of judgment in the Book of Revelation (11:15), for the construction in the Greek would have to be entirely different.

This trumpet will call the Church home.

•**VERSES 55-56** Christ removed the sting of death when He forgave our sins.

CHAPTER 16:
CONCLUSION

•**VERSE 2** This verse indicates that the Church was meeting on the first day of the week. Paul wanted all the offerings to be taken before he arrived in Corinth.

•**VERSES 6-7** Paul was very flexible about his plans for the months ahead so he could be subject to the leading of the Lord.

•**VERSES 8-9** Paul wanted to stay in Ephesus for awhile, because there was strong opposition to the Gospel there.

•**VERSES 10-11** Paul asked the Corinthians to accept Timothy and his teaching without intimidating him.

•**VERSE 13** "Quit" means acquit.

•**VERSE 19** Aquila and Priscilla met Paul when he first came to Corinth. They were among the first converts there and opened their home for Bible studies.

1. Why do unbelievers think the things of the Spirit are foolishness? (See 1 Corinthians 2:14.)

_____

_____

_____

2. According to 1 Corinthians 6:19-20, why should we honor God in our body and in our spirit?

_____

_____

_____

3. Temptation itself is not a sin; it is when we give into it that it becomes sin. What does 1 Corinthians 10:13 say God will do to help us while facing temptations?

_____

_____

_____

4. We see in 1 Corinthians 12 that there are many gifts of the Spirit. But those gifts are nothing if we don't exercise them in love. Give a definition of agape love as found in 1 Corinthians 13:4-8.

_____

_____

_____

5. Paul teaches in 1 Corinthians 10 that the experiences of the children of Israel were examples for us. Which one of these lessons in verses 6-10 can apply to your life today and why?

_____

_____

_____

THE SECOND EPISTLE OF PAUL TO THE
CORINTHIANS

AUTHOR OF LETTER:
Paul the Apostle

WRITTEN TO:
The church in Corinth.

DATE AND PLACE OF WRITING:
In Philippi around 60 A.D.

PURPOSE OF WRITING:
To give them proof of his apostleship, and to explain his intentions of coming to them.

INTRODUCTION:
When the church in Corinth received Paul's first epistle, those who were against him became more vocal, even expressing doubts about Paul's authority and apostleship. This second epistle is mainly Paul's defense and testimony of his ministry.

CHAPTER 1:
THE COMFORT OF GOD

•**VERSE 1** God, not man, calls and ordains people for the ministry. Paul's authority was from God.

•**VERSE 2** God is the source of grace and peace, and Christ is the avenue by which grace and peace flow to us.

•**VERSE 3** "Blessed" means praise be unto God.

"Mercies" also means blessings.

"Comfort" is the Greek word used for the Holy Spirit which means "One who comes along to help."

•**VERSE 4** When we experience God's help and comfort during a trial, we're better prepared to minister to others (1 Corinthians 15:32).

•**VERSE 5** Paul had endured many sufferings and had even been given up for dead.

Those who say that all Christians should be healthy don't understand God's dealings with man. Though God didn't remove Paul's thorn in the flesh, He did give him the strength to bear it (Chapter 12:7-9).

•**VERSES 6-7** Paul could see the purpose for his sufferings.

•**VERSE 8** Paul may have been speaking here of a serious illness, being fed to the lions, or some other torture he had to endure (1 Corinthians 15:32).

•**VERSE 9** When Paul thought he was dying, he found a deeper trust in God.

•**VERSE 10** It takes more faith to make a total commitment to God and to rest in whatever He chooses to do with us, than it does to demand that He heal us and put conditions on our service to Him.

•**VERSES 16-24** Paul had planned to visit Corinth on the way to Macedonia. He decided not to go when he heard of the turmoil his first letter of correction had caused.

•**VERSE 22** "Earnest" means a deposit, which shows good faith.

CHAPTER 2:
HOW TO RESIST SATAN

•**VERSES 1-2** Paul didn't want to visit the church to discipline the Corinthians, for the believers there had been a joy to him.

•**VERSE 4** It was agonizing for Paul to write his epistle to the Corinthians, for he had to settle many problems in the church in that letter.

•**VERSES 6-8** The man from the first epistle who had been involved in the incestuous affair had repented, so Paul told the Christians to forgive, comfort, and confirm their love for the man.

•**VERSE 11** To keep Satan from taking advantage of a situation to destroy us, we need to:

(1) Recognize the attacks of Satan.

(2) Resist his attacks by refusing them through the victory Christ won for us on the Cross.

(3) Rejoice in the victory over Satan.

•**VERSE 14** When the Romans won a great battle, the celebration would include a victory parade and the burning of incense. The fragrance or "savour" of the incense would fill the city.

•**VERSE 17** "Corrupt" means make merchandise. Some men used the work of God as an opportunity to prey on people.

They seek to make financial gain from the believers. Paul was aware that God was always observing him.

KEY WORD

kapeleuo = corrupt, make merchandise

CHAPTER 3:
THE NEW COVENANT

•**VERSE 5** The greatest lesson of strength we can learn is that God is our sufficiency (John 15:5; Philippians 4:13).

•**VERSE 6** The letter of the Law condemns us all to death, but the new covenant of grace by the Spirit of God gives us life.

Many people misinterpret this verse and say that Bible studies deaden us, and emotional experiences bring life to the Church. The "letter" of the Law condemns me to death.

•**VERSES 7-13** Moses covered his face so the people wouldn't see the glory of God fading from his face.

•**VERSE 14** The glory of the Law has also faded; because when Jesus Christ established the new covenant, the old covenant was no longer necessary.

We don't need the Law to establish our righteousness, for our faith in Christ does so according to God's grace and faithfulness.

•**VERSES 15-16** The Jews regard the Law as if the veil were still there; they don't see that the glory has faded away. One day they'll be able to see the Law without the veil.

•**VERSE 18** Our faces are unveiled so that we can clearly see the glory of Christ.

With our eyes on Him, we're changed into His image by the Holy Spirit.

CHAPTER 4:
THE HOPE OF GLORY

•**VERSES 3-4** The Gospel is unseen by those who are lost, because Satan has blinded their eyes. These people are often too prejudiced to reasonably discuss spiritual things.

We need to pray that God will destroy the blinding power and influence Satan has over them and that the Holy Spirit will open their eyes to the truth (2 Corinthians 10:4).

•**VERSE 7** The greatest treasure on earth is the good news of God's love for us, the Gospel; and God has graciously chosen to put this treasure into us, the earthen vessels.

•**VERSE 9** We're never forsaken by God.

•**VERSE 14** We know that the same Spirit that raised Christ from the dead will also raise us.

•**VERSE 17** Though this life is often painful, our problems will seem mild and only temporary when we see it from the spiritual side.

•**VERSE 18** We can comfort ourselves by keeping our eyes on spiritual rather than material things, for the spiritual things are eternal.

CHAPTER 5:
OUR EARTHLY TENTS

•**VERSE 1** "Tabernacle" means tent. Paul often refers to our bodies as tents temporarily housing our spirits.

•**VERSE 5** "Earnest" again means deposit. The Holy Spirit is the down payment God has given to show that He is earnest about completing the work of redemption He has begun in us.

🔑 KEY WORD

arrhabon = earnest, deposit (5:5)

•**VERSES 6-8** Death is actually moving from the tent to our new house. Paul's desire was to leave his body and join the Lord in heaven.

•**VERSE 10** When we Christians stand before the judgment seat of Christ, the motivations behind our works will be evaluated. The works prompted by base desires will be burned, and only the ones done in the right spirit will remain. We will be rewarded according to these.

Our judgment will have nothing to do with our salvation, for that was determined when we accepted Christ. There will be a different judgment for sinners before God's Great White Throne (Revelation 20:11-15).

•**VERSE 11** "Terror" means fear or reverence.

•**VERSE 13** Some people were saying that Paul was crazy; being "beside oneself" indicated a split personality.

•**VERSE 15** Colossians 3:4; Philippians 1:21.

•**VERSE 16** We want to know Christ by the Spirit, not merely know of Him through what others say.

•**VERSE 17** Many of our difficulties as Christians arise from the struggle between our new spiritual nature and the fleshly body, in which it is trapped.

•**VERSES 18-19** God wants us to participate in the reconciliation of the world to Him, the plan He was working out during the life of Christ.

•**VERSE 20** We're representatives of Christ with the authority to speak for Him.

As ambassadors, we're not at home in this corrupt world, but our hearts are at home in heaven (Hebrews 11:13-16).

•**VERSE 21** God imputed our sins to Jesus and imputes His righteousness to us. What a deal!

CHAPTER 6:
THE MINISTRY

•**VERSE 3** If a minister does something that offends people, they blame the ministry.

•**VERSES 4-5** "Approving" means proving. "Necessities" means going without. These are some of the physical strains of the ministry.

•**VERSE 6** Pureness, knowledge, longsuffering, and kindness are the emotional pressures the minister deals with.

•**VERSES 7-10** The Holy Ghost, love unfeigned, and verses 7-10 are the spiritual aspects of the ministry.

•**VERSES 14-18** This is a warning to those Christians considering marriage to an unbeliever. What fellowship has straightness with crookedness? "Belial" is Satan.

CHAPTER 7:
GODLY SORROW

•**VERSES 2-4** Paul felt free to open his heart to the Corinthians.

•**VERSES 5-7** Paul had second thoughts about the first letter he sent to the Corinthians, because he had dealt harshly with them.

He wanted them to realize that he only wrote so strictly because he loved them as a father (verse 12).

•**VERSE 10** Sorrow with repentance brings change. Sorrow alone accomplishes nothing.

Peter was sorry he denied Christ and he repented. Judas was sorry he betrayed Christ, but instead of repenting, he killed himself.

•**VERSES 13-16** Paul was delighted with the attitude and the changed behavior of the Corinthian Christians when they read his letter.

CHAPTER 8:
THE EXAMPLE OF THE MACEDONIANS

•**VERSE 1** The northern part of Greece was called Macedonia; the southern part was called Achaia. Corinth was in Achaia.

•**VERSE 2** The Macedonians were poor, but they gave freely to the saints in Jerusalem.

•**VERSE 3** "Power" means credit.

•**VERSE 4** Paul didn't want to take the gift from the Macedonians at first, because he knew how poor they were themselves.

However, he revealed that they wanted to be part of the fellowship of the body by ministering to the church in Jerusalem.

•**VERSE 5** After we give ourselves to God, He guides us in giving to others.

•**VERSE 8** Paul wasn't commanding the Corinthians to give but asking them to show their love.

•**VERSE 9** Paul uses Jesus as another example of sacrificial giving.

•**VERSES 10-11** The Corinthians had decided to send a gift to Jerusalem the year before.

Paul was telling them that the time had come to act on that decision.

•**VERSE 14** Paul sought a balance between those who had an abundance and those who were in need in the Church.

He knew the Corinthians themselves might someday need help from the other churches.

•**VERSE 18** The "brother" mentioned here is probably Luke.

•**VERSES 21-22** Paul wanted to keep the handling of the money they collected above suspicion.

CHAPTER 9:
THE SPIRITUAL LAW OF GIVING

•**VERSE 6** This is an important spiritual law. Spiritual laws are as reliable as the laws of nature.

•**VERSE 7** Giving should be between God and the individual. We shouldn't give under pressure (necessity) or grudgingly, but as we have decided in our hearts.

"Cheerful" here is also translated as hilarious.

CHAPTER 10:
PAUL DEFENDS HIMSELF

Some scholars believe that Chapters 10 through 13 are actually a second epistle, and Chapters 1 through 9 are a third epistle.

Certainly, there seems to be much in these next chapters that don't seem to follow the tone or content of the preceding chapters.

•**VERSE 1** Apparently, some of the Corinthians who disliked Paul had ridiculed his appearance. "Presence" also means outward appearance.

•**VERSE 2** It seems that one man in the church in Corinth criticized Paul and had gathered a small group around himself. He seemed to use everything against Paul—from his appearance to the collection for the church in Jerusalem.

One of the accusations against Paul was that he was guided by his flesh and not by the Spirit (2 Corinthians 1:17).

•**VERSES 3-4** Paul's methods of defense were not carnal but spiritual.

•**VERSE 5** We need to ask the Holy Spirit for help in controlling our imagination and thoughts.

•**VERSE 8** Paul didn't want to tear the people down with his authority but to build them up.

•**VERSE 15** Paul had taken the Gospel to the Corinthians, but another man was building on the foundation Paul had laid.

There are always those who come into an established work and try to draw people after themselves. This man in Corinth was trying to build himself up by tearing Paul down.

•**VERSES 17-18** Some people take unto themselves the glory due to God for His works through them.

CHAPTER 11:
PAUL'S TRIALS

•**VERSE 2** In the Jewish culture, espousal was the period between engagement and marriage. It was the complete commitment of the couple to one another. However, the marriage wasn't consummated until the wedding ceremony had taken place.

A friend of the groom was assigned to watch over the bride during the espousal period to assure her virginity until the wedding day.

Paul here pictures himself as the friend of the Groom, Jesus Christ, and Paul desires to present the Church to Christ as a chaste bride.

•**VERSE 3** Satan used half-truths to beguile Eve when he tempted her to eat the forbidden fruit.

•**VERSE 4** Other teachers had come into the Corinthian Church and had introduced a gospel of works rather than the gospel as Paul had preached it.

•**VERSE 6** The Greeks highly prized graceful and eloquent speech.

Some of the Corinthians had said that Paul wasn't a polished orator, but he said that he spoke with the authority of knowledge.

•**VERSES 7-9** Paul accepted a love offering from the Philippian church while he was living and ministering in Corinth.

•**VERSES 13-15** God will judge the false teachers who lead the sheep astray.

•**VERSES 16-18** Paul was reluctant to defend himself against the criticisms of those in Corinth who were against him, but felt compelled to protect the flock by establishing his authority.

•**VERSE 24** The 39-stripe beating was enough to kill a man. Paul endured five such beatings for preaching the Gospel.

•**VERSES 25-28** Paul went through pain, torture, hunger, weariness, shipwreck, and dangerous journeys to carry the Gospel wherever Christ led him. In addition, Paul was concerned about all the churches.

CHAPTER 12:
PAUL'S WEAKNESSES

•**VERSE 1** "Expedient" means necessary.

•**VERSE 2** Fourteen years earlier, Paul was stoned in Lystra and his friends thought he was dead. Paul himself didn't know if he was dead or alive. Perhaps this was the occasion of Paul's experience.

The "third heaven" refers to the dwelling place of God. The first heaven is the atmosphere around the earth, and the second heaven is the celestial heaven of the sun and moon.

•**VERSE 4** Paul's experience was beyond his capacity to describe it.

•**VERSE 5** Paul chose to glory in his weaknesses rather than in his experiences, ministry, or spiritual power.

•**VERSES 7-8** "Thorn" is also translated twisting stake, which indicates excruciating pain. This was the physical suffering he endured from the "thorn."

The messengers (angels) of Satan brought mental anguish. When God didn't heal him or answer right away, Paul felt spiritual pain.

•**VERSE 9** God's answer to Paul was that He would be strong in Paul's weakness.

•**VERSE 10** When we know we're weak, we allow God to work through and in us as He desires.

•**VERSE 12** The signs of an apostle were:

(1) He must have seen the risen Christ.

(2) He had to have the gift of the working of miracles.

•**VERSE 14** Paul enjoyed his financial independence from the Corinthians. He wanted to give to them, not take from them.

•**VERSE 15** Paul would gladly have given of himself for the Corinthians.

•**VERSE 16** Paul here quotes his enemies. They said that he had been crafty about money, and instead of allowing the Corinthians to support him, he was going to keep the Jerusalem collection for himself.

•**VERSES 17-18** Paul pointed out that neither he, Titus, nor the other brethren had taken any money from the Corinthians for themselves.

CHAPTER 13:
PAUL'S WARNING

•**VERSES 2-3** Paul says here that on his next visit to Corinth he wouldn't spare those who walk in an unrighteous path.

•**VERSE 5** Paul warns the Corinthians to examine themselves, to prove whether or not they are really in the faith.

Without Christ the Corinthians would be reprobates.

•VERSE 8 Paul knew that the truth about himself would be revealed in time and the liars exposed. Unfortunately, damage is sometimes done before the truth is known.

•VERSES 11-14 Paul closes his letter with some beautiful admonitions and a loving benediction.

CALVARY DISTINCTIVE

"Therefore if any man be in Christ, he is a new creature: old things are passed away; behold, all things are become new" (2 Corinthians 5:17).

It's a beautiful work of God today, to see what the world has cast off and viewed as hopeless wrecks be transformed into glorious vessels of honor.

1. We have peace in knowing that the God we serve is the God of all comfort in times of trouble. How can we use trials and tribulations to glorify God? (See 2 Corinthians 1:4-5 and 1 Corinthians 11:23a.)

_____

_____

_____

2. Although in this life we will have problems and afflictions, 2 Corinthians 4:17 says that they are working for us an eternal glory that far outweighs them all. What is the comfort that we can hold onto in verse 18?

_____

_____

_____

3. Every person will eventually face death. Why is death for the believer not something to be feared? (See 2 Corinthians 5:1-8.)

_____

_____

_____

4. What is the important spiritual law found in 2 Corinthians 9:6 and Luke 6:38? What should the attitude of our heart be as we give? (See 2 Corinthians 9:7.)

_____

_____

_____

5. Jesus told Paul, "My grace is sufficient for you, for My strength is made perfect in weakness." Read 2 Corinthians 12:9-10. What does this scripture mean to you today?

_____

_____

_____

THE EPISTLE OF PAUL THE APOSTLE TO THE
GALATIANS

AUTHOR OF LETTER:
Paul the Apostle

WRITTEN TO:
The churches in the area of Galatia.

DATE AND PLACE OF WRITING:
Written during Paul's third visit to Corinth around 60 A.D.

THEME:
Grace and justification by faith.

PURPOSE OF WRITING:
To reaffirm his apostleship.
To correct the heretical teaching that had followed his ministry.
To free them again from the bondage of the Law.
To show them that salvation is through faith and through the grace of God.

CHAPTER 1:
ORDINATION FROM GOD

•**VERSE 1** "Apostle" means one who has been sent.

The apostleship of Paul had been challenged by false teachers. They questioned his authority because he had not been ordained by men—Paul was ordained directly by Jesus Christ (Acts 9:1-22).

The resurrection of Christ is central to the message of the Gospel. His victory over death is our reason to hope.

•**VERSE 3** Grace is God's unmerited favor. The peace Paul speaks of here is the peace of God. When we know the grace of God, then we can experience the peace of God.

The title "Lord" describes our relationship to Jesus.

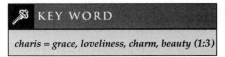

KEY WORD

charis = grace, loveliness, charm, beauty (1:3)

•**VERSE 4** Paul here describes the work of Jesus Christ for us.

•**VERSES 6-9** The Galatians were Gauls, who had conquered and settled the area of Asia Minor long before the birth of Christ. Paul traveled in Asia Minor on his missionary journeys.

The false teachers followed Paul after he left cities and challenged his authority and criticized his teaching.

"Gospel" means good news.

Paul taught the Galatians that their basis for righteousness was the grace of God. The false teachers said that a man's works made him righteous.

They were putting the Galatians under the yoke of the Law, which was really not another gospel, but a perversion of the good news that Christ had brought to man.

"Accursed" in Greek is anathema, which means cursed to the lowest hell.

•VERSES 10-12 Paul was taught the Gospel by Jesus Christ.

•VERSE 13 "Wasted" means devastated.

•VERSE 15 God's hand was on Paul's life from the moment of his birth.

He arranged for Paul to be a well-educated Jew, a Roman citizen, and a man who was immersed in the Greek culture from boyhood.

God knew what Paul needed to prepare him for the ministry.

God creates us for His pleasure (Revelation 4:11). He has a specific purpose for each one of us, and we can only be fulfilled when we're serving Him according to His plan (Psalm 17:15; John 8:29).

•VERSE 16 God wants us to reveal His Son to the world. He continually works in us through the Holy Spirit to mold us into the image of Christ (2 Corinthians 3:18; 1 John 2:6, 4:17).

"Heathen" here refers to the Gentiles.

•VERSES 17-18 Paul was prepared for the ministry by Jesus Christ for three years (Zechariah 4).

•VERSES 19-24 Paul wanted the Galatians to know that his teachings were direct revelations from Jesus Christ, not doctrine from the Church leaders.

CHAPTER 2:
JUSTIFICATION BY FAITH

•VERSE 1 Acts 15.

•VERSE 2 Paul spoke privately to the apostles, who were highly esteemed among the brethren, so that there wouldn't be a general commotion over his ministry to the Gentiles.

•VERSES 4-5 Paul had defended the gospel of grace and hadn't submitted himself to the teachers who tried to make Jews out of the Christians.

He hadn't gone to Jerusalem for guidance from the elders there, but to state his case. He felt very strongly that the Gentile Christians should maintain the liberty they had in Christ.

•VERSES 6-9 Paul explained to the Galatians that there was no established spiritual hierarchy in Jerusalem constituting a spiritual authority over the whole Church.

He wanted them to realize that the Christian Jews were no closer to God than the Christian Gentiles.

Cephas is another name for Peter.

•VERSE 13 "Dissimulation" here refers to hypocrisy.

•VERSE 16 Justification before God comes by faith in Jesus Christ (Romans 4:5).

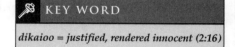

KEY WORD

dikaioo = justified, rendered innocent (2:16)

•VERSE 17 Romans 5:20-6:2, 8:22-23; 1 Corinthians 15:54-57.

•VERSE 20 The basis for our relationship with God is His unmerited grace. God wants us to trust Him for our salvation rather than rely on our own righteousness of faith (Hebrews 11:6; Ephesians 2:8).

Our salvation is the work of God: He drew us to Himself, gave us faith and imputed the righteousness of Christ to us.

Christ established the basis for salvation with His death on the cross, as we identify ourselves with Him by making Him our Lord.

We share in His death, resurrection, and life. Now we walk in the Spirit rather than in our corruption.

•VERSE 21 We do not frustrate the grace of God. When we accept His numerous gifts, we establish the grace of God in our lives.

Our righteousness isn't based on our keeping the Law, but on the righteousness of Christ through faith. The faith that brings this righteous standing before God is the faith that manifests itself in the works of God (Romans 6:2: 1 John 3:9).

We shouldn't misuse the grace of God as an excuse to continue in sin (1 Peter 2:16; Jude 4).

CHAPTER 3:
THE PROMISE TO ABRAHAM

•VERSE 1 The righteousness we have through Christ is complete; it cannot be improved upon.

•VERSE 2 We come to God on the basis of what He is, not on the basis of what we are.

The door is always open to us when we approach Him on the basis of His grace, but rarely open when we approach Him on the basis of our righteousness.

If we can fellowship with God in a love relationship, why would we ever choose a legal relationship instead?

The gift of the Holy Spirit isn't an earned blessing.

•VERSE 3 Paul relates the spirit to our faith and the flesh to our works.

Our faith produces fruit, not fleshly works. Fruit is the natural result of relationship (1 Corinthians 11:28-31; Matthew 12:33; John 15:8).

God doesn't require us to do works we hate, but He endows and equips us for a particular ministry in the Body of Christ. When we fulfill our ministry, it's natural and comfortable for us (2 Corinthians 5:14).

God doesn't acknowledge or reward the works of our flesh; He wants to see the fruit of the Spirit in our lives, which is the product of believing and abiding in Jesus (John 15:1-8).

When we received Jesus, God justified and imputed the righteousness of Christ to us. Our works of the flesh do not add anything to our relationship with God.

He is pleased by our faith (Hebrews 11:6).

•VERSE 5 The fruit is produced in our lives—not because of our righteousness, but because of faith (Acts 3:1-16; Matthew 5:16; James 5:17,18).

•VERSE 6 Abraham is acknowledged as the father of those who believe. Righteousness was imputed to him because of his faith, not because of his actions. What Abraham believed was demonstrated by what he did.

Our actions must also be in harmony with what we believe.

•VERSE 7 Abraham is the father of a spiritual race of people, rather than a physical race.

•VERSES 8-9 The covenant blessings God gave to Abraham are ours also through faith.

•VERSES 10-11 The Law condemns the man who tries to be justified by it.

•VERSE 12 The Law is concerned with works, not with faith.

•VERSE 13 The New Testament emphasizes what God has done for us.

The Church has made the mistake of emphasizing what we should do for God.

We have moved from the life of faith, grace, and spirit to the life of law, works, and flesh. We've gone from blessing and victory to a life of rejection and defeat (1 Peter 1:3-5).

The Law was intended by God to show us our inadequacy and our need of Him; it was never intended to make men feel righteous (Romans 7:7; Galatians 3:24).

• **VERSE 14** We cannot receive the Holy Spirit by the works of the Law. We receive the Holy Spirit by our faith in Jesus Christ.

• **VERSE 15** God confirmed His covenant with Abraham. The Law, which was added 430 years later, didn't void the original covenant (verse 17).

• **VERSE 16** The blessing of Abraham is Jesus Christ and the fellowship with God that He makes possible.

• **VERSES 17-18** God's covenant with Abraham concerned the Gentiles, and the Law was for Israel. Therefore, the covenant with Abraham wasn't affected by the Law.

• **VERSE 19** The Law is good and holy. Obedience to the Law provides a life of blessing. The Law is the standard that God is conforming us to.

Our relationship with God is established on faith, not on our obedience to the Law. Our faith is a constant while our experience (obedience) is a variable.

The Law was necessary before Christ came, to give man a covering for his sins so he could relate to God.

• **VERSE 21** If the Law could make us righteous, God wouldn't have sacrificed His Son (Luke 22:42).

• **VERSE 22** Romans 3:23.

• **VERSE 23** The Law kept people at a distance from God with the priest as mediator.

• **VERSE 24** The schoolmaster in the Greek culture was the household servant who escorted the child safely to the place of instruction.

The Law taught us where we failed to meet God's standards. It made us realize how our sins separated us from God, and how impossible it was for us to be righteous on our own.

The Law showed us our need for Christ. When we're justified, God imputes righteousness to us just as if we had never sinned.

• **VERSE 25** After the Law has driven us to Christ, it has finished its work in us (Micah 6:8; Matthew 5:48; John 16:7-11; Matthew 12:31-32; Isaiah 53:6).

The power of the Spirit and our love for Christ combine to keep us on the path of righteousness now.

• **VERSE 26** "Children" here means "placed as a son" (John 1:12).

• **VERSE 27** When we're baptized, we bury the old life of the flesh and begin a new life in Christ (Romans 6:3-7; John 3:6-7).

• **VERSE 28** Jesus Christ removes the distinctions that divide people into superior and inferior groups.

CHAPTER 4:
FREEDOM FROM THE LAW

• **VERSE 2** "Tutors" refers to guardians. "Governors" here refers to stewards.

The Law was a guardian for the children of Israel. They were the heirs of many promises from God, but they had to wait until the time chosen by God to enter into the full inheritance.

• **VERSE 3** "Elements" here refers to elementary things, the basic fundamentals. Being under the Law is being in bondage (Acts 15:1-31).

• **VERSE 4** God sent His Son from His presence in heaven to redeem fallen man on the earth (John 17:5).

•**VERSE 6** The Trinity works in harmony (Romans 8:16). Jesus often used the intimate word "Abba" when speaking of His Father.

•**VERSE 7** We need the restraints of the Law when we have a primary relationship with God. When we mature to a love relationship with Him, we no longer need the Law.

Where there is a strong love relationship, there is no need for laws. Love fulfills the Law (Romans 13:10; Matthew 22:37-40; John 13:35; 2 Corinthians 9:7; Ephesians 1:18).

•**VERSE 8** Romans 6:20.

•**VERSE 9** We know God only because He has revealed Himself to us (Job 11:7; John 6:44).

The Law is weak because it can only diagnose our problems; it cannot cure them.

•**VERSE 10** The days the Jews observed were the Sabbath days; the months were the new moon feasts; the times they observed were the annual festivals; and the years they observed were the sabbatical years.

•**VERSE 12** Paul begged the Galatians to walk in grace as he did, rather than live under the Law.

•**VERSES 13-14** Paul once described his physical problem as a "thorn in the flesh" (stake, literally) 2 Corinthians 12:7.

"Temptation" refers to the testing.

•**VERSE 15** Paul's reference here to the Galatians "giving him their eyes" could indicate that he had eye problems; or, he could be describing the depth of their love for him.

•**VERSE 16** 3 John 4.

•**VERSE 17** The false teachers were very affectionate toward the Galatians.

•**VERSE 19** This is the only time Paul used the endearing term "my little children" in his letters.

The Holy Spirit works in us to conform us into the image of Christ (Ephesians 4:13).

•**VERSE 20** Paul wished the Galatians to know that he was softening his tone at this point.

•**VERSE 23** Ishmael, the son of the servant Hagar, was the child produced by fleshly efforts to fulfill God's promise. Isaac, the son of Sarah, was the child of faith.

•**VERSE 27** Paul quotes this scripture to demonstrate that there will be many more converts to God through His grace than through the Law (Isaiah 54:1).

•**VERSE 28** Paul relates the Christian to Isaac, the child of promise.

•**VERSE 29** The false teachers were persecuting Paul just as Ishmael had mocked Isaac.

CHAPTER 5:
RIGHTEOUSNESS BY FAITH

•**VERSE 1** Paul here urges the Galatians to hold to the sound doctrine he had taught them, rather than being confused and caught up in every new wind of doctrine (Ephesians 4:11-14).

•**VERSE 2** Paul points out the futility of being circumcised or doing any other work to try to assure salvation or righteous standing with God.

No religious ritual can ever save us.

•**VERSES 3-4** If a man is circumcised in order to be saved, then he is responsible for the whole law, because he has established a legal relationship with God (James 2:11).

•**VERSE 5** Philippians 3:4-9.

•**VERSE 7** First Corinthians 9:24; Philippians 3:14.

•**VERSE 8** The doctrine taught by the false teachers wasn't from God but from men.

Many of the cults put people under bondage to their laws.

Their leaders are often very convincing speakers, and we need to evaluate the teachings we hear in light of what the Bible says (1 Thessalonians 5:21).

•VERSE 9 If we move just slightly away from pure doctrine, we can go further away, as we try to reconcile our beliefs.

•VERSE 11 The Cross offends people, because when Christ sacrificed Himself for the sins of every person, He became the only way to God.

People are bothered by the narrowness of one way; they prefer to think that man can somehow affect his salvation through a wide choice of roads to God.

•VERSE 13 We're no longer slaves to our flesh, sin, and Satan when we're born again (Romans 6; 2 Timothy 2:26). We're also free from the Law.

Now we must exercise our freedom so that we're not brought back into bondage (1 Corinthians 6:12).

•VERSE 16 "Walk" here refers to our manner of life.

When our spirits are in union with God, we're alive. When our spirits are not in union with God, we're dead (Ephesians 2:1-3).

One of the signs that a man isn't in fellowship with God is his conformity to the world (Romans 12:12; 1 John 2:15; 2 Corinthians 6:17).

God communicates with us through our spirits (Romans 8:16-17; John 4:23-24). The spirit confirms that we belong to God (John 14:20) and opens our understanding of spiritual things teaching and instructing us (1 Corinthians 2:14-15).

When we walk in the Spirit, we allow Him to rule our minds and control our thoughts (Romans 8:5). We feed on spiritual food to keep our spiritual man strong (Job 23:12).

If we program our minds with spiritual things, then the Spirit overflows from our lives.

When we walk in the Spirit we have fellowship with God (1 John 1:7). We have joy, peace, understanding, and patience We also have strength and power over the flesh with the ability to see the consequences of following the fleshly life (Romans 8:6).

•VERSE 17 The conflict between the flesh and the Spirit is common in the life of the believer.

God has given us instincts and desires that are part of our natural function. When our fleshly instincts try to rule us, then the struggle with the Spirit begins (Romans 7:19-25).

Sometimes it seems that we're overwhelmed by our fleshly desires (Matthew 26:41), but God uses our weak areas to show us His strength (Romans 7:24-25).

When we ask Him for help, He is right there with the power to do for us what we cannot do for ourselves.

We cannot reform our flesh; it must be crucified (Galatians 2:20; Romans 6:6). We must continually reckon our flesh dead and buried as new temptations occur.

God works on us from the inside out, not from the outside in. While we try to practice self-control, God is teaching us Spirit-control.

•VERSE 18 Romans 8:14; Psalm 40:8; 2 Corinthians 3:3.

•VERSE 19 These works of the flesh all deal with sexual sin (1 Corinthians 6:15-20; Romans 1:21-27). "Uncleanness" is immorality.

•VERSE 20 Idolatry is worshiping God in ways that He doesn't sanction. Many people offer the works of their flesh to God as worship. God doesn't reward the works of the flesh.

The meaning of the word translated "witchcraft" here encompasses the use of hallucinogenic drugs.

Wrath is an ungovernable temper given to explosions.

One who strives is self-seeking. An example is the politician who seeks office to gratify his ego rather than to serve the people.

• **VERSE 21** Our Christian life should be wholehearted and intense, not a borderline experience (1 Corinthians 9:24).

• **VERSE 22** The contrast here is between the works of the flesh and the fruit of the Spirit.

Our fruit is nurtured and cultivated by God (John 15:1,4). The Spirit is the dynamic power of God working in our lives to bring forth fruit (Acts 1:8; Romans 8:14).

The word "love" here is the Greek word *agape*, the unselfish spiritual love that comes from God. The rest of this verse describes agape (1 Corinthians 13). The fruit of the Spirit is agape (1 John 3:14).

Joy is the consciousness of God's love. Peace is more than the absence of conflict. True peace is only possible when agape exists.

Gentleness is sensitivity to the needs of others. Love is the strongest motivator for goodness. Agape causes others to have faith in our word; it makes us trustworthy.

Meekness is humility. The people who are humble don't tell you they are. Temperance is moderation.

The fruit of the Spirit should be flowing from our lives for the building up of the Body of Christ (James 1:22-24).

• **VERSE 25** Living in the Spirit begins when we are born again.

Walking in the Spirit means that we are conscious of God's presence with us at all times.

FRUIT OF THE SPIRIT

LOVE

JOY

PEACE

LONG-SUFFERING

GENTLENESS

GOODNESS

FAITH

MEEKNESS

TEMPERANCE

An awareness of God's presence helps us to be obedient to Him and to avoid evil.

If we walk in the Spirit, we will not fulfill the desires of the flesh (verse 16). Walking in the Spirit is walking in love.

• **VERSE 26** The glory and praise of men soon passes.

Making a show in the flesh provokes others and causes envy. We should conduct ourselves in a way that leads people to glorify God for our actions (John 3:29-30).

CHAPTER 6:
CHRISTIAN CONDUCT

• **VERSE 1** We are to reach out to help and lift the brother or sister who falls. We should show compassion and understanding, remembering that we also are tempted.

• **VERSE 2** Paul tells the Galatians to lift the burdens from each other in Christian love (John 13:34; Matthew 22:36-40).

The false teachers were adding to the Galatians' burdens by putting them under the Law.

KEY WORD

baros = burden, weight (6:2)

•**VERSE 3** Romans 12:3; James 1:22; 1 John 1:8; 1 Corinthians 4:7.

•**VERSE 4** Paul suggests that we examine the motivation behind our works to determine whether we did our best.

We shouldn't judge our works in comparison to the works of others, but in comparison to our ideal in Jesus Christ (Luke 18:10-14; John 16:8-11).

•**VERSE 5** Paul uses a different Greek word here for "burden" than the word he used in verse 2. The "burden" in verse 2 is the same as used in Acts 15:28. The "burden" here in verse 5 is similar to a backpack.

•**VERSE 6** The Lord blesses those who give cheerfully and willingly to Him (Malachi 3:8-12; Philippians 4:17).

Unfortunately, some people try to take advantage of Christians by begging for money, as if the work of God depended on men's donations.

•**VERSES 7-8** We mustn't make allowances for our flesh (Romans 13:14). Many people fool themselves into thinking that they can live to please their flesh and have a good relationship with God, too.

•**VERSES 9-10** We shouldn't be so concerned about our own pleasure or comfort that we overlook the needs of people all around us.

•**VERSES 12-13** Acts 15:10.

•**VERSE 14** We shouldn't glory in ourselves when God chooses to use us in some way (1 Corinthians 1:29).

We have to come to the cross in our own personal walk and experience.

We must be dead to the world and to the desires the world stirs up in us.

•**VERSE 15** Outward rituals like circumcision don't alter our standing with God. He closely observes our inward lives for signs of consecration.

•**VERSE 17** Paul was tired of defending his teachings and ministry.

His faithful and committed conduct, his willingness to suffer beatings, imprisonment for his testimony, and the abundant fruit from his ministry should have been enough to dispel any doubts that arose when false teachers attacked Paul's teachings.

CALVARY DISTINCTIVE

"Brethren, if a man be overtaken in a fault, ye which are spiritual, restore such a one in the spirit of meekness; considering thyself, lest thou also be tempted" (Galatians 6:1).

I thank the Lord for the grace that I've received, and having received God's grace, I seek to extend it to others.

STUDY QUESTIONS FOR GALATIANS

1. Since neither Jews nor Gentiles are justified by the works of the Law, how are we then justified? (See Galatians 2:16.)

_____

_____

_____

2. According to Galatians 3:24 what was the purpose of the Law?

_____

_____

_____

3. We see in Galatians chapter 4 that if we have faith in Jesus Christ, then we are God's children. What has God given to us as His children? (See Galatians 4:6, 1 John 4:13, and Ephesians 1:13.)

_____

_____

_____

4. Read over the list of the works of the flesh in Galatians 5:19-21. What does it say about the people who do such things?

_____

_____

_____

5. Our flesh and spirit are in conflict with each other. Galatians 5:16 says that if we walk in the Spirit we will not fulfill the lust of the flesh. What does it mean to walk in the Spirit?

_____

_____

_____

THE EPISTLE OF PAUL THE APOSTLE TO THE
EPHESIANS

AUTHOR OF LETTER:
Paul the Apostle

WRITTEN TO:
The church in Ephesus, and perhaps to the church of Laodicea as well.

DATE AND PLACE OF WRITING:
Approximately the year 64 A.D., during Paul's imprisonment in Rome.

THEME:
That we are in Christ Jesus.

PURPOSE OF WRITING:
To enumerate the spiritual blessings we have in and through Jesus Christ.
To tell them what God has done for them.
To promote unity in the body of Christ.
To encourage them to live as children of light.

CHAPTER 1:

THE BELIEVER'S PLACE IN CHRIST

•**VERSE 1** The theme of this book is that we are in Christ Jesus (John 15).

•**VERSE 2** Remember that "Lord" is a title, not part of the name of Jesus. "Christ" is His distinction, for He is the Messiah.

•**VERSE 3** There has to be a work of God in our lives before we can do something for Him.

We need to see our position in Christ, seated with Him in heavenly places, before we can learn to walk the Christian walk.

•**VERSE 4** The first blessing we have in Christ is that we were chosen by God.

•**VERSE 6** The second blessing is that God has accepted us through Jesus Christ.

God will not and cannot accept us apart from Jesus.

•**VERSE 7** The third blessing is that we've been redeemed by the shed blood of Christ and that our sins have been forgiven (Psalm 32:1).

•**VERSE 8** God's grace has abounded toward us.

•**VERSES 9-10** The fourth blessing is that God has made His will known to us: that Christ may be the center of all.

•**VERSE 11** The fifth blessing is that we've been given an inheritance in the Kingdom of God.

•**VERSES 13-14** After we heard the Gospel and believed, God gave us the Holy Spirit as proof of His intention to complete our redemption.

•**VERSE 15** Faith and love go hand-in-hand.

•**VERSE 16** It's important that we study Paul's prayer to learn how to pray more effectively.

•**VERSE 17** Philippians 3:10; Job 11:7.

We can only have the true knowledge of God as the Holy Spirit reveals Him to us.

•**VERSE 18** Once we know the glory that God has in store for us, the world loses its attraction. God values us highly and considers the saints a rich inheritance.

•**VERSES 19-23** What a vast source of power God is, but how little of His power we appropriate in our lives.

CHAPTER 2:
GOD'S GRACE

•**VERSE 1** "Sin" means to miss the mark. It's not necessarily willful; sometimes it's an omission. A "trespass" is a deliberate sin (transgression).

KEY WORD

hamartia = sin, to miss the mark (2:1)

•**VERSE 2** "Walked" means meandered. Meandering is aimless sauntering. "Course" here comes from the Greek word for *weather vane*.

Before Christ, we followed the tide of the world wherever it took us; Satan was in control of our lives.

•**VERSE 3** "Conversation" means manner of living.

•**VERSE 6** This is our position in Christ.

•**VERSE 7** God is going to take all eternity to show us how much He loves us.

•**VERSES 8-9** Our salvation is a gift of God through faith, not a reward for any works we've done; for God wants the glory.

•**VERSE 10** "Workmanship" comes from the Greek work *poiema*, which means handiwork or a careful work of art.

As the artist seeks to express himself in his work, so God expresses Himself in us. God goes before us and prepares the path in which we walk.

KEY WORD

poiema = workmanship
From this Greek word we get a direct transliteration into English the word poem.
A poem is a work of art, and an artist is seeking to express himself in his work.
You are His workmanship. God wants to express Himself in you (2:10).

•**VERSES 14-15** Christ has made both Jew and Greek into one and has broken down the walls of race, class, occupation, or whatever separates people. He is the common denominator, making us all equal.

•**VERSES 20-22** Our bodies are now the temples of God.

CHAPTER 3:
THE PLAN OF SALVATION

•**VERSES 9-12** God kept His plan for man hidden until He decided to reveal the mystery to His Church (1 Peter 1:12).

•**VERSE 14** Being on our knees is a symbol of submission and worship.

•**VERSES 16-21** This is Paul's second prayer in this epistle.

"Dwell" means "to settle down and make oneself at home" (verse 17).

CHAPTER 4:
WALKING IN CHRIST

• **VERSE 1** We're called to be children of the King. We represent the Father to the world.

• **VERSE 6** God controls the circumstances of our lives. So, when we complain about our situation we're murmuring against God.

• **VERSE 7** The grace of God is sufficient for each of us, no matter what we've done.

• **VERSES 8-10** When Christ died, He first went to Sheol (or Hades) to preach to those who had died in the faith, believing that God would send the Messiah (Matthew 16:4; 27:52-53; Acts 2:30-31; Isaiah 61:1).

On the third day, He led the captives into eternal life.

• **VERSE 11** An apostle had to have seen the risen Christ and had to have the gift of miracles in operation in his life.

The gift of prophecy isn't limited to foretelling future events but is also a "forthtelling" of God's message.

Evangelists are especially gifted in sharing the Gospel with unbelievers.

Pastors and teachers or "teaching pastors" feed the Word of God to the Church (John 21:15-17; 1 Peter 5:2).

• **VERSE 12** The primary purpose of the Church isn't to convert sinners to Christianity, but to "perfect"(complete and mature) the saints for the ministry and edification of the Body.

• **VERSE 14** Strong sheep won't be led away from their shepherd.

A strong church emphasizes teaching the Word, so the people have a sound scriptural base to help them discern between true and false doctrine.

• **VERSES 15-16** Each of us adds a unique part to the Body of Christ.

• **VERSES 17-19** Paul's description of the heathen Gentiles in his time is an apt description of those who are blindly following Satan today.

They're empty-headed, ignorant, beyond feeling, and motivated by greed. "Uncleanness" means sexual impurity.

• **VERSE 22** "Conversation" again means manner of life. We're to put off the way of life that our flesh ("old man") wants us to lead.

• **VERSES 26-27** We should settle our differences as soon as possible, so Satan has no opportunity to take advantage of us.

• **VERSE 29** We can tear down or build up people with our word. How much better to build up and minister grace to those around us.

CHAPTER 5:
WALKING IN LOVE

• **VERSE 4** "Convenient" means necessary. Foolish talking and jesting are jokes that refer to fornication, uncleanness, and filthiness. Dirty jokes have no place in a Christian's conversation.

• **VERSE 16** It's so easy to waste time. We need to look for ways to use our time wisely.

• **VERSE 18** Be ye being filled or continually filled with the Spirit.

CALVARY DISTINCTIVE

"And be not drunk with wine, wherein is excess; but be filled with the Spirit" (Ephesians 5:18).

We believe that every born again child of God has the Holy Spirit dwelling in him. He is under the injunction of the Scriptures to yield his body to the control of the Holy Spirit and to be constantly filled with the Holy Spirit.

•**VERSE 19** We can encourage ourselves in the Lord by repeating scriptures and singing hymns and spiritual songs (1 Samuel 30:6; Psalm 42:5).

•**VERSE 23** This verse gives God's order for the home. If we try to defy God's order, we invite unhappiness into our relationships.

•**VERSE 25** Christ demonstrated His love for the Church in a powerful way. The more a husband shows his love to his wife and seeks to make her secure in his love, the easier for her to submit to him.

•**VERSE 26** The Word of God is one of the most powerful cleansing agents within the Church.

•**VERSE 27** Righteousness isn't something we attain by our actions; it's a gift we receive by our faith in Jesus Christ.

•**VERSE 33** Women were regarded in Greek and Jewish cultures as one step above a slave.

Paul here encouraged the husbands to regard their wives as beloved companions. "Reverence" also means respect.

CHAPTER 6:
STANDING WITH CHRIST

•**VERSE 1** In Paul's time, children were often considered an annoyance and had no rights. Babies were often abandoned or sold into slavery.

•**VERSES 2-3** This is the first commandment with a promise given in the Old Testament (Exodus 20:12).

•**VERSE 4** We shouldn't tease or provoke our children in an unkind way, nor should our expectations be so high that our children become frustrated by unrealistic demands.

•**VERSES 5-8** We should seek to be outstanding employees, cheerfully doing even the lowliest task and thinking of our work as a service to the Lord.

•**VERSE 10** Our strength is in the Lord.

•**VERSE 14** Our first weapon in spiritual warfare is truth, which is always stronger than a lie.

•**VERSE 16** Faith is a powerful weapon, protecting us from the fiery darts Satan sends our way.

•**VERSE 17** The sword of the Spirit, God's Word, is a strong offensive weapon against the enemy.

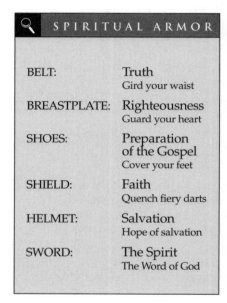

SPIRITUAL ARMOR

BELT:	Truth Gird your waist
BREASTPLATE:	Righteousness Guard your heart
SHOES:	Preparation of the Gospel Cover your feet
SHIELD:	Faith Quench fiery darts
HELMET:	Salvation Hope of salvation
SWORD:	The Spirit The Word of God

STUDY QUESTIONS FOR EPHESIANS

1. God has blessed us with all spiritual blessings in heavenly places in Christ. What blessings do you see in Ephesians 1:4-11?

_____

_____

_____

2. Salvation is a wonderful gift of God; it is not something we can earn. Why do you think God designed it this way? (See Ephesians 2:8-9.)

_____

_____

_____

3. How does God answer our prayers according to Ephesians 3:20?

_____

_____

_____

4. Ephesians 5:11 states that we are to have nothing to do with the unfruitful deeds of darkness. Write out verse 12. How can you apply this scripture in your life today?

_____

_____

_____

5. The Bible says that our warfare is not in the physical world. How are we to fight this battle as testified in Ephesians 6:13-18?

_____

_____

_____

THE EPISTLE OF PAUL THE APOSTLE TO THE
PHILIPPIANS

AUTHOR OF LETTER:
Paul the Apostle

WRITTEN TO:
The church in Philippi.
All believers everywhere.

DATE AND PLACE OF WRITING:
Approximately the year 61-62 A.D., during Paul's imprisonment in Rome.

THEME:
Joy

PURPOSE OF WRITING:

To show believers how to live in victory and joy in any circumstance.

To promote unity within the church.

To challenge the church to cling steadfastly to their faith in the Lord Jesus Christ.

To urge believers to abound in the love of Christ and experience fellowship with the Lord so that His joy and power could be theirs.

To express a personal "thank you" to his friends for their monetary gift.

CHAPTER 1:
PAUL'S PRAYER

•**VERSE 1** "Servant" is bondslave. A bondslave had no rights and was totally at the disposal of his master.

"Saint" means holy. Holy people are set apart and different from others. Paul notes that the place of the saints is in Christ Jesus.

 KEY WORD

hagios = holy, translated saint;
consecrated to Jesus Christ (1:1).

•**VERSE 2** "Grace," which also means beauty and charm, was the typical Greek salutation. The typical Hebrew salutation was and is "Peace" (Shalom).

•**VERSE 4** Third John 4.

•**VERSE 6** Hebrews 12:2.

•**VERSE 9** Paul always went to the heart of a matter in his prayers. He prayed about the causes, not the symptoms.

•**VERSE 10** Paul prayed that the Philippians would have discernment, so they would spend their time on the "excellent" things.

• **VERSE 12** Paul could see that his trials were serving a purpose in God's plan to spread the Gospel.

If Paul hadn't been confined in Rome he probably wouldn't have written the epistles.

• **VERSE 20** Paul's fervent desire was that Christ be magnified through him.

• **VERSES 23-24** Paul had mixed emotions, for he knew that when he died he'd be with Christ and that would be "far better" than to continue on earth.

However, Paul felt a responsibility to the churches under him to continue to guide them in spiritual things (2 Corinthians 5:8).

• **VERSE 27** "Conversation" again means manner of living. Paul wanted the believers to be: (1) of one spirit, (2) striving together for the faith, (3) not terrified by their enemies.

CHAPTER 2
EXHORTATIONS

• **VERSE 1** In Paul's day, people believed that the deepest emotions were felt in the pit of the stomach or bowel area. Today, we call it a "gut feeling."

• **VERSE 6** "Being" means "to be constantly established in a position." Christ is God and always has been God. "Robbery" means "something to be grasped."

• **VERSE 7** When Jesus made Himself of no reputation, He divested Himself of His heavenly glory. He emptied Himself as a pitcher turned upside down until the last drop drained out (John 17:5,14; 2 Corinthians 8:9).

Jesus took on the position of a servant when He assumed the body of flesh. He did this of His own volition and chose to submit Himself to the Father (John 6:38; 14:28; Hebrews 2:9; Matthew 26:39; 1 Timothy 3:16).

• **VERSE 8** Jesus was willing to abase Himself and to die a humble death on the Cross (Matthew 23:12; Luke 14:11).

• **VERSES 12-13** In the Greek manuscripts these two verses are one verse. God does all the work in us, giving us the will to do what He wants us to do.

• **VERSES 17-23** Caesar was so capricious that Paul had no idea whether he'd sentence him to death or release him.

• **VERSE 24** Paul was released and did visit Philippi.

CHAPTER 3:
PRESSING TOWARD THE MARK

• **VERSE 1** We should rejoice in the Lord even when we can't rejoice over the circumstances.

We don't need to praise and thank Him for sin or its effects, but we do need to have the right attitude toward Him in all things.

• **VERSE 2** Paul was warning the Philippians about the false teachers who'd try to lead them into Judaism.

The Jews called the Gentiles "dogs," so Paul turned it around and called the Judaizers "dogs."

"Concision" refers to mutilators of the flesh or those who enforced circumcision.

• **VERSE 3** Paul states that circumcision is actually a spiritual matter of the heart and not of the flesh.

• **VERSES 5-6** Paul had reason to glory in the flesh according to the Law, for he had been a Hebrew of the Hebrews.

• **VERSES 7-8** Paul was writing this letter some 30 years after his conversion on the Damascus road. He still had no regrets about giving up all that he had attained under the Law.

• **VERSE 9** The righteousness of Christ is so much better than the righteousness we earn by keeping the Law.

•**VERSE 10** We have to share in the sufferings of Christ as well as in the power of Christ.

•**VERSES 13-14** As Christians we must: (1) Forget the past and not allow ourselves to rest in our past works.

(2) Push ourselves ahead.

"Press" means persecute or give it everything we've got.

•**VERSE 20** "Conversation" again means manner of life.

•**VERSE 21** Our change will be a metamorphosis just as a caterpillar changes into a butterfly (1 John 3:2).

CHAPTER 4:
THE PHILIPPIANS' GIFT

•**VERSE 3** Exodus 32:32; Psalm 69:28; Daniel 12:1; Luke 10:20; Revelation 20:12.

•**VERSE 5** The Christian should be temperate in his attitude towards material things, because these will be so unimportant in God's kingdom.

•**VERSES 6-7** "Careful" means anxious.

The three steps to the peace of God are: (1) be anxious for nothing, (2) pray about everything, (3) be thankful for all things.

•**VERSE 8** We should keep our minds on things that edify (Proverbs 23:7).

•**VERSE 10** Paul was glad that the Philippians had sent some support to him.

•**VERSE 11** The world is trying to make us discontented with our lives and our belongings.

•**VERSE 13** This is one of the key verses of the New Testament, along with John 15:5.

•**VERSE 15** The Philippian Church was the only one that supported Paul when he left Macedonia.

•**VERSE 17** Paul didn't thank the Philippians so that he'd receive another gift from them, but to let them know that they'd share in the heavenly reward for his ministry.

•**VERSE 18** Paul had no longing or hankering for anything material; he was content with what he had.

•**VERSE 19** God's resources are infinite. He has more than enough to supply all our needs.

He doesn't always give us all our wants, because sometimes our wants aren't His will for us (Romans 8:32).

1. What were the four things that Paul prayed for the Philippians in Philippians 1:9-11?

_____

_____

_____

2. Read and meditate upon Philippians 2:6-8. We see that Jesus completely emptied Himself and was obedient unto death. What was the result? (See Philippians 2:9-11.)

_____

_____

_____

3. As Christians, what do we need to do in order to reach the goal that God has set for us? (See Philippians 3:13-14.)

_____

_____

_____

4. Sometimes it seems there is so much to worry about in our lives. What is the cure for worry found in Philippians 4:6-7?

_____

_____

_____

5. What things should we be thinking about and meditating upon? (See Philippians 4:8.)

_____

_____

_____

COLOSSIANS

AUTHOR OF LETTER:
Paul the Apostle

WRITTEN TO:
The churches in Colosse, Laodicea, and Hierapolis.

DATE AND PLACE OF WRITING:
Approximately the year 64 A.D., during Paul's imprisonment in Rome.

THEME:
The preeminence of Christ.

PURPOSE OF WRITING:
To correct heresies that were becoming popular in that community (Gnosticism, which denies the deity of Jesus Christ; and Judaism, which mixes works along with faith for salvation).

CHAPTER 1:
FAITH, LOVE, AND HOPE

•**VERSE 1** Paul had never visited the Colossian Church, but he had probably directed its establishment during his three years in Ephesus.

"Apostle" means one who is sent. God makes men into apostles, it's not something a man chooses for himself.

•**VERSE 2** Paul again uses "grace and peace" as a greeting.

•**VERSE 3** Paul had a rich, full prayer life.

Though he was a prisoner of Rome, he touched the world for God through his prayers.

He went to the heart of a problem when he prayed (Acts 9:11).

•**VERSES 4-5** This epistle is concerned with faith, love, and hope.

•**VERSE 6** It was a sad day when the Church decided it no longer needed the help of the Holy Spirit in the spreading of the Gospel.

The Church is reaching less people on a percentage basis with the Gospel today than it reached in Paul's time. The Gospel brings forth the fruit of freedom wherever it goes.

•**VERSE 7** Epaphras was a minister in Colosse. He had told Paul all about the church there.

•**VERSES 9-11** Paul prayed that the Colossians would: (1) know God's will for their lives, (2) walk worthy of the Lord, (3) be fruitful in good works, (4) increase in the knowledge of God, (5) be strengthened by His power.

•**VERSES 12-14** Paul gave three reasons to give thanks:

(1) God has made us fit to share in the inheritance of the saints.

(2) He has brought us out of darkness into His Kingdom.

(3) He has redeemed us through the blood of Christ and forgiven our sins.

•**VERSE 15** The word "image" comes from the Greek word *eikon,* a document that described a person in photographic detail.

Jesus was the "image" or manifestation of God.

The word "firstborn" comes from the Greek word *prototokos* and signifies preeminence rather than first in order of birth. "The Creator, First, Beginning of every creation" would be a correct translation.

•**VERSE 16** This verse describes Jesus as the Creator and the object of creation.

•**VERSE 17** Christ is also the sustainer of creation. "Consist" means held together (similar to cohesion).

•**VERSE 18** "Firstborn" again means first in eminence, not first chronologically.

•**VERSES 21-22** "Reconcile" means to change thoroughly from. We've been thoroughly changed from sinners to saints by Him.

•**VERSE 22-23** We can be confident that God will accept us when Christ presents us to Him, as long as we continue in the faith.

•**VERSES 26-27** The mystery that God has shown His saints is that Christ is in us, our hope of glory.

•**VERSE 28** "Perfect" means complete.

KEY WORD

musterion = mystery; enigma (1:27)

CHAPTER 2:
THE LAW IS REPLACED

•**VERSES 1-2** "Conflict" means care. Paul's prayer was that the hearts of the believers would be knit together in love and that they'd have a full assurance of Christ in them as the hope of glory.

•**VERSE 3** In Christ are hid all the treasures of wisdom and knowledge.

•**VERSES 5-7** Paul, who had become a part of their fellowship through prayer, was rejoicing in the order and strength of their faith.

•**VERSE 8** "Rudiments" means elements.

•**VERSE 9** In Christ dwells the fullness of the Godhead.

•**VERSE 10** "Head" means authority. "Principality and power" refers to the highest rankings of angelic beings.

•**VERSE 11** The "circumcision of Christ" is the spiritual work of Christ within us.

•**VERSE 12** Paul used the rituals of circumcision and baptism to demonstrate that it is Christ's work in us, not our own works, that gives us salvation.

•**VERSE 13** "Trespasses" means willful disobedience.

•**VERSE 14** The handwriting of ordinances against us is the Law. The Law condemned us but Jesus blotted it out by His death on the Cross (Romans 7:9).

•**VERSE 15** These principalities and powers are the rankings of demons and fallen angels in the satanic realm. Jesus triumphed over Satan through the Cross.

•**VERSE 18** The Gnostics taught that we need an intermediary to communicate with God and that angels serve this function.

They believed that Jesus was one of many angels who acted as an intermediary.

•**VERSES 20-22** If we're dead with Christ to the things of the flesh then the Law has no power over us.

CHAPTER 3:
THE NEW MAN

•**VERSES 2-3** Since we reckon the old man to be dead, our flesh shouldn't be able to entangle us in sin.

•**VERSE 4** Matthew 24:30; Revelation 19:14.

•**VERSES 5-10** These things of the flesh should be put to death (mortified) in us.

•**VERSES 12-17** The ancients thought that the pit of the stomach (bowels) was the area of deepest emotion. These are the deeds and emotions we should seek to encourage in ourselves.

•**VERSES 18-19** Ephesians 5:22-23. The wife is to submit to her husband as the husband is in submission to Christ.

•**VERSES 23-24** These verses give us a beautiful rule for life.

CHAPTER 4:
PAUL'S REQUEST

•**VERSE 3** Paul was chained to a Roman guard day and night during the writing of this letter.

•**VERSE 5** "Without" refers to those who are outside the Body of Christ.

•**VERSE 6** Our speech should be tasteful.

•**VERSE 9** Onesimus was once a runaway slave belonging to Philemon.

•**VERSE 11** "Jesus" was a popular name in the days of Paul; it is "Joshua" in Hebrew.

•**VERSES 12-13** Epaphras labored fervently in prayer for the Colossians, for he dearly loved them. "Zeal" means love.

•**VERSE 14** Luke, the author of the Gospel of Luke and the Book of Acts, was a physician.

•**VERSE 18** Paul probably reminded the Colossians of his chains, because he had difficulty signing his name clearly with the shackles on his arms.

CALVARY DISTINCTIVE

"And whatsoever ye do in word or deed, do all in the name of the Lord Jesus, giving thanks to God and the Father by him" (Colossians 3:17).

There's no more important attitude to have in the ministry. We need to serve as unto the Lord because we're going to find people obnoxious.

1. Paul's prayer life is a wonderful example for us. What five things did he pray for the Colossians in Colossians 1:9-11?

_____

_____

_____

2. What were the three things that Paul gave thanks to the Father for in Colossians 1:12-14?

_____

_____

_____

3. Compare Colossians 1:16-17 with John 1:1-3. What do they testify about Jesus?

_____

_____

_____

4. Colossians chapter 3 is full of rules for holy living. Write out verses 2 and 3 and memorize them.

_____

_____

_____

5. We are exhorted in Colossians 3:17 that whatsoever we do, whether in word or deed, do it all in the name of the Lord Jesus. What is the reason given in 3:23-24 for this exhortation?

_____

_____

_____

THE FIRST EPISTLE OF PAUL TO THE

THESSALONIANS

AUTHOR OF LETTER:
Paul the Apostle

WRITTEN TO:
The church in Thessalonica.

DATE AND PLACE OF WRITING:
Approximately 53 or 54 A.D. in Corinth, during his second missionary journey. (Possibly the first epistle Paul wrote.)

THEME:
The return of Jesus Christ.

PURPOSE OF WRITING:
To correct some of the misconceptions that had arisen within the church.
To encourage them in the faith and in godly living.
To affirm the hope of the coming of Jesus Christ.

CHAPTER 1:
FAITH, LOVE, AND HOPE

•**VERSE 1** This is one of the first epistles Paul wrote.

Since his apostleship had not yet been challenged by the false teachers, he didn't begin this epistle with a defense (as he did in so many others).

Silvanus is Silas.

•**VERSE 3** Faith is the work God requires of us (John 6:29).

Love motivated the works of the Thessalonian believers. They waited with patience for the return of Christ and the establishment of His Kingdom.

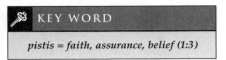
KEY WORD

pistis = faith, assurance, belief (1:3)

•**VERSE 4** God has chosen us to be His children (John 15:16; Romans 9:16).

•**VERSE 5** The power of the Holy Spirit was demonstrated in the miracles that accompanied Paul's teaching.

•**VERSE 6** The Jews had stirred up the people against Paul, so a great tumult and contention arose in the city when the Thessalonians received Christ.

•**VERSE 8** True evangelism is a by-product of a healthy church.

•**VERSE 9** Turning from idols to God is a work of faith.

It must have been difficult for the Thessalonians to give up their traditions in the worship of their pagan gods, for religion had been part of their lives for generations.

•**VERSE 10** Waiting for Jesus is the patience of hope.

There is a difference between the persecution of the Church and the Great Tribulation.

The persecution on Christians comes from others here on earth. The Tribulation is the wrath of God on the Christ-rejecting world.

It would be inconsistent for God to pour out His wrath on His Church (Genesis 18:20-32; 2 Peter 2:9).

CHAPTER 2:
THE TRUE MINISTER

•**VERSE 2** Paul was beaten and thrown into a dungeon in Philippi.

•**VERSES 3-5** God will hold the so-called evangelists and television personalities accountable for what they preach, and for the motivations behind their ministries.

 KEY WORD

akatharsia = uncleanness, referring to moral impurity (2:3)

•**VERSE 6** Paul was self-supporting, but some of the other apostles were supported by the churches.

•**VERSES 7-8** Paul was more interested in giving himself to the brethren than in gaining anything from them.

•**VERSE 11** "Charged" means challenged.

•**VERSE 12** We should walk as children of the King.

•**VERSE 13** John 15:3.

•**VERSES 15-16** This is Paul's assessment of the Jews, his brothers, who opposed Christ.

The leaders of the Jews weren't spiritual, but materialists. They crucified Christ because His teachings threatened their power and position.

Though the Jews were God's chosen people, they rejected His Son and listened to their leaders.

Since then, they have suffered more than any other people (Matthew 15:14; Luke 12:48).

•**VERSE 18** Satan sometimes hinders us in the things we want to do for God.

•**VERSES 19-20** The greatest joy and reward of any minister of God will be to see those to whom he ministered to gathered around the throne of God at Christ's coming.

Material rewards are nothing compared to this.

CHAPTER 3:
PAUL'S LOVE FOR THE THESSALONIANS

•**VERSE 3** Paul felt that the trials he experienced were part of his calling in the ministry.

•**VERSE 5** Paul sent Timothy to see how the church in Thessalonica was doing, because he was so anxious for them.

•**VERSES 6-8** Paul was comforted and uplifted by the news from the brethren.

•**VERSE 13** "To the end" means "for the purpose." When Christ comes again to establish His Kingdom on Earth, we'll be with Him (Colossians 3:4; Jude 14; Revelation 19:7-14).

CHAPTER 4:
THE CHRISTIAN WALK

•**VERSE 2** It's amazing how much Paul was able to teach the Thessalonians in the three weeks he spent with them.

•**VERSE 6** Not all people who claim to be Christians are honest businessmen.

•**VERSE 10** Many Christians are settled into spiritual complacency and aren't growing in Christ.

•**VERSE 11** Paul was aware of the damage which gossips can do when they don't mind their own business.

•**VERSE 13** The term "asleep" is used in the New Testament to describe a Christian who has moved from his earthly body to his heavenly body.

The word "moved" would be more appropriate.

The Christians wanted to differentiate this condition from the state of death for the unbeliever (John 11:26; 2 Corinthians 5:1-8; 12:2-4).

•**VERSE 15** "Prevent" means "having an advantage over."

Those who live until the Lord comes won't have any advantage over those who died earlier.

•**VERSES 16-17** Isaiah 42:13; Jeremiah 25:30; Hosea 11:10; Joel 3:16; Amos 1:2; Revelation 4:1, 10:3.

Those Christians who have died are already with Christ and will be with Him at His coming (verse 14).

We'll meet them with the Lord in the air. "Caught up" (the Greek is harpazo) here means "snatched away with great force" (1 Corinthians 15:51-52).

KEY WORD

harpazo = caught up, to be snatched away or taken by force; translated at times "by force" (4:17).

CHAPTER 5:
THE RETURN OF JESUS CHRIST

•**VERSE 2** If people aren't watching for Christ's coming, they'll suffer a loss as when a thief breaks into their home (Matthew 24:42-51).

•**VERSES 4-6** The coming of Christ shouldn't take the Christians by surprise, for we're supposed to be watching for Him (Matthew 24:42).

•**VERSE 9** God hasn't chosen us for the wrath which is coming on the earth. He's chosen us for salvation.

•**VERSE 11** We're to comfort and build up each other.

•**VERSE 18** God wants us to be thankful.

•**VERSES 21-22** We're not to despise prophecies, but neither are we to accept every prophecy without testing it (1 Corinthians 14:29).

•**VERSE 22** Avoiding even the appearance of evil is a step beyond avoiding evil itself.

We're not to give others the opportunity to doubt the sincerity of our faith by our actions, even if we know the actions to be innocent.

•**VERSE 23** We meet God in the realm of our spirit.

•**VERSE 24** Christ has called us to follow Him, and He'll present us to God as His sheep.

CALVARY DISTINCTIVE

"For the Lord himself shall descend from heaven with a shout, with the voice of the archangel, and with the trump of God: and the dead in Christ shall rise first: Then we which are alive and remain shall be caught up together with them in the clouds to meet the Lord in the air: and so shall we ever be with the Lord" (1 Thessalonians 4:16-17).

The Rapture can take place at any time. There are no prophecies that have yet to be fulfilled before the Rapture occurs.

1. Paul makes mention in chapter 1, verse 3 of their "work of faith." What does Jesus say is the work of faith? (See John 6:29.)

_____

_____

_____

2. Compare 1 Thessalonians 2:19-20 with 3 John 1:4. What is the greatest joy for a minister of God?

_____

_____

_____

3. Paul was encouraged by Timothy's report of the Thessalonians' faith. In 1 Thessalonians 3:12-13 he said a beautiful prayer for them. Rewrite this in your own words as your personal prayer to God.

_____

_____

_____

4. Why does Paul use the term "asleep" instead of "dead" in 1 Thessalonians 4:13? (Read John 11:26 and 2 Corinthians 5:1.) What would be an even better word to use?

_____

_____

_____

5. We are given a list of exhortations in 1 Thessalonians 5:16-22. Which one speaks to you the most today and why?

_____

_____

_____

THE SECOND EPISTLE OF PAUL TO THE
THESSALONIANS

AUTHOR OF LETTER:
Paul the Apostle

WRITTEN TO:
The church in Thessalonica.

DATE AND PLACE OF WRITING:
Approximately 54 A.D. in Corinth, during his second missionary journey.

THEME:
The return of Jesus Christ.

PURPOSE OF WRITING:
To correct the misconception that they were going through the Great Tribulation.
To encourage them in their faith during their persecution.
To assure them that the Day of the Lord had not yet come.
To warn them against idleness.

CHAPTER 1:
THE PERSECUTION

•**VERSE 1** Silvanus here again is Silas. "Church" comes from a Greek word meaning "the called-out ones."

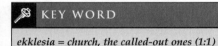

KEY WORD

ekklesia = church, the called-out ones (1:1)

•**VERSE 3** "Meet" here means proper. Faith is increased through the knowledge of God, which comes through the study of His Word. Our spiritual growth is dependent on our study of the Bible.

•**VERSE 4** The church was being persecuted, probably by the Judaizing teachers who had troubled the other young churches.

•**VERSE 5** The Thessalonians were being troubled by man, not God. God's wrath will be poured out on the world that has rejected His Son, not on His Church.

God uses our sufferings to mature us (Romans 8:17-18; 1 Peter 4:12; 2 Timothy 3:12).

•**VERSES 7-9** The punishment of those who don't know God will be banishment from both His presence and the glory of His power.

•**VERSE 11** Paul prayed for the Thessalonians, that:

(1) God would count them worthy of their calling (Luke 21:36).

(2) God would bless them as He wanted to bless them.

(3) The name of Jesus would be glorified through the witness of their transformed lives.

CHAPTER 2:
THE DAY OF JUDGMENT

• **VERSE 1** 1 Thessalonians 4:16-17.

• **VERSE 2** Paul told the Thessalonians not to be troubled in mind or spirit, nor by a letter supposedly from him claiming that the Day of the Lord had come.

The Christians were being taught that the day of God's wrath was upon them, and that they were in the Tribulation period.

• **VERSE 3** The "day" referred to here is the Day of Judgment. "Falling away" comes from the Greek word for depart. This may refer to the departure of the Church, for the Day of Judgment will come after the Rapture.

However, in 1 Timothy Paul added the words "depart from the faith" instead of "depart" alone.

 KEY WORD

apostasia = falling away; depart (2:3)

• **VERSE 4** The Day of Judgment won't come until the Antichrist has set himself upon a throne in the rebuilt temple in Jerusalem (Matthew 24:15-20; Revelation 13:14; Isaiah 16).

• **VERSE 7** "Letteth" means hinders. The Holy Spirit in the believers is hindering the Antichrist from revealing himself.

Once the Holy Spirit's restraining power through the Church is removed, the Antichrist will make his move.

• **VERSE 8** "Wicked" means lawless.

• **VERSE 13** Acts 13:48.

• **VERSE 15** The traditions Paul wanted the Thessalonians to adhere to were the teachings he gave them in person and by letter.

CHAPTER 3
EXHORTATIONS

• **VERSES 1-2** Paul asked the Thessalonians to pray:

(1) The Word of God would flow freely through Him.

(2) God would deliver him from unreasonable men.

• **VERSES 6-12** Some of the brethren in the church weren't working to support themselves.

Paul used himself as an example, for when he was in Thessalonica he paid his own expenses by working.

• **VERSE 17** Paul brought attention to his signature, so they'd be able to identify his epistles and not be misled by false letters.

CALVARY DISTINCTIVE

"And now ye know what withholdeth that he might be revealed in his time. For the mystery of iniquity doth already work: only he who now letteth will let, until he be taken out of the way. And then shall that Wicked be revealed, whom the Lord shall consume with the spirit of his mouth, and shall destroy with the brightness of his coming" (2 Thessalonians 2:6-8).

I believe that the Holy Spirit within the church is the restraining force that is holding back the powers of darkness from completely engulfing and overwhelming the world right now.

STUDY QUESTIONS FOR 2ND THESSALONIANS

1. We see that the Thessalonians were suffering persecution because of their faith in Jesus Christ. What does 2 Thessalonians 1:5, Romans 8:17-18, and 1 Peter 4:12-13 say about our sufferings?

_____

_____

_____

2. Paul was reassuring the Thessalonians that the persecution they were suffering was not the Day of Judgment. According to 2 Thessalonians 2:3-4, what two things must happen before the Great Tribulation begins?

_____

_____

_____

3. Based on 2 Thessalonians 2:13 and Acts 13:48, what choice did God make before we had faith to believe?

_____

_____

_____

4. Because the way we live is a witness to the world around us, Paul was warning Christians against idleness. What command did he give in 2 Thessalonians 3:10?

_____

_____

_____

5. There are so many wonderful attributes about the Lord for which we are thankful. What do you see about Jesus in 2 Thessalonians 3:3 and 3:16? Why are you thankful for these attributes today?

_____

_____

_____

THE FIRST EPISTLE OF PAUL TO
TIMOTHY

AUTHOR OF LETTER:
Paul the Apostle

WRITTEN TO:
Timothy

DATE AND PLACE OF WRITING:
The time is uncertain, but about the same time he wrote to Titus.

THEME:
A pastoral epistle.

PURPOSE OF WRITING:
To instruct Timothy about the government of the church.
To give Timothy instructions about conduct in God's household.
To encourage Timothy to fight the good fight of faith.

INTRODUCTION:
Most of Paul's epistles were written to churches, but First and Second Timothy, Titus, and Philemon were written to individuals.

Paul wrote to Timothy to advise and counsel him on the ministry.

CHAPTER 1:
THE CHRISTIAN AND THE LAW

•**VERSE 1** Paul indicates that God commanded him to be an apostle.

•**VERSE 2** Timothy had been a comfort and joy to Paul and a companion on many of his journeys, so Paul thought of him as a son.

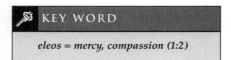

KEY WORD

eleos = mercy, compassion (1:2)

Paul usually invoked grace and peace in his epistles, but here he added "mercy."

Justice is getting what we deserve; mercy is not getting what we deserve; grace is getting the blessings we don't deserve.

•**VERSES 3-4** Paul wanted Timothy to keep the Ephesian church from getting mixed up in false doctrines.

•**VERSES 6-8** The Law actually deals with a man's heart more than with his actions, but people didn't understand when Jesus taught this.

Our righteousness is dependent on our faith in Christ, not on keeping the Law. Some Christians were tempted to cling to the traditions of the Law because it provided a sense of security.

• **VERSE 10** "Men stealers" were kidnappers who sold men into slavery.

• **VERSE 12** When God calls, He also enables. If He calls us to do something, He gives us the ability to do it.

• **VERSE 13** When we sin willfully, God chastises us. Unbelievers are dealt with differently, because they're ignorant of God's will for them.

• **VERSE 16** When a well-known sinner comes to God, it gives other sinners hope that God will forgive and accept them, too.

• **VERSE 18** There had been some prophecies concerning Timothy's ministry when he first began to serve the Lord.

CHAPTER 2:
PRAYER

• **VERSE 1** Paul lists various forms of prayer.

• **VERSE 2** We should pray for our leaders, whether we agree with them or not.

• **VERSE 5** Job 9:33; John 14:6.

• **VERSE 7** Paul was a preacher, an apostle, and a teacher.

CHAPTER 3:
BISHOPS AND DEACONS

• **VERSE 1** "Bishop" means overseer of the church.

• **VERSE 3** Greediness among church officials is the curse of the modern church.

• **VERSE 16** God was manifested in the flesh in Jesus Christ.

CHAPTER 4:
ADVICE TO A YOUNG PASTOR

• **VERSE 1** Galatians 1:8.

• **VERSE 2** Men can lie and deceive when their consciences have been dulled.

• **VERSES 4-5** Paul told Timothy that he didn't have to refuse meats which were prohibited by the Law, because God sanctifies all our food.

• **VERSE 8** There are eternal benefits in godly exercise.

• **VERSE 10** Jesus is the Savior of the world, but only those who accept Him will be saved.

• **VERSE 16** We learn a subject better when we teach it ourselves.

☘ CALVARY DISTINCTIVE

"Let no man despise thy youth; but be thou an example of the believers, in word, in conversation, in charity, in spirit, in faith, in purity"
(1 Timothy 4:12).

...we need to make certain that one of our major themes is love. That love needs to be demonstrated by our own actions, attitudes, and life. May everyone see the love of Christ manifested in us.

CHAPTER 5:
MORE ADVICE ON PASTORING

• **VERSES 1-2** Paul gives Timothy advice on his relations with believers in the church.

• **VERSE 6** The woman who "liveth in pleasure" is a woman who's forsaken the Lord to live in the world.

• **VERSE 9** "Threescore" is sixty.

• **VERSES 14-15** Paul is still talking about the young widows. Though in verse 11 it appears that he doesn't want them to marry, he's speaking of widows forsaking the Lord to marry.

He advised the younger widows to marry and care for their homes and children, rather than to stay single and be tempted to waste their lives.

•VERSE 16 "Relieve" means take care of.

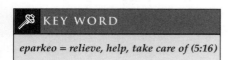

KEY WORD

eparkeo = relieve, help, take care of (5:16)

•VERSE 23 Timothy had a problem adjusting to the water in Ephesus (similar to the stomach problems we sometimes develop by drinking water in a foreign country).

CHAPTER 6:
THE TREASURE OF GODLINESS

•VERSE 1 Our behavior at work reflects on Jesus Christ and our witness for Him.

•VERSE 5 Some people see godliness as a way to make gain or acquire possessions, as the "prosperity doctrine" teaches.

•VERSE 6 Godliness itself is a treasure.

•VERSE 9 "Lusts" also means strong desires.

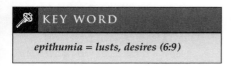

KEY WORD

epithumia = lusts, desires (6:9)

•VERSE 10 If money is the obsession of our lives, we'll be pierced with many sorrows.

•VERSE 14 This verse refers back to the commandment Paul gave in verse 12.

•VERSE 17 God has given us a beautiful world to enjoy for free.

•VERSE 19 Matthew 6:19-21, 19:21.

1. Christians are often accused of being narrow-minded in regards to our belief that Jesus is the only way to salvation. How do 1 Timothy 2:5 and John 14:6 confirm this belief is correct?

_____

_____

_____

2. Paul wants Timothy to remind the brethren about what will happen in the latter days. What does 1 Timothy 4:1-3 forewarn us about the last days?

_____

_____

_____

3. We have confidence in knowing that if God calls us to do something, He will give us the ability to do it. How do 1 Timothy 1:12 and Philippians 4:13 testify to this promise?

_____

_____

_____

4. List the requirements found in 1 Timothy chapter 3 that are common for both bishops (verses 1-7) and deacons (verses 8-13).

_____

_____

_____

5. We are warned that the love of money is the root of all evil. Write out 1 Timothy 6:6-8 and commit it to memory.

_____

_____

_____

THE SECOND EPISTLE OF PAUL TO
TIMOTHY

AUTHOR OF LETTER:
Paul the Apostle

WRITTEN TO:
Timothy, who at this time was in Ephesus.

DATE AND PLACE OF WRITING:
In Rome while in prison, approximately 64 A.D.

THEME:
A pastoral epistle.

PURPOSE OF WRITING:
To encourage Timothy to remain faithful in the work of the Gospel.
To encourage Timothy to continue in what he had learned.
To ask Timothy to come to him.

INTRODUCTION:
This is the last of Paul's letters. Here he pours out his heart to Timothy, his "beloved son."

CHAPTER 1:
EXHORTATION TO TIMOTHY

•**VERSE 2** Paul again adds "mercy" to grace and peace in the salutation.

•**VERSE 3** Paul had great power in prayer.

•**VERSE 4** Timothy had been in tears at the thought of Paul's approaching execution.

•**VERSE 6** Timothy's gift was declared by the word of prophecy, when hands were laid on him in prayer.

•**VERSE 7** Timothy had probably become fearful about the exercise of his gift.

•**VERSE 9** God has saved and called us—not because of our worthiness, but because of His grace.

•**VERSE 11** A preacher proclaims the truth to those who don't know it. Preaching is for sinners.

Teaching is for those who already know the truth of the Gospel, who need information on doctrine and how to walk the Christian life in the Spirit.

•**VERSE 15** "Asia" refers to the peninsula we know as Asia Minor (Turkey), that area around Ephesus.

False teachers had led the young Christians into the bondage of legalism and away from Paul's teachings of grace.

CHAPTER 2:
FOUR FAITHFUL SAYINGS

•**VERSE 2** This is the method by which the Gospel is to be communicated.

•**VERSES 3-4** If we become entangled with the affairs of daily life, the things of God can be choked out (Mark 4:18-19).

•**VERSE 6** We cannot minister if we haven't first received from God ourselves.

•**VERSE 8** The Resurrection is central to the message of the Gospel.

•**VERSES 11-13** Paul gives four faithful sayings:

(1) If we're dead with Christ, we'll also live with Him.

Our physical bodies may die, but our spirits will go to our new heavenly bodies (John 11:26).

(2) If we suffer, we'll also reign with Him.

Paul was suffering for Christ at the time he wrote this letter (Romans 8:18; Hebrews 11:25-26).

(3) If we deny Him, He'll deny us (Luke 12:8-9).

(4) We might not believe in Christ, but He is still who He is, and He'll faithfully perform what He has said He will.

•**VERSE 14** Paul told Timothy to remind the Christians of these faithful sayings, to avoid disputes over spiritual terminology.

•**VERSES 17-18** Paul also mentioned Hymenaeus in 1 Timothy 1:20 as a man he turned over to Satan. False teachings eat into men's souls like a cankerworm.

🔑 KEY WORD

gaggraina = canker; gangrene; it eats and rots the flesh.

Profane arguments eat away at you, like spiritual gangrene (2:17).

•**VERSE 21** "Sanctified" means set apart. We want to be set apart for our Master's use.

•**VERSE 26** Many people aren't free to see the truth of the Gospel, because they're captives of Satan who has blinded their eyes.

CHAPTER 3:
THE LAST DAYS

•**VERSES 1-7** These verses describe people in the world today.

•**VERSES 8-9** Jannes and Jambres are thought to be two of the magicians who tried to defeat Moses in Pharaoh's court.

•**VERSE 12** Christians suffer persecution for Christ, because the world is hostile to God.

•**VERSES 16-17** Scriptures must be read in context in order to receive the benefits Paul lists here.

🔑 KEY WORDS

philautos = the love of self, putting me first above all others; (phileo means love, autos means self).

philarguros = covetous, the love of money; (phileo means love, arguros means money).

alazones = boasters

huperephanos = proud; (huper means above, and phanos means appearance); appearing or feeling above others, haughty.

storgos = affection; the negative prefix (a) astorgos = without natural affection.

diabolos = false accuser, slanderer.

akrates = incontinent, without self control.

anemeros = fierce, usually used of a wild beast; men will become like wild beasts.

aphilegathos = despisers of those that are good.

CHAPTER 4:
THE CHARGE TO TIMOTHY

•VERSE 1 Christ will judge the nations when He sets up His Kingdom.

•VERSE 2 The work of the minister is to reprove, rebuke, and exhort when necessary.

•VERSES 6-8 Paul knew he'd be executed soon, and this might be his last chance to encourage Timothy in the ministry.

•VERSE 11 This is the same Mark who deserted Paul and Barnabas on the first missionary journey. He was the cause of their disagreement and parting of ways.

Now Paul has forgiven Mark and considers him a profitable servant of God.

•VERSE 13 The "cloak" is Paul's coat.

•VERSES 14-15 Paul warns Timothy to beware of Alexander.

•VERSE 16 At Paul's first appearance before Caesar none of his friends stood by him for moral support.

•VERSE 17 Jesus is the faithful friend who stands with us when everyone else forsakes us.

•VERSE 19 Priscilla and Aquila had been Paul's friends since the early days of his ministry.

CALVARY DISTINCTIVE

"Study to show thyself approved unto God, a workman that needeth not to be ashamed, rightly dividing the word of truth" (2 Timothy 2:15).

True education doesn't come from the wisdom of the world, but by the guidance and the wisdom that comes from the Holy Spirit.

1. According to 2 Timothy 1:9, why has God saved us and called us?

_____

_____

_____

2. What are the four faithful sayings found in 2 Timothy 2:11-13?

_____

_____

_____

3. We are exhorted in 2 Timothy 2:22 to flee youthful lusts. What are we to seek instead?

_____

_____

_____

4. List the characteristics of people in the last days, mentioned in 2 Timothy 3:1-5. How are we to deal with such people?

_____

_____

_____

5. What does 2 Timothy 3:16-17 say about Scripture?

_____

_____

_____

THE EPISTLE OF PAUL TO
TITUS

AUTHOR OF LETTER:

Paul the Apostle

WRITTEN TO:

Titus

DATE AND PLACE OF WRITING:

He wrote his epistle to Titus at about the same time that he wrote the first epistle to Timothy.

THEME:

A pastoral epistle.

PURPOSE OF WRITING:

To encourage Titus to establish elders and various other offices within the churches.

To tell Titus the things he should teach the people about godly living.

CHAPTER 1:

QUALIFICATIONS OF THE ELDERS

•**VERSE 2** "Eternal life" also means age-abiding life. Ephesians 1:4.

•**VERSE 4** Paul also considered Titus as his son. Paul led Titus to Christ.

Paul once again adds "mercy" to the salutation. When we realize the mercy and grace of God toward us, the result is peace.

The day Jesus becomes the Lord of our lives is as important as the day He became our Savior.

•**VERSE 5** The elders, or overseers, were to guard the churches against doctrinal impurity and to oversee the business of the church.

•**VERSE 7** "Bishop" means overseer.

A self-willed person always wants to have his own way.

A person "given to filthy lucre" is money-hungry.

•**VERSE 9** The overseers need to be doctrinally sound so they can detect and correct even the slightest deviation from the truth.

> ## 🔑 KEY WORDS
>
> *episkopos= bishops, overseers of the church, the men who oversaw the functions of the church.*
>
> *presbyteros = overseers, deacons, those who served doing the practical things that needed to be done around the church.*

•**VERSE 16** Many people profess to know God, but their lives deny Him.

CHAPTER 2:
THE LIFESTYLE OF THE CHRISTIAN

•**VERSE 1** Truth never lies in the extreme position. It's always balanced.

•**VERSE 2** The "aged men" are to be sober as opposed to drunken.

"Grave" means serious. "Temperate" means moderate. "Charity" means love.

•**VERSES 4-5** The older women are to teach the younger women about family relations and good housekeeping.

•**VERSE 7** Titus was to set the pattern for the Christians in good works, sincere doctrine, and sound speech.

•**VERSE 10** "Purloining" is stealing.

•**VERSE 12** The grace of God teaches us to:

(1) Deny ungodliness and worldly desires.

(2) Live soberly, righteously, and godly in the world.

•**VERSE 13** This verse declares that Christ is God, for the Scriptures never refer to an "appearing" of God.

•**VERSE 14** We're to be peculiar people because we have peace during a storm and answer with love, not because we're odd or strange.

CHAPTER 3:
THE CHRISTIAN IN THE WORLD

•**VERSE 2** The world is telling people to be strong and assertive, but Paul tells us to be gentle and meek.

•**VERSES 3-5** God delivered us from our former way of life by the washing of regeneration and the renewing of the Holy Spirit.

•**VERSES 6-8** God imputes the righteousness of Christ to us through faith. Our grateful response is to be careful to maintain good works.

•**VERSE 9** Many people who like to argue about scriptures aren't seriously seeking the truth. It's a waste of time to debate with them.

•**VERSES 10-11** A man involved in a heresy condemns himself.

CALVARY DISTINCTIVE

"Looking for that blessed hope, and the glorious appearing of the great God and our Savior Jesus Christ" (Titus 2:13).

I believe it is God's intention that every church age be convinced they are the last generation. I also believe that God's divine design is for the church to live in constant expectancy of the Lord's return.

1. God has given us many promises in His Word, one of which is the promise of eternal life. How can we be assured that God will keep His promises? (See Titus 1:2.)

_____

_____

_____

2. Many people claim to be Christians. How can we tell if someone is truly walking with the Lord? (See Titus 1:16 and Matthew 7:15-20.)

_____

_____

_____

3. According to Titus 2:11-12, what does the grace of God teach us?

_____

_____

_____

4. How and why did God save us? (See Titus 3:5.)

_____

_____

_____

5. Read Titus 3:3-7. What does it mean to you today that you have been made an heir according to the hope of eternal life?

_____

_____

_____

THE EPISTLE OF PAUL TO
PHILEMON

AUTHOR OF LETTER:
Paul the Apostle

WRITTEN TO:
Philemon

DATE AND PLACE OF WRITING:
Approximately 64 A.D., during Paul's imprisonment in Rome.
This letter was written at the same time that Paul wrote the Colossian epistle.

PURPOSE OF WRITING:
To ask Philemon to be merciful and gracious unto Onesimus, his runaway slave, and to receive him as a brother in the Lord.

To promise to pay any debt that Onesimus might owe him.

To ask Philemon to be preparing a place for Paul to stay, for he is expecting to be released soon from prison.

•**VERSE 1** Paul calls himself "a prisoner of Jesus Christ," not a prisoner of Rome or of the emperor.

The man who's a prisoner of Christ is free in every other way.

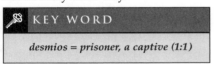

KEY WORD

desmios = prisoner, a captive (1:1)

•**VERSE 2** Apphia was probably Philemon's wife, and Archippus was probably his son.

Philemon had a church that met in his home in Colosse.

Apparently he was a wealthy man, because he had slaves. There were sixty million slaves in the world in those days. It seems inconsistent that a Christian man would own slaves.

•**VERSE 5** Our love isn't a true love until it's directed toward all the saints.

•**VERSE 7** Feelings in "the bowels" refer to deep, gut-level feelings.

•**VERSES 8-9** Paul now considered himself aged.

As a spiritual father to Philemon and an elder in the church, Paul could have ordered Philemon in this matter, but because of love he chose to make a request.

•**VERSE 11** The name "Onesimus" means profitable. Paul was word-playing with the name.

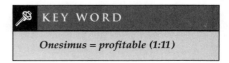

KEY WORD

Onesimus = profitable (1:11)

•**VERSE** 12 Paul asks that Philemon receive Onesimus kindly.

The usual penalty for an escaped slave was death or branding with a hot iron to mark him as a fugitive.

•**VERSES** 13-14 Paul wanted very much to keep Onesimus with him in Rome, because the young man had been very helpful in ministering to his needs.

•**VERSE** 15 Paul says that perhaps God's purpose was served in the running away of Onesimus, because while a runaway he met Paul and was converted.

•**VERSE** 17 Paul asks that Philemon receive Onesimus as he would receive Paul himself. This is real intercession.

Jesus intercedes with God for us and asks God to attribute the righteousness of Christ to us.

•**VERSES** 18-19 Jesus asks God to put all our sins and transgressions on His account.

Paul reminded Philemon that his life was saved when Paul led him to Christ, so Philemon owed him a favor.

•**VERSES** 21-22 Paul was sure that Philemon would comply with his earnest request.

•**VERSE** 23 Epaphras was also from Colosse, so perhaps he recognized Onesimus as Philemon's runaway slave.

STUDY QUESTIONS FOR PHILEMON

1. According to verse 6, what was Paul's prayer for Philemon?

_____

_____

_____

2. Meditate upon verse 18. How does this verse illustrate what Jesus has done for you?

_____

_____

_____

3. Paul's request to Philemon was gracious and merciful. How might these attributes be an example to you?

_____

_____

_____

4. Take a moment and bring to mind those that might have offended or wronged you. Write a prayer of forgiveness, asking the Lord to give you a spirit of love.

_____

_____

_____

5. Why is verse 25 necessary for the Christian walk?

_____

_____

_____

THE EPISTLE TO THE
HEBREWS

AUTHOR OF LETTER:

Not known for certain, but thought to be Paul the Apostle.

The author of Hebrews is unknown, but we know that God inspired him, just as He inspired the authors of the other books in the Bible.

WRITTEN TO:

The Jewish believers.

DATE AND PLACE OF WRITING:

Approximately 64 A.D., six years before the destruction of the temple.

THEME:

The supremacy and sufficiency of Jesus Christ.

PURPOSE OF WRITING:

To address the danger of turning away from Jesus Christ and trying to find salvation under the Jewish religious system once again.

To show that there is no other sacrifice; Christ is the One, once and for all.

INTRODUCTION:

The book of Hebrews was written for the Jews who had accepted Jesus as their Messiah. They were in danger of slipping back into the traditions of Judaism because they had not put down roots in the soil of Christianity.

The book of Hebrews appeals to the Greek mind as well as the Jewish mind. The Greeks saw everything on earth as the shadows cast by what was real, so they were always searching for reality. Hebrews presents Jesus as the reality. The Jews were searching for a way to approach God because historically they had felt too unholy to approach Him. Hebrews presents Jesus as approachable.

CHAPTER 1:

LET US DRAW NEAR TO GOD

•VERSE 1 "In many parts and in many ways, in past times God spake by the prophets unto the fathers."

1. This verse assumes the existence of God. The Bible never tries to prove His existence (Psalm 19:1-4; Romans 1:20).

2. This verse assumes that God has spoken to man. If God created man, He had a purpose for him.

Therefore, He would speak to man early in history and maintain a record of what He said.

In 4,000 places the Bible refers to itself as God's word to man.

None of the prophets or fathers had the whole truth, but each had a part. The parts came to them in different ways: in dreams, in visits from angels, in a "still small voice" (Hosea 12:10).

•VERSE 2 God spoke to us by and in Jesus, for He is God's message to us (John 14:10).

What was the message of God through Jesus? God is a God of love, grace, and mercy. He is a forgiving God who is not angry with man but wants to fellowship with man.

Jesus is superior to the prophets because He had the whole truth of God.

1. Jesus is the heir of all things. The world is not the way God created it; man's rebellion has brought it to this state.

God gave the world to man but man forfeited it to Satan. The purpose of Jesus' coming was to redeem the earth back to God. When Jesus returns, we'll see the world as God meant it to be.

2. Jesus is the Creator of all things. He created the world and He maintains it (John 1:3; Colossians 1:17).

The Bible is God's revelation of Himself to man.

God revealed Himself to the prophets and they wrote down what He told them.

However, sometimes people misunderstood the nature of God as He was revealed by the prophets, so God sent His own Son to give us a more complete revelation of Himself.

•VERSE 3 Jesus is the "outshining" (outraying, effulgence) of God's glory (1 Timothy 6:16). Through Jesus, we see God as much as man can see Him.

The express image means "impression" as in making a mold (John 14:9).

"Upholding" here is maintaining (Colossians 1:17).

"Purged" here means cleansed, (1 John 1:7) continually cleansing (1 John 1:9).

This cleansing is not a license for us to sin; rather, it frees us from the power of sin so that we need not live the life of sin anymore (Romans 6:1,2).

Jesus is seated at the right hand of the Father (Romans 8:34; John 17:24).

•VERSE 4 When we become conscious of the vastness of God, we become conscious of how nothing we are.

The Jews reached this consciousness and it caused them to hold the angels in high esteem because of their position near God.

"Being made so much better" is having become so much better in the Greek. Jesus was always higher than the angels.

At Jesus' excellent name, every knee will bow (Philippians 2:9-11).

•VERSE 5 The angels are created beings, not sons of God, as Jesus is.

•VERSE 6 "Firstbegotten" means first in honor and position, not first in order. In Revelation 5, the angels worship Jesus.

•VERSE 7 The angels are the servants of God; ministering spirits.

Jesus emptied Himself of His heavenly glory and became a servant, but that is not His heavenly position.

•VERSE 8 God calls Jesus "God," Thomas called Jesus "God" (John 20:28), John called Him "God" (John 1:1), and Paul called Him "God" (Titus 2:13, 3:4).

•VERSE 10 God calls Jesus "Lord" here, and describes the work of Jesus in creation.

•VERSES 11-12 Even the creation shall pass away (2 Peter 3:10,11).

"But Thou art the same" refers to the nature of Christ. He is our Rock in a changing world (immutability) and He is eternal (immortality).

•VERSE 13 This is the position God made for His Son, and Jesus waits now for the Father to make His enemies a footstool.

The writer of Hebrews quotes freely from the Old Testament, having a good grasp of the scriptures, seeing the many references to Jesus that run through them (Hebrews 10:7).

•**VERSE 14** This verse refers to the angels again.

CHAPTER 2:
THE HUMANITY OF CHRIST

•**VERSE 1** We should pay close attention to the words of Christ avoiding the danger of drifting away from our salvation through Him.

Backsliding usually occurs gradually, and the writer of Hebrews did not want to see the Jewish Christians slip back into the laws of Judaism with its legal bondage, and lose their joy and their first love for God (Revelation 2:4).

•**VERSE 2** The word spoken by the angels in prophecy (Daniel 10) and in giving the Law (Acts 7:53) came to pass.

•**VERSE 3** We have even more reason to carefully consider the words of Christ (John 15:1) and to receive our salvation through Him.

Jesus first spoke of salvation, and the disciples who heard Him reported what He said.

•**VERSE 4** God confirmed Jesus' words with signs and miracles, and the Holy Spirit confirmed His words by giving spiritual gifts (Acts 2:22).

•**VERSE 6** Christ visited us when He became a man.

•**VERSE 7** Man was made lower than the angels, but was put over God's creation.

•**VERSE 8** Man forfeited the earth to Satan and now creation is not subject to man.

•**VERSE 9** Jesus identified Himself with fallen man by taking on a human form and dying in our place.

He could not have died as God, so He had to become a man to suffer and die for us.

•**VERSE 10** Jesus is the object of creation as well as the Creator.

He is the captain ("trailblazer") of our salvation, for He has preceded us into glory and will lead us there.

The word "perfect" here indicates completeness, a full maturity.

•**VERSE 11** The Lord sanctified (consecrated, set apart for exclusive use) and calls us His brothers (John 15:15).

•**VERSE 12** Psalm 22, a prophetic psalm dealing with the crucifixion and resurrection of Jesus (Psalm 22:22).

•**VERSE 13** Isaiah 8:17-18.

•**VERSE 14** "Destroy" here means to put out of business. Jesus suffered and died to put Satan's power over us out of business.

We have the power to reckon our flesh (our "old man") dead and give no place to sin in our lives.

We can identify with Christ in His resurrection and enjoy life in the Promised Land for the Christian.

We claim the cities in the land by faith and rejoice in the victory over the enemy.

•**VERSE 15** Jesus came to set us free from the bondage of our flesh.

•**VERSE 16** Jesus did not take on the nature of angels because He would not have understood man as well, and as an angel He could not die.

•**VERSE 17** Since Jesus was a man, He is merciful and understanding because He knows what temptations and drives we are subject to.

CHAPTER 3:
JESUS IS SUPERIOR TO MOSES

Hebrews was written for Jews who thought that Moses was closer to God than the angels.

•**VERSE 1** "Holy brethren" does not refer to our virtue but to the righteousness God imputes to us because of our faith in Jesus Christ.

As "partakers of the heavenly calling" we look not unto our earthly situation for fulfillment but to our final home with Christ (1 Corinthians 15:19).

"Consider" means to study carefully in the Greek. It is the same word Jesus used in Matthew 6:28 when He said, "Consider the lilies of the field...."

KEY WORD

katanoeo = consider, study carefully (3:1)

"Apostle" means one who has been sent, ambassador. This is the only place Jesus is called an apostle.

An ambassador represents all the power and authority of his country (Matthew 28:18).

An ambassador speaks for his nation. Jesus spoke God's thoughts (John 14:10). Jesus is the high priest of our profession (confession).

Job asked for a daysman to bridge the gap between God and man (Job 9:33). "Priest" means bridge builder. God has built the bridge to man.

• **VERSES 2-6** Moses was a faithful servant in the house of God but Jesus was the faithful Son who built the house.

The house of God in the days of Moses was the nation Israel. The house of God that Christ built is the Church, for He dwells in us when we invite Him in.

We are to hold fast to our hope in Christ, but He also has promised to keep us (Jude 1:24; 2 Timothy 1:12; 1 Peter 1:3-5).

•**VERSES 7-9** The Holy Spirit is the author of the Bible (Acts 28:25).

God was grieved with the children of Israel for their tempting and striving, always erring in their hearts, not knowing God's ways.

They saw God's works for forty years as they wandered in the wilderness and God didn't allow them to enter the rest He had prepared in the Promised Land.

•**VERSE 12** The Parable of the Sower (Matthew 13); The Parable of the Foolish Man and the Wise Man (Matthew 7:26).

•**VERSE 13** To prevent our hearts from becoming hardened with unbelief, we need to exhort one another daily in the things of God.

•**VERSE 14** We need more of Jesus in our lives as the solution to problems that arise, not more love, faith, or other gifts. We need more of Jesus Himself in us.

•**VERSES 15-19** The story of the children of Israel is retold here to show us that unbelief can rob us of all the rich blessings God wants to bestow on us.

The Israelites took their eyes off God and saw only the obstacles before them, refusing to believe in God's beautiful provision (Hebrews 11:6).

Their unbelief kept them from entering into the rest God had prepared for them.

CHAPTER 4:
THE REST OF GOD

•**VERSES 1-4** When we enter into the rest God has for us, we are able to relax and stop worrying. We have more time to set our minds on Him and to rejoice and praise Him.

•**VERSES 5-8** The children of Israel had one day to make the choice to enter into the rest God had for them. When they tried to go in the next day by their own strength, it was too late.

•**VERSES 9-10** After God created the world, He "rested" (ceased) from His acts of creation, but His work in the world was not finished.

When man fell short of God's ideal, it was necessary that God do a work of redemption, bringing unrighteous man into fellowship with a righteous God.

Jesus came to finish the work of redemption on the Cross (John 4:34; 19:30; Isaiah 53:6-10; 2 Corinthians 5:21).

The righteousness of Christ is now imputed to us because of our belief in what He has done (Philippians 3:8,9).

We do not need to struggle and labor to increase our righteousness, because God is satisfied with the righteousness of Christ that He has given to us.

When we learn to rest and trust in what Jesus has done for us on the Cross, we glory in Him and have no chance to boast about our own righteousness.

We have to work at staying in the place of rest in God because Satan will attack and try to destroy our rest.

• **VERSE 11** The children of Israel are the example of unbelief, for they were not allowed into God's rest because of their unbelief.

God's Word helps us to know ourselves and to recognize our motivations (John 15:7; Psalm 119:9; 139:1-6; Matthew 6:1-8).

• **VERSE 13** The New Testament emphasis is on attitude more than actions. Our righteousness depends on our attitude toward Christ.

• **VERSE 14** "Profession" here means confession.

"Passed into the heavens" refers to the resurrection of Jesus and His ascension into heaven.

• **VERSE 15** Since Jesus was a man, He has mercy on us, knowing the temptations that we face.

He was tempted by Satan beyond anything man has ever experienced (Matthew 4:1-11).

CHAPTER 5:
THE PRIESTHOOD

• **VERSE 1** The high priest was a man ordained by God for men.

The Jews were very conscious of their sin and the effect of sin in separating them from God. When they saw the sacrificial animal dying for their sins, it brought the awfulness of sin forcefully to their awareness.

Usually the gift offerings were meal offerings given as peace offerings to bring them into fellowship with God, while the sacrifices were blood offerings for sin.

• **VERSE 2** The word here translated "compassion" in the Greek means "being shocked at something and wanting to say something sympathetic but being held back."

KEY WORD

metriopatheo = compassion, being shocked, sympathetic yet refrained (5:2)

Since the high priest was a man himself "compassed with infirmity," he understood the temptations and trials of other men.

God allows ministers to go through trials and testings to keep them in touch with their own humanity.

• **VERSE 3** The high priest would offer a sacrifice first for himself and then for the people.

• **VERSE 4** The ministry is a calling of God, not a career that one chooses.

• **VERSES 5-6** God ordained Christ to be the high priest of the Church. Jesus did not exalt Himself or put Himself in this position.

• **VERSE 7** In the days when He was a man, Jesus prayed unto the Father for help with the weaknesses of the flesh.

This verse describes His prayer in the garden of Gethsemane when He wept deeply and agonized over the death God was asking Him to endure.

•VERSE 8 Obedience is doing something we really don't want to do.

Even though Jesus was the Son of God, He laid down His own will and accepted the will of the Father.

•VERSE 9 The word "perfect" here again means complete, of full age.

Jesus was thoroughly prepared to become our salvation. We who obey Him and have made Him our Lord have eternal life through Him (James 1:22).

•VERSE 10 There were various orders of the priesthood. Jesus belonged to the order of Melchizedek.

The priest would stand before God to represent the people and would stand before the people to represent God. Jesus as our high priest brings us into direct fellowship with God.

•VERSE 11 The writer of Hebrews wanted to elaborate on the subject of the priesthood of Christ, but it was hard for him to simplify his teachings to be understood by the spiritually immature Christians he was writing to.

•VERSE 12 The Christians should have been ready to go into deeper spiritual matters, but they were even drifting away from the "first principles" (ABC's) of doctrine.

They had to be retaught the basics of the Christian faith (the milk) when they should have been getting into weightier material (the meat).

Their spiritual development was arrested at the infant stage. The writer was anxious to get them into deeper teaching because God's Word gives us strength and helps us to grow (1 John 2:14).

•VERSES 13-14 The translation "of full age" here is made from the same Greek word translated perfect elsewhere.

Baby Christians have no power to discern between good and evil and are therefore a prey to the wolves that sometimes enter the Church.

CHAPTER 6:
A WARNING TO SLOTHFUL CHRISTIANS

•VERSE 1 "Perfection" means maturity.

•VERSES 1-3 The author of Hebrews is trying to lead the baby Christians beyond their first steps into a closer walk with Christ.

•VERSE 4 Many people are frightened by these next verses, but if we compare scripture with scripture, we find that there is hope for us.

Here the word "once" comes from a Greek word meaning once and for all, indicating finality.

Those who were "enlightened" were brought to a knowledge of the sacrifice of Jesus for their sins.

The "heavenly gift" is the gift of salvation (Romans 6:23; Ephesians 2:8).

"Partakers" means partners.

•VERSE 5 There seems to be a state where one has only "tasted" the things of God and not fully drunk (Matthew 7:21-23).

In the Parable of the Sower (Matthew 13), the seeds that fell among the stones and thorns did not mature and produce fruit. When we produce fruit, it is the evidence that we have faith.

•VERSE 7 Herbs here means vegetables.

•VERSES 7-8 These verses may refer to the Parable of the Sower in Matthew 13.

If we allow God to mature us and produce fruit through us, we will make our "calling and election sure" and we won't have to fear the warning in verses 4-6 (2 Peter 1:2-10).

•VERSES 9-10 When we accept salvation through Christ, there are certain responses we should make.

• **VERSE 11** We should strive, agonize, and work until it is painful to do the things pertaining to godliness.

• **VERSE 12** Many Christians today are slothful in their Christian walk, and because of them the message of the Church is weakened.

The Old Testament patriarchs are held up as examples of the life of faith and patience. Our faith is often tested in the times of waiting.

Our faith is demonstrated when we have confidence while we wait for God to do something.

• **VERSE 14** God made this promise to Abraham after the testing in the sacrifice of Isaac (Genesis 22:17).

• **VERSE 15** Abraham had to wait many years for his child of promise to be born.

When he tried to help God to fulfill His promise, Ishmael was born and his descendants, the Arab nations, continue to struggle with the descendants of Isaac, the Israelites, to this day.

The four keys to the faith of Abraham are:

(1) Abraham did not consider the human possibilities (or impossibilities).

(2) He did not stagger at the promise of God through unbelief.

(3) He was strong in faith and gave glory to God.

(4) He was persuaded that God was able to do what He had promised (Romans 4:19-21).

• **VERSE 16** Men swear by God because He is greater than we are, but He swore by Himself since there is no one above Him.

• **VERSES 17-18** God gave His promise and an oath on the promise as two immutable confirmations of His word.

• **VERSES 19-20** We who trust in Christ as our refuge have the hope of redemption through Him.

Christ's death gave us access to God without having to go through an earthly high priest who had to go through the veil into God's presence.

CHAPTER 7:
SUPERIOR PRIESTHOOD OF JESUS CHRIST

• **VERSE 1** In Genesis 14:18-20, we read that Melchizedek was a priest of God long before God had established the priesthood through Aaron or Levi.

Melchizedek gave bread and wine to Abraham as a forerunner of the sacrament of communion.

• **VERSE 2** "Melchizedek" means King of Righteousness. "King of Salem" means King of Peace.

• **VERSE 3** "Without descent" refers to the fact that no genealogy was given for Melchizedek.

Jews were very careful to keep their records of genealogies, especially where the priesthood was concerned.

Since Melchizedek's appearance in the Bible is so mysterious (having neither beginning of days nor end of life), some people think He may have been Jesus Christ.

The titles, King of Righteousness and King of Peace certainly would apply to Jesus. Also, in the prophetic Psalm 110, which speaks of Jesus, verse 4 states, "Thou art a priest forever after the order of Melchizedek."

• **VERSE 4** The Jews traced their faith back to Abraham as the founding father.

• **VERSE 5** The priests received a tithe from the people rather than an inheritance of land.

•**VERSE 6** Melchizedek received a tithe from Abraham, and also from Levi, in the sense that Levi descended from Abraham.

The author is seeking to establish the superiority of Melchizedek over the Levitical priesthood, knowing the issue of Christ as our high priest was a sensitive one.

He could see that the weak and immature Hebrew Christians might easily slip back into the security of the traditions of Judaism.

•**VERSE 7** The one who gives the blessing is greater than the one who receives it.

•**VERSE 11** If the Levitical priesthood could bring people into a perfect relationship with God through the Law, there would have been no need for God to speak of another priesthood when He spoke through David in Psalm 110:4.

•**VERSE 12** If the priesthood changed, then the Law governing it would have to change also.

•**VERSES 13-14** Jesus was from the tribe of Judah, and Moses did not include that tribe when he spoke of the priesthood, so Jesus could not be a priest under the Law.

The author of Hebrews was acquainted with the concerns of the Hebrew Christians and wanted to resolve their difficulties so they could enter in more fully.

•**VERSE 16** "Carnal" means fleshly.

The order of Melchizedek is contrasted with the order of Levi rather than compared to it.

The Law made men priests, but Jesus did not need the Law to make Him a priest since He had the power of eternal life and, thus, an unchanging priesthood.

•**VERSES 18-19** The Law was given to the Jews, not to the Gentiles.

When the Gentiles became Christians, some of the Jewish Christians thought the Gentiles should keep the Law, but the Church elders decided not to yoke the Gentiles with a burden they found impossible to bear (Acts 15).

The purpose of the Law was to show our sin and to demonstrate that we cannot hope to approach God on the basis of our own righteousness (Galatians 3:24).

Since we have come to God by our faith in Jesus, we have no place to boast of ourselves (Galatians 6:14).

We seek to obey and please God because we love Him, not because of the Law (1 Corinthians 6:12).

•**VERSES 21-22** God made Jesus a priest forever by an oath, but the Levites were made priests by birth.

•**VERSE 22** God's oath made the new covenant through Jesus even more sure than the old covenant.

The new covenant depends on what Jesus has done, not on what we have done. It is based on His love and faithfulness, not on our works (Hebrews 9:13-14).

Jesus is the proof of God's love for us.

•**VERSE 23** This verse refers again to the Levitical order.

The priesthood was not continual because of human frailty; as the old priests died their sons took their places.

The people could not be sure of their priests because the priests brought their own concepts into their positions. The priesthood was subject to change.

•**VERSE 24** The priesthood of Jesus is constant and does not pass from one man to another.

•**VERSE 25** The salvation through Jesus can reach to anyone, anywhere. Jesus stands before God and represents and intercedes for us. He does not have to go through a veil or make sin sacrifices for Himself or for us (Romans 8:31-34).

The heart of the message of the New Testament is that Jesus is a living Lord.

•**VERSE 26** Jesus is holy, harmless (sensitive), undefiled, unstained, (unsullied by sin), separate from sinners.

He never sinned but He was always approachable. The sins of others never sullied Him, and He is made higher than the heavens (John 17:5).

•**VERSE 27** Every morning and evening the priests had to offer sacrifices for the sins of the people.

Jesus did not have to offer for Himself because He was sinless.

The Levitical sacrifices were shadows that looked forward to the ultimate, once and for all sacrifice of Jesus.

He became the Sacrifice and the High Priest, but He only had to be offered once to bring eternal salvation to the world.

CHAPTER 8:
THE NEW COVENANT

•**VERSE 1** "Sum" here means chief or total.

Jesus is in heaven at God's right hand (Matthew 26:64; Acts 7:56; John 17:5).

•**VERSE 2** Jesus is a minister in heaven, not in the earthly temple.

•**VERSES 3-4** Jesus did not serve as a priest on earth, but in heaven.

•**VERSE 5** The priests were only representing in earthly form the heavenly scene about the throne of God (Colossians 2:14-18).

•**VERSE 6** The Law barred the door to God but Jesus opened it for us.

The covenant of God with the Jews is different from His covenant with those who come to Him through Christ (Romans 11:25-29).

The old covenant was conditional upon man's doing something, but the new covenant is based on man's believing what Christ has done.

•**VERSES 8-9** God spoke of a new covenant since the people were not keeping the old covenant properly and He could not accept (regard) them.

•**VERSE 10** The new covenant would have its laws written in people's hearts, not on tablets of stone.

The old covenant failed because the urgings of the flesh superseded the urgings of the spirit in man.

The new covenant is based on God, making us new creations so that we are Spirit-controlled rather than body-controlled.

God makes His will the desire of our hearts (Psalm 40:8).

•**VERSES 11-13** Jesus spoke of the new covenant in Mark 14:22-25.

Soon after Hebrews was written, the temple was destroyed and the sacrifices of the old covenant ceased.

CHAPTER 9:
THE OLD AND THE NEW COVENANTS

•**VERSE 1** The "ordinances" concerned the way the priests were to conduct their duties and the way the people were to come to offer their sacrifices and gifts to God.

•**VERSES 6-9** The earthly ceremonies were symbolic representations of heaven.

•**VERSE 10** "Until the time of reformation" means until the time of setting things right.

•**VERSES 11,12** "Building" here also means creation.

Jesus did not go into the earthly model (the temple), but into the actual heavenly scene the temple represented.

KEY WORD

ktisis = building, creation (9:11)

He did not go into the holy of holies on earth, but directly into the presence of God.

He did not need to sprinkle the blood of bulls and goats in order to enter into God's presence, and He did not go in once each year, but once forever.

•VERSES 13-14 The purpose of both covenants was to bring man into relationship with God.

Sin is disobedience to God; the exercise of my will in conflict to the will of God.

Sin separates a man from God (Isaiah 59:1,2; 1 John 1:6-10). God set up the animal sacrifices for sin in the first covenant (Hebrews 9:22), but the blood of bulls and goats only covered sin; it did not do away with it.

Jesus was the perfect sacrifice of the second covenant (1 Peter 1:19), whose death finally put an end to sin.

When we accept the sacrifice that Jesus made for our sins, our conscience is cleaned and we are free from the laws of "dead works" in the first covenant.

•VERSE 15 Jesus is the mediator Who brings us to God (Job 9:33; John 10:7,8, 14:6). We are promised eternal redemption and an eternal inheritance if we believe in the work God has done for us.

•VERSES 16-17 A man's last will and testament is not in force until the man dies.

•VERSES 18-20 The sprinkled blood indicated that the covenant with God was in force because the substitutionary animal had been slain.

•VERSE 22 Second Corinthians 5:21; Isaiah 53:6.

•VERSE 25 Jesus offered His own blood, not the blood of animals, when He made His sacrifice.

•VERSE 26 The Old Testament atonement for sin was an annual covering, but the New Testament atonement

through Jesus is putting away sins once for all. His one sacrifice was sufficient to wipe out our sins forever.

•VERSE 27 Romans 6:23; Ezekiel 18:20.

•VERSE 28 Christ experienced the wages of sin for us.

Jesus is returning to establish the Kingdom of God on the earth. His second coming will have nothing to do with sin or reconciling man to God because He resolved the sin issue with His death.

CHAPTER 10:
THE PERFECT SACRIFICE

•VERSE 1 "Image" here means clear likeness.

The Law was not an image of heavenly things but a shadow.

•VERSE 2 If the Law could make people perfect, they wouldn't need to keep offering sacrifices.

•VERSES 3-4 The sacrifices reminded the people of their sin every time they offered them. Their guilty consciences were not cleansed by the sacrifice (Psalm 51).

•VERSES 5-7 The author of Hebrews quotes Psalm 40:6-8 from the Greek Septuagint (the translation of the Old Testament from Hebrew into Greek by 70 scholars), and has Christ say the verses.

Psalm 40:6 speaks of "opening" the ear, which was the piercing of a bondservant's ear when he wanted to stay with his master.

It is more important to God that we obey Him than to offer sacrifices to Him (1 Samuel 15:22).

The "volume of the book" is the Old Testament. There are over 300 prophecies in the Old Testament that refer to Jesus and His birth, life, and resurrection. There are another 300 that refer to His Second Coming.

Jesus taught and demonstrated that the Law is actually spiritual.

•**VERSE 9** When Jesus did the will of God, He did away with the first covenant and established the second.

•**VERSE 10** "Sanctified" means set apart for God. We are sanctified through Jesus Who did the will of the Father when He sacrificed His body.

•**VERSES 12-13** Jesus is now in heaven at the Father's right hand, resting in the finished work of the Cross, and waiting for the day that God will give Him the ultimate victory over His enemies.

•**VERSE 14** God sees us in the fully mature, completed state when we are presented to Him by Jesus Christ—not in the imperfect state we are in now.

•**VERSES 15-16** This new covenant works from the inside out since God puts His thoughts and desires in our hearts.

The old covenant worked from the outside in and consisted of a list of do's and don'ts that made carnal man rebel (Jeremiah 31:33,34).

•**VERSE 17** The word "sin" means to miss the mark.

Iniquities are a combination of sin and transgression. A transgression is a willful disobedience.

Sin can be a failure to be or to do something, whereas transgression is deliberately not being or doing something (Psalm 32:1; Romans 8:1).

•**VERSE 18** Since the blood of Jesus had done away with all our sins, there is no need for offerings to be made to obtain forgiveness.

•**VERSE 19** We have boldness to enter into the presence of God because of the work of Christ for us.

The high priest only dared to go into the presence of God one day a year, and that after many sacrifices had been made and much blood was shed.

•**VERSE 20** "New" here refers to newly slain.

Under the old covenant, a man could approach God immediately after the animal had been slain for his sins and before he could commit new ones.

He always felt most comfortable in his relationship with God right after the sacrifice had been offered.

Christ's death works in our lives as a perpetual sacrifice, so that each time we commit a sin, it is as if an animal were immediately sacrificed to cleanse us from that sin.

•**VERSE 21** Jesus is our high priest.

•**VERSE 22** We don't have to fear God's rejection when we come before Him, as the Jews feared when the high priest went into the holy of holies to offer the sacrifices for them (John 6:37).

The sacrifice of Christ rids us of a guilty conscience and continually cleanses us (Romans 8:1; 1 John 1:7).

•**VERSES 22-24** Verse 22 begins a series of admonitions beginning with "Let us." Since Jesus made His sacrifice for us, we should draw near to God, hold fast our faith, and be considerate of one another.

•**VERSE 23** The new covenant depends on the promises of God, not our works.

•**VERSE 24** It is important that Christians take thought and care for one another and exhort each other to good works.

•**VERSE 25** Regular gathering with other Christians helps to keep the whole body of believers functioning and developing properly.

"The day approaching" refers to the second coming of Christ. We need more strength as the times grow more troubled.

•**VERSES 26-29** These verses should be read carefully.

Verse 29 defines "willful sin."

The only sin that will condemn a man is the sin against God's love and His provision for our salvation through the sacrifice of Jesus on the Cross (Matthew 7:14, 12:31,32, 26:39; John 10:7, 14:6)

The only sacrifice God will accept for our sins is the sacrifice He prepared for us in Jesus. We need only to accept the sacrifice of Jesus as our salvation.

•**VERSES 30-31** Second Peter 3:9; Ezekiel 33:11.

•**VERSES 32-33** Many of the Hebrew Christians were persecuted for their faith in Christ.

•**VERSE 34** The Hebrew Christians were disinherited by their families.

They took the "spoiling of their goods" joyfully seeing the material world in its proper perspective and the spiritual viewpoint (Mark 8:36, 10:29,30).

•**VERSE 35** We are not to cast away our boldness to enter God's presence since there is a great reward in free and intimate fellowship with Him.

•**VERSE 36** The return of Jesus Christ is being delayed by God so that all those who want to accept His salvation will have the opportunity (2 Peter 3:3-9; James 5:7,8).

•**VERSES 37-38** The author of Hebrews quotes from Habakkuk 2:1-4, who was also tired of the evil he saw all around him.

CHAPTER 11:
THE HALL OF FAITH

•**VERSE 1** This verse defines faith. "Substance" here means the confident expectation.

Faith rejoices without seeing or understanding what God is doing (2 Corinthians 4:18).

•**VERSE 2** The "good report" was that their faith was a witness of their relationship with God.

•**VERSE 3** God created the world from materials that are invisible to the naked eye.

•**VERSE 4** The Hall of Faith begins here. These are people who were known for outstanding faith. Abel's sacrifice was offered in faith, Cain's was not.

•**VERSE 5** Just as Enoch was spared from the judgment of God upon the earth during the Flood, so the Church will be spared from the Tribulation.

In pleasing God, Enoch fulfilled the purpose for which man was created (Revelation 4:11).

•**VERSE 6** We limit the work of God in our lives through unbelief (Psalm 78:41).

When we realize how mighty God is, our problems are put in perspective.

•**VERSE 7** When God warned Noah about the rains to come, Noah accepted His word by faith, though it had never rained before. He so believed God's word that he was motivated by fear to build the ark.

Noah's building of the ark condemned the people around him for their unbelief, and made him an heir of righteousness.

Noah's faith prompted him to positive action. Faith and works go hand-in-hand. Righteousness by faith produces works that are consistent with what we believe, whereas the righteousness in God's eyes is the result of our faith, never our works.

•**VERSE 8** Abraham is called the father of those who believe. His first step of faith was to leave the land of his father to journey to the Promised Land.

•**VERSE 9** Abraham lived in tents in the Promised Land and owned very little land, yet believed that God had promised all the land to him for his descendants.

•**VERSE 10** Abraham's heart was in the City of God, not in earthly treasures or buildings.

THE HALL OF FAITH

ABEL

ENOCH

NOAH

ABRAHAM

SARAH

ISAAC

JACOB

JOSEPH

MOSES

RAHAB

GIDEON

BARAK

SAMSON

JEPHTHAH

DAVID

SAMUEL

THE PROPHETS

•VERSE 11 The birth of Isaac was based on God's faithfulness in performing that which He had promised—not on Sarah or Abraham's faith.

•VERSE 12 Sarah was past childbearing age (over 90) and Abraham was over 100 years old, "as good as dead," and yet God gave them a child and innumerable descendants.

•VERSE 13 The members of the Hall of Faith all died without receiving the promised Savior and the eternal Kingdom, but their faith in the promises of God saved them. They saw the promises and held on to them.

•VERSES 14-15 The Old Testament saints could have returned to the lands they left if their hearts were still there, but they believed that God had a better place for them and they were content to be strangers and pilgrims on the earth.

•VERSE 16 The spirits of the Old Testament saints could not go into heaven until Jesus died for their sins, so they went into Sheol (Hell).

Jesus taught that Sheol was divided into two parts, with Abraham the head of the part for those who believed in God's promises (Luke 16:19-31; Psalm 16:10; Isaiah 61:1; Matthew 27:52,53).

•VERSE 17 Though Abraham had another son, the son of his fleshly attempt to fulfill God's promise, God did not recognize the other son (Genesis 22:1-14) just as He ignores our sins as we believe in Jesus (Romans 4:8).

God was only testing Abraham's obedience and faith and He never intended for Isaac to actually be sacrificed.

•VERSES 18,19 God had told Abraham specifically that Abraham would have descendants through Isaac, and since Isaac did not have children at this point, Abraham knew that God would restore Isaac to life if necessary (Genesis 22:5).

There are parallels between Abraham offering up Isaac and God sacrificing His beloved Son.

Abraham thought of Isaac as dead for the three-day journey to Mount Moriah. Jesus was dead for three days. Isaac carried the wood for sacrifice on his back. Jesus carried the cross on His back.

Both sons were submitted to the will of their fathers. Both sacrifices took place on Mount Moriah. Abraham had called the place Jehovah Jireh "the Lord will provide" and prophesied, "In the mount of the Lord it shall be seen" (Genesis 22:14).

•VERSE 20 Though Isaac was not known as a spiritual man, he is listed in the Hall of Faith because of the prophetic blessings he pronounced upon his sons.

•**VERSE 21** Jacob claimed Joseph's two sons as his own, thereby giving the double portion, the birthright, to Joseph.

Jacob's eldest son was the child of the wife who was forced on Jacob, while Joseph was the first child of Jacob's chosen bride.

When Jacob blessed Joseph's sons, he purposely crossed his hands to give the greater blessing to Ephraim, the younger son. The tribe of Ephraim was greater than that of Manasseh.

•**VERSE 22** When Joseph was dying, he asked that his bones be returned to the Promised Land when the children of Israel finally returned, believing they would someday leave Egypt and live as a nation in the land God had given to them.

•**VERSE 23** The parents of Moses hid him by faith and defied the Pharaoh's decree.

As Christians we are to obey the laws of the land unless they conflict with God's laws, and then we must obey God rather than man.

•**VERSES 24-25** Moses rejected possible rulership in Egypt when he chose to join the children of Israel in their difficulties.

•**VERSE 26** Moses valued the worst aspect of the godly life more than the best the world had to offer. He chose the afflictions of being a child of God rather than the pleasures and riches of Egypt.

•**VERSE 27** The men of faith always see more than those who rely on their natural intellect.

•**VERSE 29** By faith the children of Israel crossed the Red Sea and followed Moses into the wilderness.

Our lives inspire other people to trust God or to distrust Him. God sometimes allows His children to get into places of testings and trials that are very frightening.

In impossible circumstances where we have nowhere to turn but up, God wants us to stand still and watch Him work and then to go forward in faith.

•**VERSE 30** God promised Joshua that every place he put his foot in the Promised Land would be his. The people followed Joshua by faith.

The defeat of Jericho demonstrates that God is not confined to our rational ways of doing things (Isaiah 55:8).

The faith of the children of Israel was:

(1) Daring, because there was no turning back.

(2) Obedient, because they did not understand why they were to march around the city.

(3) Patient, because the walls did not fall down for the first several days.

(4) Anticipating, because they knew God would act on the seventh day when they shouted.

When we meet the enemy in an entrenched stronghold against us, we need this kind of faith to claim the victory.

•**VERSE 31** When God used Rahab to help the spies, it demonstrated:

(1) The sovereignty of God, because He chose Rahab and her family out of all the people of Jericho.

(2) The grace of God, because He chose Rahab despite her profession.

Rahab believed in the reports she had heard about the children of Israel and their God, and by faith she believed that they would conquer mighty Jericho.

Since the Israelites promised to spare all those in her house, Rahab's house became a house of faith.

•**VERSE 32** God often chooses men who lack confidence in their own abilities to do His work because He is made strong in our weakness.

•**VERSES 33-34** These verses refer to the men of faith listed in verse 32 and to other men of Israel.

•**VERSES 35-37** The men of faith suffered various punishments at the hands of unbelievers, thus assuring themselves a special place in the heavenly kingdom.

•**VERSE 38** Those men who are pleasing to God are often displeasing to the world.

•**VERSES 39-40** The members of the Hall of Faith did not receive the promised Messiah, so our relationship with God is even better than theirs was, because we are able to approach Him through His Son.

CHAPTER 12:
THE PATIENCE OF THE SAINTS

•**VERSE 1** This verse refers back to verse 36 of Chapter 10 where the author began to encourage the believers to be patient.

Chapter 11 listed the Old Testament saints (the great cloud of witnesses) who waited patiently for God to keep His promise in His good time.

We are waiting in faith for God to keep His promise of the second coming of Jesus Christ. God is waiting for the perfect time.

God has a plan for each of our lives— the race that is set before us. We are to remove any weights and sins that would impede our progress or slow us down.

Some activities are not sin but they do encumber us and make the race more difficult. Our choices are not always between right and wrong but are sometimes deciding whether something will be a hindrance in our race (Philippians 3:13,14; 1 Corinthians 6:12).

•**VERSE 2** Jesus not only began our faith but He finished it, too.

Our salvation depends upon the finished work of Christ and not upon any work of ours. Suffering is something we all experience.

When trials come, we don't need to fear that we are out of God's will. Instead, we should allow God to refine us through our sufferings and look beyond the pain to the eternal work He is doing in us (2 Corinthians 4:16-18; 1 Peter 1:6,7 and 4:12,13).

CALVARY DISTINCTIVE

"...let us lay aside every weight, and the sin which doth so easily beset us, and let us run with patience the race that is set before us" (Hebrews 12:1).

What we're called to do we need to do quickly. There's an urgency to our work. We need to get the message out because we don't have much time. The Lord is returning soon!

•**VERSES 3-4** We are exhorted to consider what Jesus had to suffer, both physically and mentally, during His time here on earth.

"Contradiction" is also translated rebellion.

Jesus was persecuted and we will be also (John 15:20; 2 Timothy 3:12).

•**VERSE 5** The Jews who chose to follow Christ were persecuted by their families, friends, and the government, and were beginning to grow discouraged.

God chastens His children, so when we are chastened, we have the comfort that we are His own. His concern is for our eternal benefit, not our temporal ease.

We are not to despise the chastening of the Lord or to become bitter when He rebukes us. The chastening of God is corrective, not punitive. We should accept correction without getting stubborn or rebellious, for God's chastening is motivated by love.

•**VERSES 7-8** If we have never been chastened, then we should be concerned. Those who do not belong to God are often able to get by with things that we are chastened for because God has different rules for His children than He does for them.

•**VERSES 9-10** God chastens us to make us fit material for heaven.

•**VERSE 11** He chastens us to keep us on the right path and to protect us from the bitter fruit of our errant ways.

When we are chastened, we should discover the reason for it and look ahead to the peaceable fruit that will result.

Sometimes we wonder whether a trial is chastening from God or buffeting from Satan. Sometimes God allows Satan to buffet us as a form of chastisement. He allows us to experience the bitter fruit of a path we have followed.

When we pray and ask God to remove a trial, if He takes it away then it was not of God, but if it persists then we know He wants to teach us something through it.

•**VERSES 12-13** The exhortation is to get back on the straight path and start running again.

•**VERSE 14** "Follow" here is pursue. "Holiness" here is separated. We should be separated from the world for God's exclusive use.

KEY WORD

hagiasmos = holiness, sanctification, separated (12:14)

•**VERSE 15** Bitterness often comes when we cannot understand the ways of God.

Our trials can make us bitter or better. If we are bitter, we make those around us miserable too.

•**VERSES 16-17** Esau was not crying tears of repentance; he was crying because he had lost the blessing.

Esau had shown his spiritual indifference when he sold his birthright for the food his brother made.

•**VERSE 18** Our relationship to God under the new covenant is not material, but spiritual (John 4:22).

•**VERSES 19-21** The people under the old covenant asked Moses to mediate with God for them because the evidences of His presence were so terrifying to them.

•**VERSE 23** Our names are written in the heavenly register which gives us the rights of citizenship in the Kingdom.

•**VERSE 24** The blood of Jesus cries out for God's mercy and grace to be extended to us, while Abel's blood cried out for vengeance.

•**VERSE 25** Jesus is the One we are to listen to (Mark 9:7).

Moses spoke for God on earth, and those who did not obey the laws from God were lost.

Since Jesus came directly from heaven to give God's message to us, we should consider His message even more carefully.

•**VERSES 26-28** If our lives revolve around material things, then when God shakes the earth to destroy it, we will lose everything.

We should keep a light touch with the world as we develop and strengthen our spiritual man (James 1:27).

CHAPTER 13:
APPLICATION OF SPIRITUAL TRUTHS

•**VERSE 1** "Continue" here is abide (John 13:35; 1 John 3:14).

•**VERSE 2** We demonstrate our love for others when we are friendly to strangers at church.

Entertaining in biblical days included taking a person into one's home.

•VERSE 3 There are Christians in prison in other countries whose only "crime" is loving our Lord Jesus and who need our prayers and help (1 Corinthians 12:26).

There are so many ways that we can minister love to our neighbors if we will take the time and let His love flow through us (1 Corinthians 13:13).

•VERSE 4 God made Eve to be Adam's companion to bring completeness, love, and beauty to his life in marriage (Genesis 2:20-24; 1 Corinthians 6:15-19; 2 Corinthians 6:14).

•VERSE 5 "Conversation" here means manner of life.

•VERSE 7 Those who teach us the Word of God have spiritual authority over us, but not to the point of the Nicolaitanes, who lorded over the lay people (Revelation 2:6,15).

•VERSE 8 Jesus has the same divine characteristic of immutability (changelessness) that God has. We are anchored to Him in this changing world.

•VERSE 9 We do not need "new truth." The sound doctrine of God's Word is enough.

Our standing with Christ is based upon His grace, not upon outward observances, such as eating or abstaining from meat.

•VERSE 10 The altar we have is spiritual, and the high priests have no right to serve or partake there.

•VERSES 11-12 The animals' bodies were taken outside the camp to be burned, and Jesus was also sacrificed outside the city walls.

•VERSE 13 When we go "without the camp" we are going outside the system of Judaism to find Jesus. The Jews find it particularly difficult to bear the reproach of Christ.

•VERSE 14 We are looking for the glorious City of God.

•VERSE 15 As Christians, we also offer sacrifices to God, but sacrifices are from our hearts rather than a tradition (Isaiah 1:11-15).

God wants joyful, willing sacrifices, not grudging service. We can also offer God "a broken spirit and a contrite heart" (Psalm 51:17), and our bodies (Roman 12:1).

•VERSE 16 We offer the sacrifice of praise to God and the sacrifice of doing good to others.

"Communicate" here means to help out, to distribute what we have to those in need (James 2:14-17; 1 John 3:18; Proverbs 19:17).

•VERSE 17 This verse has been carried to extremes, with a "shepherd" who oversees all a person's activities.

Actually, a teacher should teach us to submit to God, not to himself. If we know God's Word and follow it, our teacher can give a good account of us.

•VERSE 18 Pastors and teachers need prayer too.

•VERSE 20 Paul is the only New Testament author to use the term "God of Peace." He also used the term "Lord Jesus" more than any other author.

We make our peace with God when we accept God's salvation through Christ, but the peace of God is a further step.

We need to appropriate the peace of God in every situation by committing ourselves totally to Him.

Jesus is the Good Shepherd (Ezekiel 34; John 10:1-29).

The everlasting covenant is between God and Christ, for God promised to raise Jesus from the dead.

•VERSE 21 "Perfect" here again is complete, of full age.

God does the work in us, so we do not have any room to boast (Ephesians 2:10).

We are the instrument in His hands.

•VERSE 22 "Suffer" here is give heed, allow with obedience.

•VERSE 23 Timothy was Paul's frequent companion.

STUDY QUESTIONS FOR HEBREWS

1. The book of Hebrews begins by stating that in these last days, God has spoken to us by His Son. What 9 things do you learn about Jesus in chapter 1, verses 2-4?

_____

_____

_____

2. Hebrews 4:16 tells us that we can come to the throne of grace with confidence and receive mercy and help. Why does the Lord have such mercy upon us? (See Hebrews 4:15.)

_____

_____

_____

3. Under the old covenant, sins could only be covered by the blood of animal sacrifices but not done away with completely. Meditate on Hebrews 9:15 and rewrite it in your own words.

_____

_____

_____

4. According to Hebrews 11:1, what is the definition of faith?

_____

_____

_____

5. Hebrews chapter 11 (the Hall of Faith) gives us many examples of Old Testament saints. How are we to run the race? (See Hebrews 12:1-3.)

_____

_____

_____

THE EPISTLE OF
JAMES

AUTHOR OF LETTER:
James, the brother of Jesus and Jude.

WRITTEN TO:
The twelve tribes scattered abroad.

DATE AND PLACE OF WRITING:
One of the earliest epistles; at least two years before Paul's first epistle.

THEME:
The faith that works.

PURPOSE OF WRITING:
To encourage them during their difficulties.
To instruct them in practical Christian living.

CHAPTER 1:
PATIENCE IN TRIALS

•**VERSE 1** The author of this epistle is known as James the Great, not James the brother of John and the son of Zebedee.

This is the James who had a major role in the leadership of the early Church. He presided over the council called to settle the dispute about the Gentile converts (Acts 15:13-29).

He is considered by scholars to be the son of Joseph and Mary, a half-brother of Jesus Christ (Mark 6:3).

"Servant" means bondslave.

•**VERSE 2** "Divers temptations" means various testings.

•**VERSE 3** Patience is developed through trials while we wait in faith for God to act.

🔑 KEY WORD

hupomone = patience, enduring (1:3)

•**VERSE 5** God doesn't chide us when we ask for wisdom; instead, He gives it to us freely (Proverbs 4:5-6).

•**VERSE 12** Revelation 2:10.

•**VERSE 17** God is immutable: He doesn't change.

•**VERSE 18** John 1:12-13.

•**VERSE 22** We need to obey God's Word when we hear it.

•**VERSE 27** True religion is evidenced in actions.

CHAPTER 2:
FAITH AND WORKS

• **VERSE 9** "Convinced" means convicted.

• **VERSE 13** We'll be judged according to the mercy we show others.

• **VERSE 18** Works don't save us, but they're the evidence of the faith we have.

• **VERSE 20** Faith manifests itself in action.

• **VERSE 26** The body without the spirit is the scriptural definition of death. The spirit doesn't die; the body does. Faith without works is like a dead body.

CHAPTER 3:
THE UNRULY MEMBER

• **VERSE 1** "Masters" means teachers. Teachers in the Church will be held accountable for their teachings when they come before God.

KEY WORD

didaskalos = masters, teachers (3:1)

• **VERSE 4** A helm is the wheel controlling the rudder of a ship.

• **VERSES 7-8** Only God can tame our tongues as we submit to the control of the Holy Spirit.

• **VERSE 13** "Conversation" means manner of life or way of living.

• **VERSES 14-16** The wisdom of the world produces confusion, strife, and evil works.

• **VERSES 17-18** The wisdom of God produces peace, harmony, and good works.

CHAPTER 4:
THE LOVE OF THE WORLD

• **VERSES 2-3** Often we don't receive the things we ask of God because the motivation in our hearts is wrong.

• **VERSE 4** James here addresses the Church as the Bride of Christ. He accuses her of spiritual adultery for her love of the things of the world.

• **VERSE 5** The Spirit of God wants our love and commitment for Himself exclusively. When He sees us devoting ourselves to the world and material things, He is jealous of our misplaced devotion.

• **VERSE 7** We don't have to succumb to the lure of worldly things when Satan holds them before us. God will protect us if we ask for His help.

• **VERSE 8** God wants us to be concerned with Him and with spiritual things. He knows that the worldly things which tempt us would only leave us dissatisfied.

• **VERSE 15** We should preface our plans with the condition, "If the Lord wills...."

CHAPTER 5:
THE LATTER RAIN

• **VERSE 3** Many people are trying to protect themselves financially by hoarding gold and other valuables in these uncertain times.

• **VERSE 7** Though we continually see evil men afflicting and mistreating good men and going unpunished, James encourages the Church to wait patiently for the Lord's coming.

He reminds us that God is also waiting patiently to gather the "precious fruit."

The "early rain" refers to the first outpouring of the Holy Spirit upon the Church after Christ's ascension into heaven (Acts 1:8, 2:4).

The "latter rain" is the final outpouring of the Holy Spirit before the harvest is reaped. We're experiencing the latter rain now.

• **VERSES 10-11** The prophets are an example to us of the patience in enduring affliction.

•**VERSE 12** A person who habitually lies will often make an oath in order to convince people that he's telling the truth.

•**VERSE 13** Sometimes we're afflicted as the result of God's chastening in our lives. We should pray and ask God what He wants us to do when we're afflicted.

KEY WORD

kakopatheo = afflicted, suffer trouble (5:13)

•**VERSE 14** There's a difference between sickness and affliction. We're to ask the elders to pray for us in our sickness.

•**VERSES 16-18** Elijah is an example of a righteous man whose earnest prayers brought results.

•**VERSE 20** Our sins are all put away from us when we're born again and become new creatures in Christ.

1. According to James 1:2-4, why should we consider it joy when we face various testings?

_____

_____

_____

2. We know that our works don't save us, but according to James 2:18 what do our works prove?

_____

_____

_____

3. Although the tongue is a small part of the body, it can cause big problems. Only God can tame our tongues as we submit to the control of the Holy Spirit. Meditate upon James 3:10 and write it here.

_____

_____

_____

4. According to James 4:11-12, why should we avoid speaking evil of one another?

_____

_____

_____

5. James gives us some practical instructions in 5:13-14 when we find ourselves in various situations. What should we do if we are afflicted, happy, or sick?

_____

_____

_____

THE FIRST EPISTLE OF
PETER

AUTHOR OF LETTER:
Simon Peter

WRITTEN TO:
The Jewish and Gentile believers that were scattered due to persecution in Jerusalem.

DATE AND PLACE OF WRITING:
Babylon

PURPOSE OF WRITING:
To bring us into spiritual maturity, and into a life of strength and blessing and hope in Christ Jesus.

CHAPTER 1:
REDEMPTION

•**VERSE 1** Peter's epistles weren't written to a specific church, but to the Jewish believers in general.

"Strangers" refers to the Jews who had been scattered abroad by the Diaspora.

Paul was considered the apostle to the Gentiles. Peter was the apostle to the Jews.

•**VERSE 2** Romans 8:29. "Sanctification" means "set apart for a sacred purpose or religious use."

•**VERSE 3** The phrase "begotten us again" means born again. "Lively" means living; John 14:19.

•**VERSE 4** Matthew 6:19-20.

•**VERSE 5** God's power keeps us from straying from Him.

•**VERSES 6-7** Second Timothy 3:12.

The testings God allows in our lives aren't to destroy us, but to prove our worth. The testings are important to our Christian development.

•**VERSE 8** Even though we've never seen Jesus, we love Him and rejoice in our belief in Him.

"Unspeakable" means indescribable.

KEY WORD

agalliao = rejoice, glad, exceeding joy

•**VERSES 10-12** The prophets didn't understand the diverse prophecies that were given to them concerning the Messiah.

God's grace and plan of redemption are beyond the comprehension of the angels too.

•**VERSE 17** "Fear" is awe or reverence. We should be in awe of our glorious God!

•**VERSES 18-19** "Vain conversation" refers to an empty manner of living. The traditions of man can be bondage.

We were redeemed as though purchased in a slave market by Christ. He didn't pay for us with gold or silver, but with His own blood.

A "spot" is an inherited, congenital defect. A "blemish" is an acquired defect.

•**VERSE 20** The plan of redemption existed before the foundation of the world was laid.

•**VERSE 22** "Unfeigned" love is love without hypocrisy.

•**VERSE 23** John 1:12-13.

"Being" also means having been.

CHAPTER 2:
CHRISTIAN CONDUCT

•**VERSE 1** "Guile" is covering one's true feelings.

KEY WORD

dolos = guile, deceit, covering one's true feelings (2:1)

•**VERSE 2** To grow up spiritually we must be fed the Word of God.

•**VERSE 5** Hebrews 13:15.

•**VERSES 6-8** Jesus is the cornerstone on which our faith is built.

•**VERSE 9** The world thinks Christians are peculiar because we praise and love Jesus Christ and spend hours at Bible studies instead of doing things the world considers fun.

•**VERSE 11** We're not a part of this world anymore. We're pilgrims longing for a new land.

•**VERSES 21-23** Christ is our example of the way we should respond when persecuted.

•**VERSE 24** Isaiah 53:4-7.

CHAPTER 3:
MORE ON CHRISTIAN CONDUCT

•**VERSES 1-2** "Conversation" means behavior.

•**VERSES 3-4** True beauty is in the heart, not in the outward appearance.

•**VERSE 7** Nothing will hinder our prayer life more than problems in our marriage relationship.

•**VERSES 10-12** These are the rules for a long and happy life:

(1) Keep the tongue from speaking evil.

(2) Keep the lips from speaking deceit.

(3) Avoid evil.

(4) Do good.

(5) Seek peace.

God's eyes are on the righteous, and His ears are open to their prayers.

•**VERSE 15** "Sanctify" is consecrate. "Fear" means reverence.

We should be conducting ourselves so that people in the world are compelled to ask what makes us different. When they ask, we should be ready with a sound and reasonable answer.

•**VERSE 18** "Quickened" means made alive.

KEY WORD

zoopoieo = quickened, made alive, given life (3:18)

•**VERSE 19** Christ descended to Hades after His death on the cross. He preached to the souls there until His resurrection (Isaiah 61:1; Acts 2:22-36; Ephesians 4:8-10; Hebrews 11:39-40).

•**VERSES 21-22** The true baptism is in the heart. Unless we've allowed the Holy Spirit to work in our hearts, baptism is a meaningless ritual.

•**VERSE 22** There are rankings of angels in authority, power, principalities, and might.

CHAPTER 4:
PERSECUTIONS

•**VERSES 1-4** People speak evil of Christians because we don't follow the same empty pursuits as the world.

•**VERSE 8** "Charity" means love.

•**VERSE 11** We should minister so that the glory goes to Jesus Christ, not to ourselves.

•**VERSES 12-13** As soon as a trial comes, we begin to question why we have to suffer. Instead, we should rejoice—not at the trial, but because we're partakers in Christ's suffering and will also share in His glory.

•**VERSE 14** Matthew 5:10-12.

•**VERSE 18** We often forget that it's a miracle that God chose to give the gift of salvation to sinful mankind.

•**VERSE 19** 1 Peter 2:23.

CHAPTER 5:
EXHORTATION TO THE ELDERS

•**VERSES 1-2** This commission to the elders is the same one Jesus gave to Peter: "Feed the flock of God" (John 21:15-17). Feeding builds a strong flock. A ministry with a strong emphasis on money should raise questions about the motivations of the minister.

•**VERSE 3** Ministers are to be examples to the people, not "lords" over them.

•**VERSE 7** God wants us to give all our burdens to Him.

•**VERSES 8-9** The Bible never tells us to yield to Satan or to give up, but to resist him in the faith (James 4:7).

•**VERSE 14** The love ("charity") Peter speaks of is spiritual love (agape).

CALVARY DISTINCTIVE

"As every man hath received the gift, even so minister the same one to another, as good stewards of the manifold grace of God" (1 Peter 4:10).

The word "ministry" actually means service. We have been called to be servants. We are to be servants, first of our Lord, but also of His children.

1. First Peter 1:3-4 states that because of the resurrection of Jesus Christ from the dead we have been born again into a living hope. Referring to John 14:19, what is that living hope?

_____

_____

_____

2. 1 Peter 2:5 encourages that we are being built into a spiritual house, a holy priesthood, to offer up spiritual sacrifices acceptable to God through Jesus Christ. What are those spiritual sacrifices that are acceptable to Him? (See Hebrews 13:15.)

_____

_____

_____

3. God has given us the rules for having a long and happy life. List these five rules found in 1 Peter 3:10-11.

_____

_____

_____

4. We are going to experience trials in this life, so we shouldn't be surprised. How should we respond according to 1 Peter 4:13 and 4:16?

_____

_____

_____

5. First Peter 5:9 exhorts us to resist the devil and to stand firm in the faith. List some practical ways you can do this in your life today.

_____

_____

_____

THE SECOND EPISTLE OF
PETER

AUTHOR OF LETTER:

Simon Peter

WRITTEN TO:

To those who have received "like precious faith."

DATE AND PLACE OF WRITING:

Rome, six years after writing the epistle of First Peter.

PURPOSE OF WRITING:

So that after Peter's death, they would remember his teachings every time they read the letter.

To remind them of the necessity of making their calling and election sure; the necessity of developing and growing in their walk and relationship with the Lord.

To warn of false prophets.

To remind them that Jesus will return.

CHAPTER 1:
KNOWING GOD

•**VERSE 1** "Servant" again is bondslave. The bondslave was totally at his master's disposal, but the master had complete responsibility for the welfare of his slave.

We're to obey all the commands of Jesus, and He promises to meet all our needs.

Jesus had many disciples, but He chose only a small number to be His apostles. Peter was one of the men He chose.

•**VERSE 2** The better we know God, the more we realize the extent of His grace toward us.

We have peace, because our standing with God isn't based on our righteousness but on His promises and faithfulness.

•**VERSE 3** The more we know God, the more we experience His divine power in our lives. This power enables us to live the life of godliness and to resist the weaknesses of our flesh.

"Virtue" also means purity. God doesn't want us to ever make a truce with our flesh in the areas that give us the most trouble. Instead, as we grow in our knowledge of Him, He cleans out those areas (John 15:2-3).

KEY WORD

arete = virtue, purity (1:3)

•**VERSE 4** When we're born again, we have a new nature (2 Corinthians 5:17). Through the promises in the Word we're able to share in this divine nature (Romans 8:1).

The world and its systems are corrupted by the lust and greed that motivate people (James 4:1-3).

•**VERSES 5-7** The Christian walk is a continual progression toward the divine nature.

Rather than resting on a plateau, we should constantly be moving ahead. This way there's a great distance between where we were last year and where we are now in our spiritual maturity.

•**VERSES 8-9** If we stop developing spiritually, our lives become barren, and we become blind to our true condition.

•**VERSE 10** Jude 24.

•**VERSE 13** "Meet" means necessary.

We need to be stirred up from time to time so that we don't become satisfied with our spiritual growth, but continue to press ourselves to further progress (Psalm 17:15).

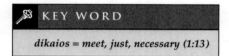

dikaios = meet, just, necessary (1:13)

•**VERSE 14** "Tabernacle" also means tent. Paul used the same word to refer to the body as the temporary home for the spirit (2 Corinthians 5:1).

•**VERSE 15** Peter hoped that his letter would continue to stir and motivate the believers after his death.

•**VERSE 16** Our courts accept the witness of two or three people to establish a fact.

There were hundreds who testified that they saw Jesus Christ risen from the dead. Many of them were martyred for their testimony.

•**VERSES 17-18** Matthew 17:5.

•**VERSE 19** Peter cites the prophecies in the Old Testament as an even greater witness of Jesus Christ than his own eyewitness testimony.

The Old Testament contains over 300 prophecies of the details of the birth, life, and death of the Messiah.

Jesus Christ fulfilled every prophecy. Prophecy is like a light shining in the darkness of history. The light focuses on Jesus Christ, the "day star" in our hearts.

•**VERSE 21** The prophecies in the Old Testament were inspired by the Holy Spirit.

CHAPTER 2:
DIVINE JUDGMENT

•**VERSES 1-3** The mark of the false teacher is his desire to make merchandise (profit) of the flock. The true teacher doesn't minister with an eye on any money he could make.

•**VERSES 6-9** Just as God delivered Lot and his family from the judgment on Sodom and Gomorrah, so God will deliver His Church from the Great Tribulation.

•**VERSES 10-22** The characteristics of those who are about to be judged are described in these verses.

•**VERSE 10** Those in the world speak evil of "dignities," using the name of God or Jesus Christ blasphemously.

•**VERSE 15** The way of Balaam was to profit from the gift God had given him.

•**VERSE 17** Hell (Hades) isn't the eternal place of the damned; it's the place where the unsaved go until the Day of Judgment.

After being judged, the damned souls will be cast into Gehenna, the Lake of Fire (Revelation 20:13-15). This is a place of darkness (Matthew 8:12).

•**VERSE 18** "Vanity" means emptiness.

•**VERSE 19** Whatever controls our lives has us in bondage. Sometimes we're in bondage to very small things.

CHAPTER 3:
THE RETURN OF CHRIST

• **VERSE 4** Peter prophesied that people would doubt Christ's imminent return and would claim that things were continuing as they had from the beginning.

This sounds like the uniformitarianism taught by the evolutionists.

• **VERSES 5-6** Evolutionists are willfully ignorant of the evidences of nature that refute their beliefs. They don't accept the biblical account of the flood that covered the earth.

• **VERSE 7** Our Earth is reserved for destruction by fire.

• **VERSE 8** God isn't bound by time, for He dwells in the eternal now (Revelation 4:8).

• **VERSE 9** James 5:7.

• **VERSE 10** The destruction of the Earth as prophesied here sounds like nuclear fission. The Bible tells us that Christ holds everything together (Colossians 1:17). When He lets go, the world will blow apart.

• **VERSE 11** The spiritual world is the only one that will last.

• **VERSE 13** The end of the world doesn't dismay us, for we're looking forward to a new heaven and a new earth.

• **VERSE 15** God's long-suffering has been the salvation of many people.

• **VERSE 16** Peter read Paul's epistles and confessed that some things in them were difficult to understand. Some people had misinterpreted Paul's teaching and were twisting God's grace as a license to go out and sin, to their own destruction.

CALVARY DISTINCTIVE

"And delivered just Lot, vexed with the filthy conversation of the wicked: (For that righteous man dwelling among them, in seeing and hearing, vexed his righteous soul from day to day with their unlawful deeds); The Lord knoweth how to deliver the godly out of temptations, and to reserve the unjust unto the day of judgment to be punished" (2 Peter 2:7-9).

The basic principle is that the Lord of the Earth is righteous. He's fair and He won't destroy the righteous with the wicked. When God is the source of the judgment, then God will deliver the righteous out of the judgment.

1.   What seven things are we taught concerning barrenness and unfruitfulness in the knowledge of our Lord Jesus Christ? (See 2 Peter 1:5-8.)

_____

_____

_____

2. Just as God delivered Lot and his family from the judgment due to Sodom and Gomorrah, so God will deliver His Church from the Great Tribulation. How does 2 Peter 2:9 confirm this?

_____

_____

_____

3. Peter mentions that with the Lord a day is like a thousand years, and a thousand years are like a day. Why is the Lord patient concerning His return? (See 2 Peter 3:8-9 and 3:15.)

_____

_____

_____

4. Seeing that judgment will come, what manner of persons ought we to be? (See 2 Peter 3:11-12.)

_____

_____

_____

5. In light of the fact that the day of the Lord will come as a thief in the night, write a prayer asking the Lord to help you live your life with that expectancy.

_____

_____

_____

THE FIRST EPISTLE OF
JOHN

AUTHOR OF LETTER:
John the Apostle

WRITTEN TO:
All believers

DATE AND PLACE OF WRITING:
Around 90 A.D.

THEME:
God is light, God is love, and God is life.

PURPOSE OF WRITING:
That your joy may be full (fullness of joy).

That you sin not; to bring you to a life of victory over sin; to give you power over sin (freedom from sin).

That you may know that you have eternal life (assurance of salvation).

To deal with those false prophets and their false testimony concerning Jesus Christ.

To remind them that Jesus will return.

INTRODUCTION:
John was the last living apostle, the only one who wasn't martyred for Christ.

The heresy of Gnosticism was gaining a foothold in the Church when John wrote this letter. The Gnostics didn't believe that God created the "evil" material world, but that a distant emanation of God did. They believed that Jesus was a phantom when He lived on the Earth and didn't have a body of flesh.

Gnosticism was further developed by Arias, who started the Arian heresy. Arias denied the deity of Christ and claimed that He was only a created being. The Arian heresy is the basis of the Watchtower Society's belief system (Jehovah's Witnesses).

John sought to correct the heresy by emphasizing the deity of Jesus Christ in his writings.

CHAPTER 1:
FELLOWSHIP WITH GOD

• VERSE 1 Christ was with God from the beginning (Micah 5:2).

The Hebrew word for "everlasting" means beyond the vanishing point. "Looked upon" means gazed steadfastly upon.

• VERSE 2 John makes a strong declaration of the eternity of Jesus Christ.

• VERSE 3 "Fellowship" in Greek is koinonia, variously translated oneness, in common, communion. Jesus came to bring us into koinonia with God.

• VERSE 4 The first reason John gives for writing this epistle is that our joy may be full (John 15:11, 16:24).

Happiness is a variable, related to our circumstances. Joy in the Lord is a constant, based on the relationship we have as His children.

• VERSE 5 John describes God as light in a philosophical and moral sense. He is completely pure, with no trace of darkness (John 3:19). Light exposes and dispels darkness (John 1:9).

• VERSE 7 The blood of Jesus Christ is continually cleansing us from all sin.

• VERSE 8 The word "sin" refers to man's sinful nature, which is dominated by the body's needs and appetites. We have to struggle to keep our carnal nature under control of the Spirit (1 Corinthians 9:27).

• VERSE 10 Romans 3:23.

CHAPTER 2:
ABIDING IN CHRIST

• VERSE 1 John's second reason for writing this letter is that we sin not.

God requires perfection from us (Matthew 5:48), but our perfection is through our belief in Christ (John 6:28-29).

The strength and life of the Spirit in us conforms us to the image of Christ.

Christ intercedes with God for us when we sin.

Jesus acts as our attorney and defends us (Hebrews 7:25) when Satan brings accusations against us (Revelation 12:10).

When Satan accuses us, we tend to draw away from God because of a sense of shame and unworthiness.

When the Holy Spirit convicts us, we're drawn to God to make things right with Him.

🔑 KEY WORD

parakletos = advocate, comforter, one who comes alongside to help you, one who stands up for you, one who will speak up for you (2:1).

• VERSE 3 John 14:21; Romans 2:13; James 1:22.

The word "know" here in the Greek means to know by experience. If we know God by experience, we'll keep His commandments.

• VERSES 5-6 We know that we're in Christ, because God's love is being perfected in us as we abide in Him.

• VERSES 9-11 We need to be honest with God and confess our feelings of hatred for another person, so that God can replace our hatred with His love.

• VERSES 13-14 "Fathers" are those who have been in the faith a long time.

"Young men" are those who are strong in the faith through the Word of God.

The Word of God is our strongest defense against sin and temptation (Psalm 119:11).

Jesus answered the temptations of Satan with the Word of God (Matthew 4:1-10).

We need a daily cleansing in the Word so we'll have the strength and power to refrain from sin (John 15:3).

KEY WORD

ginosko = to know by experience (2:13)

•**VERSE 15** "World" doesn't refer to nature but to the worldly system created by man.

•**VERSE 16** This is the world we're not to love:

(1) The lust of the flesh.

(2) The lust of the eyes (the desire to see that which is perverse).

(3) The pride of life (the desire to rule over others).

•**VERSE 17** The things of the world will pass away (2 Peter 3:11).

•**VERSE 18** Many false prophets and teachers are deceiving people today (Matthew 24:11; 2 Peter 2:3,14).

•**VERSE 19** A healthy church can purge itself of poisons.

•**VERSE 20** "Unction" means anointing. The word "know" comes from a Greek word meaning to know by intuition.

We know some things intuitively by the anointing of the Holy Spirit.

KEY WORD

eido = to know by intuition, knowledge by spiritual intuition, the Holy Spirit (2:20)

•**VERSE 22** "Christ" means Messiah.

•**VERSE 27** The Holy Spirit teaches us to abide in Christ (John 16:13).

•**VERSE 28** This is our promise of eternal life if we abide in Jesus Christ.

CHAPTER 3:
GOD'S LOVE

•**VERSE 2** Everyone has a god, master passion, or guiding principle. We become like the god we serve (Psalm 115:4-8).

Worshiping any false god is a degrading experience. Worshiping the true and living God is an elevating experience.

•**VERSE 3** Watching for the return of Christ is a purifying force in the Church.

•**VERSE 6** "Sinneth not" means does not practice sin.

•**VERSE 8** He who is living in continual sin is of the devil; for the devil has continually sinned from the beginning.

Christ was sent to the earth to destroy Satan's work in our lives (John 16:7-11; Romans 6:6).

•**VERSE 9** "Commit sin" means practice sin. "His seed" refers to Christ's seed (1 Peter 1:23).

•**VERSE 11** Our faith in Christ should produce love in our hearts for each other.

•**VERSE 16** We cannot really know God through nature, because nature is fallen. Though nature does speak to us of God, the only way we can know of God's love is through Jesus Christ (Romans 5:8).

•**VERSE 23** These are the commandments the child of God is required to keep (Matthew 5:44-46).

•**VERSE 24** Romans 8:9.

CHAPTER 4:
EXHORTATION TO LOVE

•**VERSE 1** "Beloved" means those who are loved divinely in God.

Every one of the New Testament writers warned the believers about false prophets and teachers.

• **VERSES 2-3** The way to discern a false prophet is to see what the prophet says about Jesus Christ.

If he denies the deity of Jesus, then he isn't of God.

• **VERSES 7-8** The word "love" is agape, the spiritual love we cannot have apart from God (1 Corinthians 13).

• **VERSE 12** We cannot love as God wants us to love, apart from His agape love working through us.

We're instruments through which God's divine love is manifested.

• **VERSE 17** We represent God to the world.

• **VERSE 18** If we know how completely God loves us, we don't need to fear. He won't allow anything to take place in our lives which doesn't serve a good purpose.

CHAPTER 5:
PRAYING ACCORDING TO GOD'S WILL

• **VERSE 1** We love God and should love all those who are begotten by Him.

• **VERSE 4** The Bible tells about those who are overcomers of the world and about those who are overcome by the world.

• **VERSE 6** John 3:5.

• **VERSE 9** Man's witness is accepted in a court of law. A man can be convicted or exonerated on the testimony of witnesses.

If the witness of man is accepted as true, how much more ought we to accept the witness of God.

• **VERSES 11-12** God has given us the gift of eternal life through His Son. We cannot have the gift without accepting the Son. This is God's record. Any religious leader who tells you that you can have eternal life without Jesus Christ is speaking against what God has said.

• **VERSES 14-15** We receive the things we ask for that are according to God's will.

We should not attempt to dictate to God and command that He give us what we ask for.

Prayer doesn't change the mind of God or the purposes of God. The purpose of prayer is to get God's will done.

• **VERSE 16** The "sin unto death" is the willful rejection of Jesus Christ.

• **VERSE 18** "Sinneth not" means does not practice sin.

The word "himself" isn't in this verse in the Greek. The word is "him."

Since Greek doesn't have capital letters, the translators had to choose which ones to capitalize. I think the word "he" here refers to Jesus and should be capitalized, for Jesus protects us from Satan.

• **VERSE 21** It's so easy to make idols of material things.

☧ CALVARY DISTINCTIVE

"Beloved, now are we the sons of God, and it doth not yet appear what we shall be: but we know that, when he shall appear, we shall be like him; for we shall see him as he is. And every man that hath this hope in him purifieth himself, even as he is pure" (1 John 3:2-3).

Believing that Jesus will return at any time keeps a purity in our lives. The Lord could come today!

STUDY QUESTIONS FOR 1ST JOHN

1. We know that all have sinned and come short of the glory of God. What is the exhortation in 1 John 1:9 to ensure fellowship with God?

_____

_____

_____

2. We are not to love the world or the things that are in the world. What are those things? (See 1 John 2:16.)

_____

_____

_____

3. We are comforted in knowing that if we keep God's commandments, we dwell in Him and He in us. What are His commands that we need to obey in 1 John 3:23?

_____

_____

_____

4. How did God show His love toward us? (See 1 John 4:9 and John 3:16.)

_____

_____

_____

5. John said that he wrote these things to you who believe in the name of the Son of God, so that you may know that you have eternal life. Write out 1 John 5:12.

_____

_____

_____

THE SECOND EPISTLE OF
JOHN

AUTHOR OF LETTER:
John the Apostle

WRITTEN TO:
The elect lady and her children.

DATE AND PLACE OF WRITING:
John is probably in his nineties.

THEME:
Truth

PURPOSE OF WRITING:
To deal with those false prophets and their false testimony concerning Jesus Christ.

To encourage them to abide in the commandment to love one another.

To encourage them to abide in the teaching that they've received concerning Jesus—that He is one with the Father, and that He is God manifested in the flesh.

•**VERSE 1** John refers to himself as "the elder."

We don't know the identity of the "elect lady" to whom this letter is addressed.

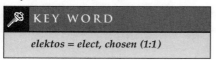

KEY WORD

elektos = elect, chosen (1:1)

"Truth" is central to the message of this letter.

•**VERSE 5** The commandment to love was given to the believers at the beginning of Christ's ministry.

•**VERSE 6** The commandment is to walk in love (John 13:34).

KEY WORD

peripateo = walk, to live, follow, be occupied with (1:6)

•**VERSE 7** This should be translated "who confess not that Jesus Christ is coming in the flesh."

Jehovah's Witnesses don't believe that Christ will come again in the flesh.

•**VERSE 10** The doctrine John refers to is that Jesus is coming in the flesh and that we should worship the Father and the Son.

1. Second John 1:6 says that we should walk in His commandments. What is the commandment that Jesus gave? (Also see John 13:34.)

_____

_____

_____

2. Who does verse 7 say is a deceiver and an antichrist?

_____

_____

_____

3. According to verse 4, why was John rejoicing?

_____

_____

_____

4. Read the exhortation in verse 8. What has the Lord called you to do in your life right now that would warrant a full reward in heaven?

_____

_____

_____

5. What is John's warning in verses 9 and 10?

_____

_____

_____

THE THIRD EPISTLE OF

JOHN

AUTHOR OF LETTER:

John the Apostle

WRITTEN TO:

Gaius

DATE AND PLACE OF WRITING:

Ephesus

Believed to be the last of John's writing; written after he wrote the book of Revelation.

THEME:

Truth

PURPOSE OF WRITING:

To deal with one of the men in the church who would not accept or receive any prophets coming in.

To tell Gaius that he did well in accepting and giving hospitality to these itinerant prophets and evangelists.

To encourage Gaius to receive Demetrius, an itinerant prophet who was coming.

•**VERSE 1** John is "the elder" again.

•**VERSE 2** This is John's personal wish for Gaius. Some people misquote it as God's general will for all His children.

•**VERSES 5-8** Itinerant prophets went from church to church to minister to the body of believers.

The apostles had written a book of advice for the churches on how to know the true prophets from the false ones.

Gaius had been sharing the hospitality of his home with the itinerant prophets.

This was especially important in those days, because most inns were dirty and the innkeepers were often dishonest.

•**VERSES 9-10** Diotrephes didn't read John's letter to the church, because he didn't want to be under anyone else. Also, he wouldn't give any help to the itinerant prophets.

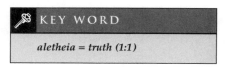

KEY WORD

aletheia = truth (1:1)

1. We know that we should follow that which is good, not that which is evil. What does verse 11 say about good and evil?

_____

_____

_____

2. John rejoiced that we walk in the truth. What does that mean to you?

_____

_____

_____

3. Define the word, "hospitality." How could hospitality be a witness for Jesus Christ?

_____

_____

_____

4. There are many rich Christians in the world today who do not practice the gift of hospitality. What does John say in verses 9-11?

_____

_____

_____

5. In verse 12, John had a good report to say about Demetrius. What kind of a report do you think someone would write about you?

_____

_____

_____

THE EPISTLE OF
JUDE

AUTHOR OF LETTER:
Jude, the brother of James and Jesus.

WRITTEN TO:
Those sanctified by God.

PURPOSE OF WRITING:
To write to them concerning their common salvation.
To encourage them to earnestly contend for the faith that was delivered to them.
To warn against false teachers that had crept in.
To exhort them to keep themselves in the love of God.

• **VERSE 1** "Servant" means bondslave.

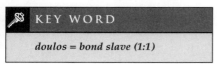

KEY WORD

doulos = bond slave (1:1)

Jude was a half-brother of Jesus and the brother of James, who authored the book of James (Mark 6:3).

"Sanctified" means "set apart, consecrated for God's exclusive purposes."

• **VERSE 3** "Needful" means necessary. Philippians 3:13-14.

• **VERSE 4** Jude also gives a warning about false prophets, who use God's grace to cover their unrighteousness.

• **VERSES 5-6** It's possible for us to experience God's delivering power in our lives without ever entering into the full blessing which God has for us.

• **VERSE 9** It appears that Michael the archangel was given the task of burying the body of Moses, and that Satan came along to try to take the body.

It's better for us to put the Lord between ourselves and Satan than to take on Satan by ourselves. We shouldn't say things against Satan, for he was once God's anointed.

David was careful in his dealings with Saul, for God had anointed Saul to be Israel's king (1 Samuel 24:6-10).

Michael said, "The Lord rebuke thee" to Satan, and we'd be wise to keep our distance also.

•VERSE 11 The "way of Cain" was the way of hatred. Cain hated his brother, because Abel was righteous.

The error of Balaam was thinking that God would totally reject His people and destroy them.

The doctrine of Balaam was the introduction of idols into the worship of God.

The gainsaying of Core occurred when Korah (Core) challenged Moses, because he was jealous of Aaron's priestly duties (Numbers 16).

•VERSE 13 The judgment for people who love darkness and hate the light is banishment to total darkness for eternity (Matthew 8:12, 22:13, 25:30).

•VERSE 20 Jude contrasts spiritual men with the carnal men described in verses 4-19.

We're to keep ourselves in the love of God, so He can bestow on us everything He wants to bless us with.

The attitudes described in verses 4-19 move us away from the place of blessing.

We build ourselves up in the faith by the study of God's Word.

It's hard to trust God when we don't know Him; but the better we know Him, the more we trust Him.

We pray in the Holy Spirit:

(1) by asking the Holy Spirit to direct our prayers, (2) when we groan (Romans 8:26-27), (3) by praying in unknown tongues (1 Corinthians 14:2).

•VERSE 21 We also keep ourselves in the love of God by looking for the return of Jesus Christ. Things are put in perspective when we keep His return in our minds.

•VERSES 22-23 People come to Christ for different reasons. Some people hear of God's love for them and respond to Him in love. Other people are afraid of hell and come to Him through fear.

It's better to draw people to God through love than through fear, so we should emphasize His love when we witness to unbelievers.

•VERSE 24 Jesus Christ keeps us from falling when we stay in the love of God.

Christ presents us to God faultless, as pure and holy as He is, with great joy.

CALVARY DISTINCTIVE

"Now unto him that is able to keep you from falling, and to present you faultless before the presence of his glory with exceeding joy" (Jude 24).

I am only blameless as I am in Christ Jesus.

STUDY QUESTIONS FOR JUDE

1. Jude exhorts in verse 3 to contend for the faith. What does Paul say about this in Philippians 3:13-14?

_____

_____

_____

2. Jude 1:20 urges to build ourselves up in the faith and to pray in the Spirit. What does Romans 8:26-27 and 1 Corinthians 14:2 say about praying in the Spirit?

_____

_____

_____

3. How do we keep ourselves in the love of God according to verse 21?

_____

_____

_____

4. Jesus Christ keeps us from falling when we stay in the love of God. How will Christ present us to God? (See Jude 24.)

_____

_____

_____

5. In verse 20 we are given an exhortation "to build up the most holy faith, praying in the Holy Ghost." Why did Jude write this? (See verses 18 and 19.)

_____

_____

_____

THE BOOK OF
REVELATION

AUTHOR OF LETTER:

John the Apostle

WRITTEN TO:

The seven churches in Asia.

DATE AND PLACE OF WRITING:

Approximately 96 A.D. when John was exiled on the island of Patmos.

THEME:

The unveiling of Jesus.

PURPOSE OF WRITING:

To tell them of the things he saw (Chapter 1).

To show His servants the things which are (Chapters 2-3).

To show His servants the things which shall be hereafter, or after these things (Chapters 4-22).

CHAPTER 1:
THE REVELATION OF JESUS

• **VERSE 1** The word "revelation" in Greek is apocalypse and means unveiling.

This book is the unveiling of Jesus Christ in His relationship to the Church, to judgment, and to what is to come. The route by which the revelation came to John is given here.

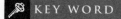 **KEY WORD**

apokalupsis = revelation; literally means the unveiling (1:1)

• **VERSE 3** The revelation was meant to be read in the churches. It refers to itself as a prophecy. The various interpretations of Revelation:

(1) The Preterist view: symbolizes the struggles of the Church against Rome.

(2) Historic view: symbolizes the historic problems the Church has had with the world.

(3) Spiritual view: a spiritual allegory without direct application to actual events.

(4) Futurist view: it is a straightforward account of what is to come. (I hold this view.)

See verse 19 of this chapter for the key to understanding the Book of Revelation.

•**VERSE 4** Seven is the number of completeness: seven days in a week, seven colors in a rainbow, seven notes on the scale, etc.

•**VERSE 5** "First begotten" refers to Jesus being first in prominence, not first in time, to be raised from the dead.

Jesus, the faithful witness, is our example to be a representative of God in our walk and in our talk.

•**VERSE 6** The Church will reign with Jesus during the Kingdom Age.

•**VERSE 8** Since this statement is also made by Jesus in verse 11 we see that He is eternally co-existent with the Father.

•**VERSE 10** "The Lord's Day" may refer to a particular day of the week, or John may mean "unto the day of the Lord," which would refer to his being taken by the Spirit to the days of the end times.

•**VERSE 12** The seven candlesticks refer to the Old Testament tabernacle when Israel was God's light in the world. In the revelation, the Church had taken that place.

•**VERSE 13** Jesus often referred to Himself as "the Son of man." This term is used interchangeably with "Son of God" in referring to Jesus.

•**VERSES 14-17** The only description of Jesus in the New Testament is here: Jesus in glory.

•**VERSE 19** John was to write about what he had seen (Chapter 1), the things which were (Chapters 2 and 3), and the things which would be "after these things" (Chapters 4 through 22).

•**VERSE 20** "Angel" means messenger, usually a supernatural being carrying divine messages.

The messages of Christ to the seven churches are applied in three ways:

(1) Local application: written to the churches at that time.

(2) Historic application: there are seven periods of Church history.

(3) Personal application: universal message to His churches.

CHAPTER 2:
EPHESUS, SMYRNA, PERGAMOS, THYATIRA

•**VERSE 2** "I know thy works"—Jesus is aware of what we do and our motivations.

•**VERSE 4** The labor of the church at Ephesus was not motivated by love.

•**VERSE 5** Jesus will not stay in a loveless church.

•**VERSE 6** The Nicolaitanes established a priesthood over the laity.

KEY WORD

Nicolaitan = Niko means priest; laitan means laity; the establishing of a priesthood (2:6).

•**VERSES 8-11** Jesus did not call the church of Smyrna to repentance because He knew they would be purified by the sufferings they would endure.

In verse 10 Jesus spoke of death, because many of them were to be martyred.

•**VERSE 14** Pagan idol worship often involved sexual orgies.

•**VERSE 17** The white stone is the stone of acceptance; the black stone signifies rejection.

•**VERSES 20-23** The unrepentant church of Thyatira will go through the Tribulation because of her spiritual fornication.

CHAPTER 3:
SARDIS, PHILADELPHIA, LAODICEA

•VERSES 1-5 Sardis is the dead Protestant church that kept too many of the pagan rituals and holidays of the churches of Thyatira and Pergamos after the Reformation.

•VERSE 7 Philadelphia is the faithful church in the last days.

•VERSE 8 Philadelphia has a little strength, places importance on God's Word, and has not denied Jesus as God's Son.

•VERSE 10 God's promise to keep His Church from the Tribulation.

•VERSE 14 Jesus is the origin of God's creation, the creative force of God.

•VERSE 17 The Laodiceans were lukewarm because they trusted in materialism. They thought they were rich and secure, but Jesus said they were "poor, blind, and naked."

•VERSES 19-20 The cure for the lukewarm church: (1) chastening, (2) to be zealous for God and to repent, (3) to open their hearts to God.

CHAPTER 4:
THE THRONE OF GOD

•VERSE 1 After these things—the things of the Church—the Rapture will take place when the trumpet calls, "Come up hither."

🔑 KEY WORD

meta tauta = hereafter, after these things
(1:19) (4:1)

🔍 THE 7 CHURCHES

CHURCH OF EPHESUS
• STRENGTHS:
Patience, Cannot bear evil, Tested
False Apostles, Perseverance,
Labor for the Lord, Endurance,
Hate The Deeds of the Nicolaitanes
• WEAKNESS:
Left their first Love

CHURCH IN SMYRNA
• STRENGTHS:
Endures Tribulation & Poverty,
Persecution, Perseverance Under
Suffering
• EXHORTATION:
Do Not Fear, Be faithful unto death

CHURCH IN PERGAMOS
• STRENGTHS:
Hold fast to the Name of the Lord,
Faithfulness Despite Corruption
• WEAKNESS:
Some Practice The Doctrines
of Balaam and the Nicolaitanes.

CHURCH IN THYATIRA
• STRENGTHS:
Works, Love, Service, Faith, Patience
A Few Undefiled Members
• WEAKNESSES:
Allows False Teaching Leading to
Sexual Immorality, and Idolatry.

CHURCH IN SARDIS
• STRENGTHS:
A Few Undefiled Members
• WEAKNESSES:
False Reputation, Spiritual
Deadness, Imperfect Works
• EXHORTATION:
Strengthen the Things That Remain.
Remember What Was Seen & Heard,
Hold Fast & Repent.

CHURCH IN PHILADELPHIA
• STRENGTHS:
Some Strength, Has Kept The Word,
Has Not Denied His Name
• EXHORTATION:
Will be Kept From The Trial, Hold fast.

CHURCH OF LAODICEA
• WEAKNESS:
Lukewarm, Spiritual Blindness
Pride, Self Dependence, Deluded,
• EXHORTATION:
Be Zealous, Repent, Receive
The Lord's Correction and His
Righteousness

•VERSE 4 The 24 elders may be specially created beings representing the Old and New Testaments or the Church in heaven. The song they sing in Chapter 5:9-10 is the song of the Church and similar to John's statement in Chapter 1:6.

•VERSE 5 "The seven Spirits of God": Isaiah 11:2 describes the sevenfold working of the Spirit in Christ.

•VERSE 6 "Beasts" here means living creatures, cherubim (Ezekiel 1 and 10).

•**VERSE 7** The appearances of these creatures may represent the four aspects of Christ in the Gospels: lion, calf, man, and eagle.

CHAPTER 5:
THE SEALED BOOK

•**VERSE 1** "Book" is scroll in the Greek in this verse.

•**VERSES 1-5** The scroll contains the title deed to the earth. When Jesus gave His life on the cross, He redeemed the earth back to God, but God hasn't taken possession of it yet.

•**VERSES 9-10** The song of the Church (see Chapter 1:6). This song places the Church in heaven during the Tribulation.

•**VERSE 11** 100 million plus millions will praise the Father and the Son.

CHAPTER 6:
THE SEALS ARE OPENED

•**VERSE 1** "Beasts" refers to cherubim again.

•**VERSE 2** I believe the white horse rider is the Antichrist, because he appears on the scene at the beginning of the Tribulation and wars and famine follow after him. When Jesus comes, peace and plenty will follow.

•**VERSE 8** One-fourth of the earth's population will die as a result of the opening of the first four seals.

•**VERSES 9-11** Those who refuse to take the mark of the beast during the Tribulation will be martyred and will ask God to avenge their deaths.

•**VERSE 13** "Stars of heaven" may refer to meteorites.

•**VERSES 16-17** Since this time will mark the unleashing of God's wrath, we know His Bride, the Church, will not be on earth (Romans 5:9; 1 Thessalonians 5:9).

THE 7 SEALS

1st SEAL:
  • White horse • Rider with bow and a crown • He went forth to conquer
2nd SEAL:
  • Red horse • Rider with a great sword and power to take peace from the earth, that men should kill each other
3rd SEAL:
  • Black horse • Rider with a pair of balances • "A measure of wheat for a penny and three measures of barley for a penny"• "Don't hurt the oil or wine"
4th SEAL:
  • Pale horse • Rider named Death, Hell followed him • Power given to them to kill a fourth part of the earth with the sword, hunger, death, and the beasts of the earth
5th SEAL:
  • Souls under the altar, slain for the Word of God and their testimony, cry out • Told to rest until their brethren were also slain in like manner
6th SEAL:
  • A great earthquake • Sun becomes black • Moon becomes as blood • Stars of heaven fall to earth • The heaven departs • Mountains & islands moved • Men say "Hide us, for the great day of God's wrath is come."
7th SEAL:
  • Silence in heaven for half an hour • Seven angels before God given seven trumpets

CHAPTER 7:
THE REMNANT IS SEALED

•**VERSE 3** The Lord will not allow the angels to hurt the earth until He has protected the remnant of Israel.

•**VERSES 4-8** The 144,000 people from the tribes of Israel are simply those the Bible says they are. Various cults try to identify themselves as the 144,000, but God even named the twelve tribes to make clear whom He meant. Ephraim and Dan aren't included in this list of the tribes, but Levi and Joseph are.

•**VERSES 9-10** These are the same martyrs we saw in Chapter 6.

•**VERSES 13-14** The reasons I believe this group is not the Church:

(1) John didn't recognize them. If this was the Church, John would know them, because he never had trouble recognizing the Church.

He would also have recognized this group if they were the Old Testament saints, because he had seen Moses and Elijah with Christ and knew them (Matthew 17:1-8).

(2) The position of this group in heaven is not that of the Bride but that of servants. The Church will be the Bride of Christ and in an exalted position.

•**VERSE 16** They had suffered on earth during the Tribulation.

CHAPTER 8:
THE TRUMPET JUDGMENTS

•**VERSE 2** These seven angels are perhaps the archangels. Gabriel and Michael are two of the archangels.

•**VERSES 3-5** The ceremonies in the tabernacle were patterned on the heavenly ceremonies.

•**VERSES 7-11** These catastrophic events resemble environmental pollution.

CHAPTER 9:
MORE TRUMPET JUDGMENTS

•**VERSE 4** The men with the seal of God on their foreheads are the 144,000 from Chapter 7.

•**VERSE 6** For five months, no matter how badly injured they are, people will not be able to die.

•**VERSE 11** "Abaddon" and "Apollyon" both mean destroyer. This is Satan, the king of the demons.

•**VERSE 14** Euphrates is the river that ran through the ancient city of Babylon.

Babylon was the center from which all the satanic cults originated.

•**VERSE 16** An army of 200,000,000.

•**VERSES 20-21** The people left alive after these plagues will continue to worship Satan.

"Sorceries" comes from the Greek word pharmakia which is the use of drugs for hallucinatory purposes.

CHAPTER 10:
THE SECOND COMING

•**VERSE 1** "Angel" means messenger. This angel is Jesus—the description here matches the one in the first chapter.

The rainbow symbolizes God's covenant with man

•**VERSE 2** The little book is the scroll which has now been unsealed; it is the title deed to the earth.

•**VERSE 3** This is the Second Coming of Christ. Other references to this loud cry are: Isaiah 42:13, Jeremiah 25:30, Hosea 11:10 and Joel 3:16.

•**VERSE 9** "Eating" or reading the book was pleasant, but digesting or absorbing it was bitter.

•**VERSE 11** Some scholars believe that this verse indicates that John will be one of the two witnesses of Chapter 11.

CHAPTER 11:
THE TWO WITNESSES

•**VERSES 1-13** This passage breaks the sequence of events and tells the story of the two witnesses.

•**VERSE 1** The Antichrist will allow the Jews to rebuild their temple

•**VERSE 2** The Jews will lose control of Jerusalem for 42 months.

•**VERSE 3** These two witnesses are primarily to the Jews.

Sackcloth was worn by the prophets as a sign of mourning for the condition of the nation. 1,260 days equals three and one-half prophetic years.

•VERSE 4 Zechariah 4 contains a vision of the olive trees and the candlesticks. God explained that He would abundantly supply His power to those who would call on Him.

The implication is that the two witnesses will be supplied with God's power in a mighty way.

•VERSE 5 Elijah was able to call down fire from heaven on those who sought to arrest him.

•VERSE 6 Elijah went to King Ahab and predicted a drought. Moses dealt with Pharaoh of Egypt when God sent the plagues.

Some Bible scholars think Moses and Elijah will be the two witnesses for the above reasons.

Also, in Malachi 4:5, God promised to send Elijah before the Great Day of the Lord; and in Matthew 17:11, Jesus said that Elijah would come and restore all things.

•VERSE 7 Only when they had finished their testimony could the beast touch them.

•VERSE 8 The city of Jerusalem will be so corrupt that God will call it spiritually Sodom and Egypt.

•VERSE 9 In John's time it would have been impossible for all the people of the earth to see the two dead bodies. Today, television will make it possible.

•VERSE 15 We take up the story in sequence again.

The kingdoms of the world which Jesus Christ purchased back for God will be in His control again.

•VERSE 18 Daniel 12:1-3 also speaks of the judgment of all men.

CHAPTER 12:
THE DRAGON CAST OUT

•VERSES 1-2 The "woman" is the nation Israel. She wears a crown of twelve stars, symbolizing the twelve tribes and reminiscent of Joseph's dream (Genesis 37:9).

•VERSE 3 The "dragon" is Satan, that old serpent.

•VERSE 5 The "man child" of Israel could be the 144,000 who will be taken to heaven in the middle of the Tribulation.

When we next see the 144,000, they are in heaven before God's throne (Chapter 14:3).

Most scholars agree that the "man child" is Jesus Christ.

•VERSE 6 When the image of the beast is set up in the temple, Israel will flee to the city of Petra (Isaiah 16:1-4). Sela is Petra.

•VERSE 9 Isaiah 14:12-17.

•VERSE 10 Satan is the one who accuses us before God.

•VERSE 11 The victory over Satan is won through the blood of Christ.

•VERSE 14 "A time, and times, and half a time" is three and one-half years.

•VERSE 15 The "flood" is an army.

CHAPTER 13:
THE BEAST AND THE FALSE PROPHET

•VERSE 1 The beast will rise out of the ten nations of the European Community ("ten horns").

•VERSE "Seat" means throne. Satan will give the beast his power, throne, and authority.

•VERSES 3-4 An attempt to assassinate the beast will put out one of his eyes and paralyze an arm (Zechariah 11:17).

•VERSE 7 "The saints" refers to Israel.

•**VERSES 11-15** This "beast" is the false prophet who leads the people to worship the beast and to erect an image in his honor.

•**VERSES 16-18** The number of the name of the beast is 666. People will have to have a mark on their heads or hands in order to buy and sell.

CHAPTER 14:
THE 144,000 IN HEAVEN

•**VERSE 4** The 144,000 follow the Lamb, but the Church as the Bride of Christ will be with the Lamb.

•**VERSE 6** These angels will preach the Gospel to all people in all nations.

•**VERSES 7-11** The people will be warned about the consequences of taking the mark of the beast or worshiping him.

•**VERSE 13** Those who are killed by the beast for refusing to take his mark will be spared from further suffering in the Tribulation.

•**VERSES 14-20** The Battle of Armageddon will take place in the Valley of Megiddo in Israel. The valley will be filled with blood from the slaughter.

CHAPTER 15:
THE SEVEN LAST PLAGUES

•**VERSES 2-3** This throng may be the 144,000, for they sing the song of Moses.

•**VERSE 8** These plagues mark the culmination of God's wrath upon the earth.

CHAPTER 16:
THE PLAGUES ARE POURED OUT

•**VERSE 2** "Noisome" means running. The burns from radiation are running sores.

•**VERSES 5-7** The Lord's judgments will be righteous.

•**VERSE 9** The ozone blanket around the earth is being depleted. Without it the ultraviolet rays will not be filtered out, so people could be badly burned from the sun.

•**VERSE 12** Russian scientists are constructing a dam in Syria across the River Euphrates.

The "kings of the east" will probably be a coalition of forces from China, Japan, and India. They will travel down the dry riverbed to reach Megiddo for the Battle of Armageddon.

•**VERSE 14** The kings of the earth will be driven by demon powers to the Battle of Armageddon.

•**VERSE 21** A "talent" weighs about 200 pounds.

CHAPTER 17:
THE PULLING DOWN OF BABYLON

•**VERSE 1** The "whore" is the false church system that was very powerful and ruled over many nations ("many waters").

•**VERSE 3** The "seven heads and ten horns" describe the Antichrist.

•**VERSE 5** Suggested reading for history students: The Two Babylons by Alexander Hislop. This book connects ancient Babylon with the corrupt church.

•**VERSE 6** "Admiration" here means wonderment.

•**VERSE 7** This church system will help the beast gain power.

•**VERSE 9** The seven heads are the seven mountains upon which the city of Rome is built.

The "woman" (false church) is based there.

•**VERSES 10-11** When John was writing, the sixth king was on the throne of the Roman empire; five had died and one was yet to come. The beast will be one of the seven.

Caesar Nero was the fifth emperor of Rome and was called "The Beast" by the early Church.

After he rejected Paul the Apostle's witness, his actions were those of a demon-possessed man.

In my opinion, the demon who possessed Nero will possess the Antichrist.

•VERSE 12 The "ten kings" are nations of the European Community (see Daniel 7).

•VERSE 13 The European Community will need a strong leader, and will give their power to the Antichrist.

•VERSE 18 Rome will come to prominence again during the reign of the Antichrist.

CHAPTER 18:
COMMERCIAL BABYLON FALLS

Though spiritual Babylon is identified as Rome, commercial Babylon isn't identified with a particular city.

With the transfer of the world's wealth to the Middle East, some believe that the original Babylon will be rebuilt.

•VERSES 1-10 The destruction of commercial Babylon will be swift. In one hour it will be utterly burned.

Since the onlookers will be standing afar off for the fear of her torment, perhaps there will be radiation contamination.

•VERSES 20-24 While those on earth are mourning the fate of Babylon, heaven is rejoicing.

•VERSE 23 This verse speaks of the merchants.

"By thy sorceries were all nations deceived" suggests a Madison Avenue-type advertising, which makes people slaves to the acquisition of things.

CHAPTER 19
PRAISING GOD IN HEAVEN

•VERSE 7 The "Lamb" is Jesus Christ, and the "Wife" is the Church, and the wedding is finally taking place.

•VERSE 8 The "righteousness of the saints" is their faith in Jesus Christ.

•VERSE 10 John was so overwhelmed by what the angel was revealing to him that he began to worship the angel, who immediately stopped him.

When the Holy Spirit speaks, He exalts Jesus Christ, never the instrument or the man. This is the sign of the true movement of God's Spirit.

"The testimony of Jesus is the spirit of prophecy" meaning that all prophecy has to do with Jesus Christ. He is the heart and soul of the Scriptures.

•VERSE 14 This army on white horses is the Church.

•VERSE 15 The Word of God is sharper than a two-edged sword.

•VERSE 19 This is the "war" of Armageddon.

•VERSE 20 "Lake of fire" is referring to the Greek Gehenna.

CHAPTER 20:
THE JUDGMENTS

•VERSE 3 "The bottomless pit" is also called the abussos or shaft, which goes from the surface to the center of the earth.

Hades, in the center of the earth, where dead men go; the abussos is where the demons go.

🗝 KEY WORD

abussos = abyss, bottomless pit (20:3)

•VERSE 4 Those on the thrones of judgment may be the Church.

•**VERSE 6** The Church will be in heavenly bodies and, thus, will not be subject to the deceptions of Satan.

•**VERSES 7-9** Many people will choose to follow Satan, though they will have lived on earth during the reign of Christ.They will rebel against the "rod of iron"—the enforced righteousness that will characterize His reign.

•**VERSE 10** "Forever and ever" is from the ages to the ages.

•**VERSES 11-15** The Great White Throne Judgment will not be for the Church.

•**VERSE 12** The books that will be opened suggests that accounts of our actions are kept in heaven.

CALVARY DISTINCTIVE

"Behold, he cometh with clouds; and every eye shall see him, and they also which pierced him: and all kindreds of the earth shall wail because of him. Even so, Amen" (Revelation 1:7).

The Second Coming of Jesus will be to establish God's Kingdom upon the earth. But prior to that Second Coming there will be an event when the church will be caught up to be with the Lord.

CHAPTER 21:
A NEW HEAVEN AND EARTH

•**VERSE 11** "Jasper stone" is the diamond.

•**VERSE 12** The number twelve is used often in the new city.

•**VERSE 16** The new city will be about 1500 miles in a cube, so it may be built on many levels.

•**VERSES 19-20** These stones were in the breastplates of the Jewish priests.

•**VERSE 23** God will provide the light source for the new city.

CHAPTER 22:
THE SOON RETURN OF CHRIST

•**VERSE 13** Jesus is speaking in this verse. The attributes of God are His, too.

•**VERSE 19** Any man who adds to or subtracts from this book will be plagued and will lose his place in heaven.

1. In Revelation 1:19 we see the key to understanding the outline of the book. What are the three things John is to write about, and what chapters are they found?

_____

_____

_____

2. What are the three different sets of seven judgments unleashed upon the earth found in Revelation chapters 6,8,9,11, and 16?

_____

_____

_____

3. After the Lord returns and is victorious over the beast and his followers, what does Revelation 20:6 say the Church will be doing?

_____

_____

_____

4. What is the ultimate fate of Satan as stated in Revelation 20:10?

_____

_____

_____

5. Describe from Revelation 21:1-4 what every Christian is looking forward to and what God has in store for us.

_____

_____

_____

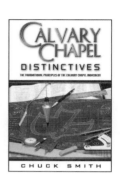

CALVARY CHAPEL DISTINCTIVES

Calvary Chapel values both the teaching of God's Word, as well as the work of the Holy Spirit. It is this balance that makes Calvary Chapel a distinct and uniquely blessed movement of God. 250 pages. **Study Guide Available.**

SIX VITAL QUESTIONS OF LIFE

Pastor Chuck considers biblical answers to six vital questions asked by the Apostle Paul in Romans 8:31-39. As you study these questions, ponder them in your heart, and consider the biblical rationale, you can be certain your relationship with God will be transformed! 80 pages.

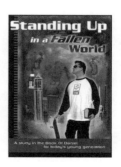

STANDING UP IN A FALLEN WORLD

Based upon the book of Daniel, this book by Chuck Smith inspires today's young adults to take a stand for righteousness, and to seek to overcome this fallen world and its evil ways. 102 pages. **Study guide available.**

HARVEST
Pastors from ten Calvary Chapels share how God broke through the barriers of evil, pride, and anger to carry out His plan. Many insights into evangelizing and trusting God's Word make this book a valuable resource for every believer. 160 pages.

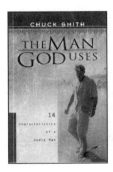

THE MAN GOD USES
Do you want to be used by God?
In his warm personal style, Chuck Smith examines the personal characteristics of the people God used in the Book of Acts. "The Man God Uses" will lead you into a deeper spiritual walk, while helping you to understand God's plan for your life. 144 pages.

WHY GRACE CHANGES EVERYTHING
Through remarkable insight gleaned from the Bible and his own life, Pastor Chuck unfolds the mystery of grace. The reader will be refreshed and encouraged by the depth of God's grace toward us. Also available in Spanish. 218 pages. **Study Guide Available.**

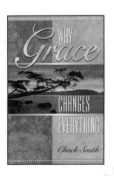

WHAT THE WORLD IS COMING TO

This book is a complete commentary on the book of Revelation and the scenario for the last days. Our world is coming to an end fast, but you don't have to go down with it! 215 pages.

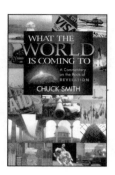

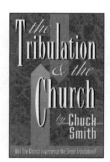

THE TRIBULATION AND THE CHURCH

Will the church of Christ experience the Great Tribulation? This book expounds upon biblical prophecy and future events while looking at the role of the Church. 72 pages.

THE FINAL CURTAIN

This recently updated book deals with such subjects as Bible prophecy, the Middle East, Russia, and the role of the Antichrist. Also included is a helpful glossary with terms relating to the Bible and prophecy. 96 pages.

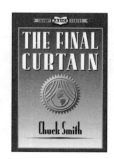

TO ORDER CALL 1-800-272-WORD (9673)